THE TRANSFORMED SELF
The Psychology of
Religious Conversion

EMOTIONS, PERSONALITY, AND PSYCHOTHERAPY

Series Editors
Carroll E. Izard, *University of Delaware, Newark, Delaware*
and
Jerome L. Singer, *Yale University, New Haven, Connecticut*

Current Volumes in this Series

THE COGNITIVE FOUNDATIONS OF PERSONALITY TRAITS
Shulamith Kreitler and Hans Kreitler

THE EMOTIONAL BRAIN: Physiology, Neuroanatomy,
Psychology, and Emotion
P. V. Simonov

EMOTIONS IN PERSONALITY AND PSYCHOPATHOLOGY
Carroll E. Izard, ed.

FREUD AND MODERN PSYCHOLOGY, Volume 1: The Emotional
Basis of Mental Illness
Helen Block Lewis

FREUD AND MODERN PSYCHOLOGY, Volume 2: The Emotional
Basis of Human Behavior
Helen Block Lewis

GUIDED AFFECTIVE IMAGERY WITH CHILDREN AND ADOLESCENTS
Hanscarl Leuner, Günther Horn, and Edda Klessmann

LANGUAGE IN PSYCHOTHERAPY: Strategies of Discovery
Robert L. Russell, ed.

THE POWER OF HUMAN IMAGINATION: New Methods
in Psychotherapy
Jerome L. Singer and Kenneth S. Pope, eds.

THE PSYCHOBIOLOGY OF EMOTIONS
Jack George Thompson

SAMPLING NORMAL AND SCHIZOPHRENIC INNER EXPERIENCE
Russell T. Hurlburt

SHYNESS: Perspectives on Research and Treatment
Warren H. Jones, Jonathan M. Cheek, and Stephen R. Briggs, eds.

THE TRANSFORMED SELF: The Psychology of Religious Conversion
Chana Ullman

A Continuation Order Plan is available for this series. A continuation order will bring delivery
of each new volume immediately upon publication. Volumes are billed only upon actual ship-
ment. For further information please contact the publisher.

THE TRANSFORMED SELF
The Psychology of Religious Conversion

Chana Ullman
The Hebrew University of Jerusalem
Jerusalem, Israel

PLENUM PRESS • NEW YORK AND LONDON

Library of Congress Cataloging in Publication Data

Ullman, Chana.
　The transformed self: the psychology of religious conversion / Chana Ullman.
　　p.　　cm. — (Emotions, personality, and psychotherapy)
　Bibliography: p.
　Includes index.
　ISBN 0-306-43134-3
　1. Conversion. I. Title. II. Series.
BR110.U43　1989　　　　　　　　　　　　　　　　　89-8498
291.4′2 — dc20　　　　　　　　　　　　　　　　　　　CIP

© 1989 Plenum Press, New York
A Division of Plenum Publishing Corporation
233 Spring Street, New York, N.Y. 10013

Printed in the United States of America

Dedicated to my parents;
and in the memory of my friend,
Shula Sommers, Ph.D.

Preface

This book is about the dramatic experience of religious conversion. The phenomenon of religious conversion lies at the crossroad of several disciplines. As the title of this book indicates, my own interest in religious conversion is not sociological, historical, nor anthropological. My primary interest is not even in the domain of the psychology of religion. That is, this book is not a comprehensive review of the social psychological factors that shape religious beliefs in general and religious conversions in particular.

Rather, my primary interest is in the experience of conversion as an instance of a meaningful, sudden change in the course of individual lives. Religious conversion is examined in this book primarily from the point of view of the psychology of the self. My aim is to elucidate the experience of religious conversion as a change in the self and to raise suggestions for the study of the self that derive from the data on religious conversion.

This interest dictated the scope as well as the methods of the present investigation. Namely, I have chosen to study individuals who have indeed changed visibly as a result of their conversion. My inquiry was based on self-report, assuming the importance of the person's own point of view. Finally, my inquiry was semi-clinical, based on the assumption of an underlying structure to the varieties of conversion experiences.

I am grateful to the people I have interviewed, for allowing me into their lives. I have substituted fictional names and when necessary disguised other potentially revealing characteristics. I hope I have succeeded in protecting their anonymity.

This book is partly based on data collected for my doctoral dissertation at Boston University. Augusto Blasi, my dissertation adviser, was a steadfast source of suggestions, criticism, and support not only at the initial stages of the research but also long after my dissertation was completed. His ideas continue to inspire my work and I am grateful to him for countless enlightening discussions. Abigail Stewart's enthusiasm as well as unfailingly constructive advice have carried me through the various stages of the research and various versions of this book. I am also grateful to Sigmund Koch for encouraging and helping to consolidate my interest in the experience of religious conversion and to Henry Weinberg for his help at the initial stages of this project.

I am indebted to Lisa Ullman, Amia Lieblich, Avishai Margalit, Michael Gorkin, Ester Goldmintz, and Yoram Bilu for reading and offering valuable comments on drafts of this manuscript. I also owe an acknowledgment and gratitude to Suzanne Gordon for sharing with me data she collected on born-again Christians. Carroll Izard's careful review of my manuscript resulted in several suggestions for extensions and revisions from which this final version greatly benefited.

My close friend and colleague Shula Sommers died at the age of 41 as this book was in press. She would probably disagree with some of the ideas expressed here, but arguing with Shula was always thought-provoking and illuminating. I believe this book could have been better had she had the chance to review the final version.

Finally, I am taking the risk of closing with a well-worn cliché, for in this case it seems a simple expression of the truth: This book could not have been written without the intellectual and emotional support of my husband, Shimon Ullman.

Chana Ullman

Contents

Introduction

In the winter of 1959, an eight-year-old boy by the name of Yossele Schumacker disappeared from his grandparents' home in Jerusalem. The boy's parents, Ida and Alter Schumacker, Russian Jews who had immigrated to Israel two years earlier, had little doubt that their son was being held by his ultra-Orthodox grandparents. Since their immigration, there had been mounting tensions between the Schumackers and the grandparents, particularly over the religious education of Yossele. Ida and Alter were practicing Orthodox Jews while in Russia, but in Israel they had gradually abandoned their religious practices; Alter had declared himself a communist and intended to return to Russia. The grandfather, Nachman Starkesh, who had himself served seven years in a Russian gulag for his defiance of Soviet laws opposed to his religious beliefs, could not allow it. He feared that disconnected from his grandparents the child would become an "atheist."

In January of 1960, the Israeli court ordered Nachman Starkesh to return the boy to his parents. Starkesh preferred imprisonment. Despite the court's assertion that nothing should be done against the child's wishes, neither Nachman nor the scores of other Orthodox Jews that the police investigated divulged any information about the boy's whereabouts. Yossele's disappearance soon became an intensely debated public dispute. The "Yossele affair" became a symbol for the rifts between the majority of secular Israeli Jews and the community of Orthodox Jews who were, in this case as in many others, defying the laws of the state for what they considered the authority of a divine law.

As the emotions intensified, the Israeli Secret Service took over the investigation. In the summer of 1962, more than three years after his disappearance, Yossele was finally found in New York, living with an Orthodox family as their "Argentinian nephew." As the details unfolded, it became clear that one woman had masterminded the intricate conspiracy that had kept Yossele in hiding. It was Ruth Ben-David Blau who had smuggled the boy out of Israel, disguised as her daughter, and who had accompanied him through several stations and forged identities in Europe and in the USA.

Ruth Ben-David Blau's part in the affair captured the public's imagination. It was intriguing not only in the light of the extraordinary initiative and ingenuity this Orthodox woman had shown in this struggle with secular authorities, but also in the light of her background. Ruth was a convert, a newcomer to Orthodox Judaism. She had been born in France, to Catholic parents. In her autobiography (*The Guardians of the City*, 1979) she outlines the story of her life. She describes her father as an atheist, a tyrannical and unstable man who had been a constant source of distress for his wife and daughter. Her mother, on the other hand, is portrayed with love and admiration, and Ruth refers to her as her closest ally. The mother was "a believer" and raised Ruth as a Catholic. Prior to her new life as a Jewish woman, Ruth herself had been briefly married and divorced; she had studied history at the Sorbonne and had been an active member of the French Resistance during World War II. In 1951, while in her early 30s, raising alone her only son, she converted to Judaism. She gradually became more Orthodox in her observance of the Halacha, the Jewish religious law. During a visit to Israel, she became familiar with the Neturai-Karta (in a literal translation, "The Guardians of the City"), the most extreme Hassidic sect in Jerusalem, and after immigrating to Israel with her son, she decided to live in their midst. It was then that she was approached by one of the leaders of Neturai-Karta and was asked to employ her experience as a Resistance fighter in the service of saving Yossele's soul.

Ruth's story raises conflicting attitudes. From her autobiography she emerges as a woman of great courage and dedication. One cannot help but admire her willingness to sacrifice personal comforts and safety in her pursuit of principles. At the same time, one is struck by the rigidity and the one-sidedness of her account, by the distortion of facts to make these fit into her new world view, and by her ruthlessness towards those who belong to a different camp. She then seems a captive, a blind follower of a zealous community, unable to reflect and unable, in consequence, to bring her own actions under moral scrutiny. The reader of Ruth's autobiography is also struck by the missing links in her story. Reading the story of her life, one still knows little about her conversion. In her efforts to glorify her present salvation she seems to gloss over her Catholic past and the circumstances that had led her to abandon it. The life she led seems disconnected and her conversion remains an enigma.

How can one explain the shift experienced by this woman, seemingly well entrenched in her own French culture, a shift that had led her to a new religion, a new country, a new nationality, and, indeed, a new self? What processes can account for this transformation?

This book is an attempt to answer these questions and to rearrange the puzzle raised by the life stories of religious converts like Ruth. Through telling the stories of converts in various religious groups and examining the recurring themes that dominate their lives, I will present a psychological analysis of the phenomenon of religious conversion.

The phenomenon of religious conversion raises questions that reach beyond the delineated terrain of the psychology of religion. As in Ruth's case, at least on the face of it, religious conversion is the occasion of a dramatic change in a person's life and in core elements of a person's self. The phenomenon of conversion is intriguing as it seems to violate our expectations of stability and continuity in major components of people's self-definition: their ideological affiliations and beliefs, their social ties, and their lifestyle. What is the nature of this transformation? What are the processes that are powerful enough to precipitate it? Are there long-term predispositions that render some people more prone to experience it? Describing these processes and predispositions is the major objective of this book.

To answer these questions I have studied the immediate as well as long-term antecedents of religious conversion in four religious groups. My study focused on the conversions of predominantly white, middle-class, young adults who have actually changed their religious denomination as a result of their conversion or who have at least acted upon it by joining a new religious organization. My investigation proceeded by two lines of inquiry: In one I compared religious converts with religious nonconverts similar in age and education, looking for the possible factors that differentiated these two groups. In the second line of inquiry I examined converts' accounts of their conversion process itself, of its immediate antecedents and consequences. Examining the recurring themes that dominated these accounts, I isolated the factors that seemed to be primary precipitants of the change.

As my findings accumulated, I underwent a miniconversion myself. They challenged not only my assumptions about the important precipitants of the change, but also my definition of the transformation itself. What I initially considered primarily a change of ideology turned out to be more akin to a falling in love.

Converts' accounts of their religious conversion were rich in complexity and nuance and reflected the varieties of religious experiences, but a common pattern united them. The picture that emerged from my data is that conversion pivots around a sudden attachment, an infatuation with a real or imagined figure which occurs on a background of great emotional turmoil. The typical convert was transformed not by a religion, but by a person. The discovery of a new truth was indistinguishable from a discovery of a new relationship, which relieved, at least temporarily, the upheaval of the previous life. This intense and omnipresent attachment discovered in the religious experience promised the convert everlasting guidance and love, for the object of the convert's infatuation was perceived as infallible. It was this relationship that had come to dominate converts' lives as well as their self-perception and that was powerful enough to affect a change in it. The new relationship seems to have provided an "alliance" reminiscent of the one that psychotherapists search for in their efforts to help their clients change. Indeed, just as it blinded the converts to other aspects of their past or present experience, the "love affair" discovered in the religious conversion sometimes seemed to succeed where traditional psychological therapies have failed: in touching the subjective experience of the self and allowing a new start.

The major thesis presented here is, then, that conversion is best understood in the context of the individual's emotional life. It occurs on a background of emotional upheaval and promises relief by a new attachment. This argument is elaborated and illustrated by presenting the differences found between converts and nonconverts and by explicating the common threads and recurring themes in the lives of religious converts.

We begin, in Chapter 1, by presenting the empirical investigation on which the bulk of this book is based and by summarizing the major findings. From the stories of the converts in my sample, the experience emerged as a haven of last resort. In the brief account that Ruth Ben-David Blau gives of the circumstances of her own conversion, she describes the year preceding it as a long "nightmare" dominated by financial hardship and heavy debt, by isolation and strains in the few relationships she did have. The converts in my study similarly centered on prolonged distress as characteristic of the period preceding their change. It was a search for psychological salvation that was prevalent in their accounts, and an appreciation of a haven discovered in a new relationship that dominated their conversion testimonials.

The relationship that emerged as central in the conversion experience was likely to take one of three major forms. These forms of attachment are described in the subsequent chapters. The types of conversion described here are not mutually exclusive. Rather, each chapter elucidates major themes that are more prevalent in some conversion experiences than in others. These conversion experiences are described with an attempt to understand the particular phenomenon of religious conversion. At the same time, the data are also viewed with regard to their implications for the study of the self.

First, and most frequently, conversion stories rested on an infatuation with a powerful authority figure, a leader, a prophet, a mentor. "I fell in love with the rabbi," a Jewish convert said. "I was transformed by his authority, his dynamism." This figure was perceived as an omnipotent father who supplied order and protection, and the transformation that occurred relied primarily on the new structure and guidance provided by him.

Chapter 2 describes the conversions that center on this attachment to a perfect father. Ruth Ben-David Blau's description of her father as a tyrant was echoed repeatedly in various versions in my interviews with contemporary religious converts. Consider the following from a Catholic convert: "My father never appreciated me as a son and I never appreciated him as a father." From a young woman devotee of the Hare Krishna movement: "My father did not understand; anything you did was wrong and I started hating him." I will describe this relationship with the absent, ineffectual, or hostile father and suggest possible ties between the lack of benevolent paternal presence and the actual conversion experience.

Second, there was a relationship with a group of peers who lavished acceptance and love. "I never had found any time of fulfillment with any group of people as I had with this group," said a convert to the Baha'i faith. Chapter 3 describes the attachment to a new group of peers. Conversion is in most cases the occasion of turning away from previous affiliations to become a member of a new community. As it offers an emotional haven, the new faith also offers a tie to a new social network. The shift from despair to hope, from distress to happiness, the emotional rapture which appears to be the *sine qua non* of the conversion experience often occurs in the presence of a group. Members of the new community wittingly or unwittingly shape the converts' change of heart. Do the expectations and dynamics of groups affect the conversion experience itself? Do religious groups force their "ready-made" construction of reality upon the person who simply happens to be present at their gatherings? These questions are addressed in this chapter, which examines the interaction between the dynamics of groups and the desires of the potential convert. I will examine here the powerful direct or indirect processes through which groups exert their influence on their members, as well as the limitations of the view of conversion as a process of "thought reform" induced by groups.

Chapter 4 describes the infatuation with the group from a different angle: as a developmental phase related to the internal as well as external demands of adolescence. I will describe here the psychological characteristics of adolescence that seem to contribute to the heightened frequency of conversions at this stage. In particular, this chapter centers on the formation of identity during adolescence and outlines some of the implications of the data on adolescent conversions for the study of identity.

Third, conversion stories revealed a passionate attachment to an unconditionally loving transcendental object. It was, as described by a Christian convert, "an intangible blanket of love" that nevertheless became for the convert as real and as concrete as a next-door neighbor.

Chapter 5 centers on those conversion experiences in which the object of infatuation is an imagined figure which is nevertheless perceived by the convert as a familiar companion. For some of the converts in my study, the traditional transcendental object of devotion becomes an unconditional provider of the self's needs. Their transformation derives from a merger with this perfect object, which becomes the internal protector of a previously fragile self. Several recurring themes in conversion experiences are described in this chapter: the sense of being chosen for a special mission, the experience of fusion with an idol, and the conviction of personalized miracles, that is, special messages to the self that are revealed in common daily events. These themes are discussed in the light of clinical literature on narcissism and some empirical research on the development of self-worth.

A psychological analysis of religious phenomena raises the difficult but inevitable question of its value. The question has two parts. One derives from the reductionistic nature of the analysis: In charting common patterns in the emotional lives of converts of different religious persuasions and relating these part-patterns of personal history to the religious turnabout, are we distorting or omitting the spirit of the religious experience? The second part of the question more clearly derives from the nature of the major argument presented here: In describing conversions as an infatuation and as a search for psychological salvation, are we condemning the religious seeker and devaluing the religious experience? Are there motives that the religious conversion satisfies other than the avoidance of negative emotions? What of a religious quest that is fueled by a vision of a better world, by a search for moral principles, or by the hope of gaining truth?

The psychological analysis attempted here does not aim at providing a complete explanation of religious experience but at providing an understanding of individual lives, in particular, the life of the person who abruptly changes religious affiliation. In so doing, this book may merely touch on the question of the nature of religious beliefs and of religious experience, but it is my hope that it renders coherent lives that otherwise seem disconnected fragments of a puzzle, and that it sheds light on some of the general processes through which the self is formed.

The second part of the question is the focus of Chapter 6, which presents conversion experiences that seem a response to questions of meaning. I will also briefly address this question here: In *The Varieties of Religious Experience* (1902), William James suggests that one should distinguish the judgment about the origin of the phenomenon from a judgment about its value. James is scornful of those who "finish off" the apostle St. Paul by identifying him as an epileptic and "snuff out" St. Teresa by describing her as a hysteric. The value of the experience cannot be decided by examining its causes. Religious phenomena, James argues, should be judged by their fruits, not by their roots.

This book is an attempt to understand conversion, not to judge it. My primary concern is the psychological roots of conversion, although I will not refrain from a judgment about its psychological fruits, when those are clear. Identifying the psychological patterns and tracing their evolution in the person's history are no more a dismissal of religion or religious sentiments than a dismissal of any other human striving. For, like religious converts, we all are to some extent products of our roots, moved by similar desires and fears.

The present study of religious conversion is necessarily limited to a particular sample of converts which may not be representative of all conversions. At the same time there are general lessons to be drawn from the experience of these converts that may shed light not only on the psychology of religious conversion but on the psychology of our own selves. The limits of generalizability of the present findings as well as the general implications that may be drawn from them are summarized in the final chapter.

1

Haven of Last Resort
Conversion and the Search for Relief

Thomas, the protagonist of Milan Kundra's story *The Unbearable Lightness of Being* (1983), describes his thoughts following the religious conversion of his estranged son:

> I used to admire believers. I thought they had an odd transcendental way of perceiving things which was closed to me. Like clairvoyants, you might say. But my son's experience proves that faith is actually quite a simple matter. He was down and out, the Catholics took him in and before he knew it, he had faith. So it was gratitude that decided the issue, most likely. (p. 308)

Thomas's words reflect a presumption that I shared. I embarked on the study of religious conversion assuming that people who had undergone a major shift in beliefs and whose lives have consequently taken a different course had examined more profoundly and more intensely beliefs that most of us take for granted. I expected that converts had reexamined the ground rules dictated by the circumstances of their upbringing. My study of religious conversion was partly designed to examine the evidence of this kind of a search for meaning. Like other social scientists interested in religion (e.g., Bateson and Ventis, 1982; Hierich, 1977), I expected a deliberate or latent reexamination of previous beliefs to be evident in the events precipitating the change. I anticipated encountering people who were discontented with ambiguities in their previous beliefs, who were preoccupied with what is right or wrong, with universal questions of meaning, and who were enlightened by a sudden resolution of these questions. As my findings accumulated, it became clear that a preoccupation with ideas was not germane to the religious turnabout. More often, a preoccupation with the self, and a state of emotional turmoil rooted in the particular circumstances of the person's life, dominated the process. "Objective" questions about the principles or the theology that underlay the old or new creeds were absent from the stories of most of the converts I interviewed. Their accounts centered on urgent needs anchored in the particular circumstances of their lives, and they described the fulfillment of these needs as the primary consequence of their religious conversion. For most of the born-again Christians, the repentant Orthodox Jews, the Hare Krishna devotees, and the Baha'i converts I interviewed, the conversion provided primarily a confirmation of their own selves through a promise of everlasting acceptance. In the following pages, I will review the material that supports these claims. But before turning to these data, I will describe the research that provided most of them.

DEFINING CONVERSION

   Psychological studies of religious conversion were numerous at the turn of the century, but interest in the phenomenon dwindled in the course of the following decades. This waning interest reflected not only the *Zeitgeist* within academic psychology which called for experimental manipulation of observable behavior, but also a decline in frequency of religious conversions within Christian religions (Clark, 1929). More recently, with the emergence and flourishing of new religious groups and with the increase in visibility and clout of born-again Evangelical Christians, the phenomenon has reclaimed the attention of psychologists. Rigorous empirical studies of the experience are, however, still scarce.

   In this scattered psychological literature on religious conversion, the term refers to a wide range of experiences. In some contemporary studies and in most of the early studies of the phenomenon, religious conversion referred to an abrupt religious experience involving an increased commitment within the framework of the person's own religious group. This experience typically occurred against the background of an already devout religious life, and these studies center, almost invariably, on Christian converts (Allison, 1968; Coe, 1900; James, 1902; Kildhal, 1958; Leuba, 1912). In other studies, conversion designates a change from one religious affiliation to another, in most cases to culturally deviant groups, or from a nonreligious background to an intense commitment to religious beliefs (Deutsch, 1975; Galanter, 1982; Levine, 1984; Salzman, 1953). Converts who participated in the present investigation have actually changed their religious affiliation following their conversion, or they have, at least, acted upon their new religious commitment by joining a new organization or a new community. Conversions of this type involve the most easily discernible changes in beliefs and attitudes. The changes are not only in degree of commitment but also in the content of the new beliefs the person adopts. In these cases the experience results in some obvious behavioral manifestations: changes in worship practices, joining a new organization, change in diet, etc. These conversions are, therefore, easier to detect and to distinguish from a stable, lifelong religious commitment. The present sample is not entirely representative, however, of present-day converts, especially born-again Christians, who grow up in Fundamentalist or Evangelical religious communities and whose conversion represents an enhancement rather than a transformation of previous religious beliefs.

Religious conversions may vary in the abruptness of the change, in the intensity of the experience, in the presence of a mystical revelation, or in the extent to which they are experienced as an act of will or of "self-surrender" (Clark, 1929; James, 1902; Starbuck, 1899; Salzman, 1953). These phenomenologically different experiences are all considered in this study. Excluded from this book, however, are conversions in which identifiable external circumstances can easily account for the change. For example, conversions in which marrying a spouse of a different faith is a primary motive or conversions that serve the deliberate purpose of gaining some material advantage such as the conversion of Jews who feared discrimination in an anti-Semitic environment, are transformations of a different kind. In other words, I consider the perception of the experience as voluntary and as profoundly important for the person involved and the presence of sincere devotion as essential to the phenomenon.

THE SUBJECTS

Forty religious converts and thirty nonconverts, men and women from four different religious groups, participated in the research which provided the impetus for this book. At the time of the study, the converts were Roman Catholics, Orthodox Jews, Hare Krishna devotees, or Baha'i followers. All of them had previously been Jewish or Christian. Most of them were white, and from middle-class backgrounds. Their ages ranged from 20 to 40 years. They had 12 to 20 years of schooling and had converted 1 month to 10 years prior to participating in the study. These religious converts were compared to 30 men and women, similar in ages and in educational background, who reported no changes in religious beliefs or practices throughout their lives. The nonconverts in the comparison group were Jews and Christians who were contacted through the same religious organizations used to recruit the Jewish and Catholic converts.

Additional anecdotal data that are cited in this book were derived from interviews with converted members of an Evangelical Christian community in the New England area and with Baalei-Teshuva, namely, Jews who returned to Orthodox Judaism and now reside in Israel.

THE RELIGIOUS GROUPS

The religious groups included in this study are diverse in beliefs and practices and varied in degree of isolation from mainstream American culture. They also vary in the degree to which the life with the religious group dominates the experience of individuals in it.

Catholic converts who participated in my study were affiliated with the Newman House, a university-based religious center for Catholic students, or with a divinity school. Some were also members of a charismatic church. Members of this church emphasized the "gifts of the Holy Spirit" as manifested in people's lives by miraculous occurrences, such as spiritual healing or the ecstatic experience of "speaking in tongues." They were practicing their religion regularly and were involved in various religiously motivated activities. Other Christian converts cited in this work were residents of a New England community of Evangelical Christians. The majority of these converts were not only residing in the religious community but also working for Christian organizations. Orthodox Jews were affiliated with a university Hillel, which is a center for Jewish students, or with a Hassidic community in the same area. They were strict in following the Orthodox law and took part in the affairs of the Orthodox community (e.g., attending study groups). Additional Jewish converts cited in this work were students of a Yeshiva for *Baalei Teshuva* ("repentant Jews") in Jerusalem.

Converts to the Baha'i faith were regular participants in fireside talks—small group gatherings for purposes of witnessing and proselytizing. The Baha'i faith is a religion founded in Persia by Mirza Hoseyn Ali (known as the *Bahaullah*, "Glory of God"), who declared himself the messenger of God in 1863. The faith spread to virtually every country in the world, including the USA, during the ministry of Bahaullah's eldest son (approximately 1900–1921). The Baha'i religion is, thus, relatively new in this country and is foreign to its culture. Converts to this faith are different from the Jewish and Christian converts studied here in that they did not stay within the Judeo-Christian tradition and in that they constitute a small minority in the USA. The Baha'i faith is clearly different, however, from the other nontraditional groups studied here. There are no clergy, no sacraments, nor a single leader of the faith. The Baha'i community is governed by elected assemblies at the local and national levels and by an internationally elected governing body known as the Universal House of Justice. The faith espouses the essential unity of all religions, and the prophets of the major religions are all viewed as "manifestations" of God. Like the Jewish and Christian converts of this study, the Baha'i followers are relatively free to pursue independent lives and independent interests or careers and are involved in their larger social milieu. Members are guided, however, by the priorities delineated by the group. Baha'i converts are encouraged, for example, to participate in missionary work overseas and to choose careers in the helping professions—medicine, nursing, education—

which the religion regards as most valuable. Although Baha'i converts meet frequently in small groups, mandatory group activities are confined to a monthly festive gathering.

Devotees of the International Society of Krishna Consciousness who participated in this study were all members of a large Krishna Consciousness Temple in the Boston area. The Hare Krishna movement was founded in 1967 by Bhaktivendanta Swami Prabhupada, a businessman who became a Hindu mystic and who started his mission for Krishna in New York City. The group represents the extreme end of a continuum: Relative to the other converts in this study, Hare Krishna devotees are required to have the most extensive and rigid participation in group life. Living arrangements are communal and every minute of the devotee's day is tightly scheduled. Sexual contacts are prohibited except for the purpose of procreation within prearranged marriages. Every Krishna Consciousness Temple is run by a president who is both administratively and spiritually in charge. The president of the Temple in which I interviewed, for example, demanded to be interviewed and tested first, so that he could see "what the study was about" before allowing the participation of other devotees. Residents of the Temple spend their time selling literature, proselytizing, chanting, studying their version of the Bhagavad Gita, and working at the Temple or for the Temple. No outside interests are allowed. In comparison to the other converts, Hare Krishna devotees are most clearly at odds with the larger culture, not only in beliefs and practices but also in appearance. Devotees are readily recognizable on the streets of major U.S. cities: All wear saffron robes, the men shave their heads, and all are required to take new Hindu names.

The men and women who participated in this study thus span a wide range of religious experiences. Some were members of well-established religious institutions, whereas others embraced relatively deviant perspectives and lifestyles. While all were sincerely and regularly practicing their religious beliefs, some had made their religious commitment a total way of life, whereas others continued to pursue secular interests and goals as well. All of them viewed their religious conversion as a major turning point in their lives. This sample of converts can be seen as representative of a large segment of the population of contemporary religious converts: those predominantly white, urban youth from lower-middle to upper-middle socioeconomic backgrounds who have changed their religious affiliation within the past three decades.

This sample cannot be seen, however, as representative of all converts. For example, it is not clear whether the patterns observed here would also characterize samples of born-again Christians drawn from rural communities who have been exposed to Fundamentalist religion throughout their lives or samples drawn from very low socioeconomic backgrounds or from different racial groups. Clearly, conversions within an altogether different cultural framework (e.g., the wave of Islamic Fundamentalism currently sweeping the Arab world or conversions to the more extreme fringe groups, such as satanic groups) are beyond the scope of this study.

THE INSTRUMENTS

Some of the measures used in this study were designed to examine cognitive factors possibly involved in the process of religious conversion. These include a scale measuring Ambiguity Tolerance (MAT-50, Norton, 1975), a scale measuring existential concerns, and a story reproduction task designed to measure degree as well as manner of attempts to reconcile ambiguous stimuli (see Ullman, 1982, for a detailed description of these measures and the rationale for including them). Converts and nonconverts were compared on these measures.

The data that were most relevant to the arguments presented in this book were collected by interviews with converts and nonconverts (see Appendix 1). The interviews with converts proceeded in chronological order starting with childhood and adolescence, then exploring the two-year period prior to conversion and the conversion process itself, and concluding with the present, postconversion life. The interviews with nonconverts proceeded similarly, using identical questions when possible.

Some of the interview questions provided additional information about factors that can be defined as cognitive. For example, I compared converts and nonconverts with respect to their interest in religious, political, or other questions that reached beyond the cir-

circumstances of their own lives (e.g., concern over social injustice, unresolved specific religious doubts) and with respect to voluntary membership in religious or political organizations during adolescence. Rigidity of the present belief system was also compared for converts and nonconverts. Rigidity was assessed by the interviewee's attitudes toward and frequency of contacts with religious groups different from their own, by the degree of proselytizing during the interview, and by their attitudes toward religious doubts. (See Appendix 2 for scoring criteria of interview variables.)

Other variables derived from the interview allowed a comparison of converts and nonconverts with respect to their emotional well-being during childhood and adolescence. For example, interview questions referred to the person's perception of both parents, of relationships within the family, of degree and nature of general psychological stress and to specific traumatic events during childhood and adolescence. These data also allowed a comparison of the frequency of explicit references to several fundamental emotions (Izard, 1977) in the accounts of converts and nonconverts (see Appendix 3).

Still other variables, describing the immediate antecedents to the change of heart, applied to converts only. I have examined the two-year period preceding conversion for the presence or absence of a cognitive quest (which was again narrowly defined as preoccupation with political, religious, or existential questions), for the presence or absence of direct group influence in the conversion process, and for the presence or absence of several indicators of emotional distress (e.g., specific traumatic events, psychiatric symptoms, heavy drug use) and of several discrete emotions appearing in the description of events leading to the conversion. Converts' accounts of the immediate consequences of their experience were similarly examined, namely, as reflecting solutions to specific, previously unresolved questions, and/or as reflecting relief from psychological distress, as well as in terms of the discrete emotions explicitly mentioned by converts in describing the consequences of their experience. Finally, the interviews with converts also provided information about their perception of long-term changes following their conversion.

The interviews were tape-recorded and then transcribed. A sample of the interviews, including 50 percent of the interviews with converts and 25 percent of the interviews with nonconverts, was scored by at least two independent judges using a detailed scoring manual. It was impossible to delete all the references to the person's conversion or religious group from the entire interview without markedly distorting the content. But code numbers were assigned to all the protocols, and while scoring the cognitive measures and the interview variables referring to the respondent's background, the scorers did not know the person's group. The coders found their task relatively easy because statements in the interview were often extreme. Indeed, the degree of agreement among judges of the interviews was high, ranging from .78 to 1.00.

CHILDHOOD AND ADOLESCENT TURMOIL

Of the 40 religious converts who participated in my study, only 6 (15 percent) were judged as describing a normal or happy childhood. By contrast, the proportion of nonconverts in the same category was 73.3 percent. About one-half of the religious converts (47.5 percent) were judged as describing an extremely unhappy childhood. These were converts in the religions new to this culture as well as converts in the Jewish and Christian groups. Among the nonconverts, there were only four (13.3 percent) who were similarly judged (see Table 1).

The emotion most frequently cited by converts as describing their childhood was anguish/distress (40 percent vs. 13 percent in the control group). The emotion most frequently cited by the control subjects as describing their childhood was happy (76 percent vs. 25 percent in the converts group). Contrary to what might have been expected on the basis of traditional conceptions of religious conversion, neither the emotion of guilt/remorse nor shame/humiliation differentiated the groups. (See Table 2.)

Religious converts, significantly more often than the nonconverts, also reported specific, disturbing, traumatic events during their childhood. About one-third of the converts had experienced early divorce or early parental death. Another third described such gross traumatic incidences as witnessing a parent attempt suicide, violent fights at home requiring police intervention, or recurrent mental breakdowns of parents. In the comparison group, on the other hand, similar early losses or severe traumatic events during childhood were

TABLE 1.   PSYCHOLOGICAL WELL-BEING DURING CHILDHOOD AND
ADOLESCENCE: CONVERTS VERSUS NONCONVERTS[a]

	Converts	Nonconverts	χ^2
Childhood stress—			
General	47.5 (19)	13.3 (4)	22.11*
	(Severe)	(Severe)	
Specific	32.0 (13)	6.6 (2)	6.26*
	(Severe trauma)	(Severe trauma)	
Adolescent stress—			
General	65.0 (26)	6.6 (2)	29.84*
	(Severe)	(Severe)	
Specific	17.5 (7)	13.3 (4)	.54
	(Severe)	(Severe)	
Drug use	57.5 (23)	26.6 (8)	8.39*
	(Moderate to	(Moderate to	
	strong)	strong)	
Psychiatric history	35.0 (14)	6.6 (2)	7.32*
Adolescent ideology			
Existential concerns	45.0 (18)	50.0 (15)	.02
Group membership	25.0 (10)	40.0 (12)	.71

[a]The first figure given is a percentage; the figure following in parentheses is the number of participants in the cell.
*$p < .05$.

described by two persons (6 percent). Reports of these tumultuous
childhood experiences came, most often, from the Hare Krishna devotees, but they were by no means confined to converts in this group.
The other converts still differed significantly from the people in the
comparison group in the amount and nature of childhood stress that
they recalled.

A young woman who converted from Christianity to Judaism
described her early life as a long series of desertions and neglect:

> My mother and father divorced when I was five. I did not see my
> mother until many years later, right before she died. She was 20 years
> younger than Daddy and she left him for another man and we stayed
> with him. He remarried three times, each wife successively richer, and he
> died bankrupt. But he was always off having parties, dating these women
> he was going to marry, or he was off at sea . . . so I really had no parents,
> my parents were always gone.

Another young woman, who converted to the Baha'i faith and
who was, at the time of the interview, completing her graduate work

TABLE 2.   DIFFERENT EMOTIONS DESCRIBING CHILDHOOD AND ADOLESCENCE[a]

	Childhood			Adolescence		
	Converts	Nonconverts	Z	Converts	Nonconverts	Z
Happy/joyous	25.0 (10)	76.0 (23)	5.1*	2.5 (1)	60.0 (18)	6.3*
Distress/anguish	40.0 (16)	13.0 (4)	2.88*	55.0 (22)	16.0 (5)	3.9*
Anger/rage	15.0 (6)	10.0 (3)	0.71	32.0 (13)	13.0 (4)	2.37*
Fear/terror	15.0 (6)	6.0 (2)	1.5	17.5 (7)	0 (0)	2.91*
Shame/shyness	25.0 (10)	16.0 (5)	1.12	17.5 (7)	10.0 (3)	1.0
Guilt/remorse	5.0 (2)	10.0 (3)	0.8	5.0 (2)	6.0 (2)	0.25

[a]The first figure given is a percentage; the figure in parentheses is the number of participants in the cell.
*$p < .01$.

in education, described her prevailing mood during childhood as unhappy and angry. She recalled, for example, her mother's obsession with her children's weight, which involved them in daily struggles with her and in attempts to manipulate their weight, placing stones in their pockets, to avoid the angry reprimands and punishments that awaited them for the slightest weight loss. She recalled hating both her parents and dreaming about "chopping my parents to little pieces." Her childhood was, then, an agonizing time:

> I was pretty unhappy, questioning everything that anybody did, doubting everything, very bitter, very resentful, trying to keep to myself and avoid anybody else.

Describing their adolescence—their high school and college years—religious converts again center on the unhappiness and pain they suffered throughout this period. About two-thirds (65 percent, versus 6.7 percent in the control group) were judged as describing an extremely difficult adolescence.

Describing their adolescence, converts and nonconverts differed markedly in their explicit references to the following discrete emotions: happy/joyous (25 percent of converts vs. 60 percent of nonconverts); distress/anguish (55 percent of converts vs. 16 percent of nonconverts); anger/rage (32 percent of converts vs. 13 percent of nonconverts); and fear/terror/anxiety (17.5 percent of converts vs. 0

percent of the nonconverts). Interestingly, the two groups did not differ in their references to guilt/remorse and such references were infrequent in the entire sample (see Table 2).

Most converts described their adolescence as a period of isolation and confusion that seemed more severe than typical adolescent turmoil. This was the case for Ben, a Jew turned Christian:

> [I was] depressed about everything. I did not know who I was, where I was, what I was supposed to be. All I knew was that I did not do well in school and that was why people did not like me. . . . I was a loner.

Or for Rachel, a convert to the Baha'i faith:

> I was angry, very unhappy, sometimes desperate. To break that I'd look for exciting things to do—sports, romance. My unhappiness was very intense and I did not know how to handle it or talk about it. I was afraid to deal with it.

Or a female convert in the Hare Krishna movement:

> At that age (12–13) a young girl becomes attracted to boys so I started having boy friends . . . but because it was not guided properly and stuff like that, you know, I got into the whole sexual thing, getting into sex life. . . . I was associating with boys a lot and also with girls who were into the same thing as me and we started getting into drugs . . . all we would do together was smoke drugs and cigarettes and drink beer. I wanted to give up drinking and the kind of people I was associated with but there was nobody else to associate with.

An ambience of instability and unhappiness characterizes converts' accounts of their childhood and adolescence. But it may be argued that religious converts tend to exaggerate their preconversion "suffering" or "sins" so as to glorify their present salvation (e.g., Heirich, 1977). Was the devotee of Krishna just cited indeed steeped in sex life at the age of 12–13? It may be that her words simply reflect the movement's denunciation of any form of sexual contacts—indeed, of any close contacts—between men and women. This tendency to denounce the old life as an abomination is evident in some accounts of religious conversions in which relatively innocent transgressions of youth are elevated to the status of major crimes and deplored by a repentant convert.

This is the case, for example, in the view of a youth rendered by Count Leo Tolstoy in *A Confession* (1961/1884), the startling autobiographical account of his religious conversion.

Tolstoy's story begins with his youthful falling away from the Christian Orthodox doctrine in which he had been brought up. He does not tell us much about the circumstances of his childhood. Other sources reveal, however, a childhood marred by early losses. Tolstoy's mother had died, giving birth to his younger sister, when he was two years old. His father died seven years later, and the young Tolstoy and his siblings were left to the care of relatives and guardians.

The remainder of Tolstoy's youth was not atypical, however, of the life led by aristocratic Russian families of the 19th century. Until the age of 16, when he entered the University of Kazan, he had been educated by private tutors. Tolstoy's description of the years of his young adulthood reveals nagging doubts and contradictions, false starts and conflicting aims. His youth, by his own account, had been spent in university education, idle sports, drinking, and gambling, and also in futile attempts to organize his estates on philanthropic principles and to improve the life of the peasants. Although the life he had led was common enough among young Russians of similar social origin, Tolstoy saw his existence as sordid and empty:

> I cannot think of those years without horror, loathing, and heartache. Lying, robbery, adultery of all kinds, drunkenness, violence, murder. There was no crime I did not commit and in spite of that people praised my conduct and my contemporaries considered and consider me to be a comparatively moral man. (p. 8)

It may be that a similar proclivity to denounce preconversion life as sinful and immoral rather than the experience of real sufferings colored the conversion stories I heard. This tendency may partly account for the differences that I observed between converts and non-converts in their recollections of childhood and adolescence. But several characteristics of my interviews with religious converts indicate that exaggerated moral indignation and a denunciation of the "sinful" past is but a fragment of the picture, for, unlike Tolstoy, many of the religious converts in my study did not describe their preconversion life as "sinful" but simply as unhappy. Explicit references to guilt or shame were infrequent and did not differentiate converts and non-converts. Converts did not center on behaviors judged by their present standards as "immoral" but on events that may be judged as abnormal or harmful by any standards. Their childhood recollections included detailed and often poignant accounts of specific traumatic events in addition to the reports of general misery. Furthermore, as will be elaborated in the next chapter, their recollections reflected differentiated attitudes toward important figures, some of whom they loved or admired, rather than a global, undiscriminating rejection of previous life, which might simply reflect the rhetoric of glorifying the present.

Finally, the emotional distress of their childhood and adolescence had seriously affected the functioning of some of these religious converts. Of the original sample of 40 converts that I interviewed, 14 (35 percent) reported specific psychiatric symptoms; of those, 6 reported severe and chronic psychiatric problems requiring intervention (e.g., hospitalization, discharge from military service on grounds of emotional instability), and 8 others from the four religious groups (20 percent versus 6.6 percent in the comparison group) had sought outpatient treatment at some point in their lives for a variety of psychiatric symptoms. Other recent studies report similar findings. In a survey of 237 American members of the Unification Church (the "Moonies"), 39 percent of the converts reported that they had had serious emotional problems in the past, with 30 percent of them seeking professional help and 6 percent requiring hospitalization. About one-quarter of the converts said that they had had serious drug problems in the past. The responses of these members of the Unification Church indicated "neurotic distress" which had declined over the course of their membership in the church, but which was still significantly higher than the "neurotic distress" of a matched comparison group (Galanter, Rabkin, Rabkin, and Deutsch, 1979). Galanter (1982) also reports similar findings for members of the Divine Light Mission. Writing about the similarities between the counterculture movement of the 1960s and the religious cults of the 1970s, Braden-Johnson (1977) characterized people attracted to the new religious groups as "very disorganized adolescents who have made at best a marginal adjustment to life" (p. 41). Similarly, Deutsch (1975), summarizing his interviews with 14 followers of Meher Baba's cult, writes that all his subjects (with one exception) described themselves as having been basically unhappy for many years prior to their involvement with the group. He reports that chronic or recurrent feelings of depression, anxiety states, low self-esteem, and poor heterosexual relationships were common symptoms.

Clark (1979) described 60 percent of the members of the religious cults he studied as "substantially and chronically disturbed" for many years prior to their involvement in the group, and Etemad (1978) similarly characterized cult members as predominantly "depressed, inadequate or borderline antisocial youth." Comparing members of the International Society for Krishna Consciousness with members in traditional religious churches, Poling (1986) found a higher incidence of parental death as well as a higher level of alienation among family members as characteristic of the Hare Krishna devotees.

With the exception of Poling's study, the research cited above included only converts in the new religious groups. Members of these groups indeed provide the most blatant examples of mental anguish and chronic emotional difficulties prior to conversion.

For example, Hare Krishna devotees in my study tended more often than the other converts to have used drugs throughout their preconversion life, and reports of emotional difficulties which required hospitalization were more frequent among converts in the Krishna Consciousness and Baha'i groups. The converts in the Jewish and Christian groups, on the other hand, were more likely to report seeking outpatient help for their difficulties and they spoke more often of a particular disruptive event—a car accident, a violent crime—that they had experienced just prior to their conversion (Ullman, 1988). These differences, while far from being conclusive, may point to a more frequent and more chronic pattern of difficulties and to a long-term process of turning away from mainstream culture among those who turn to the "foreign" religious groups.

Among Jewish and Christian converts, on the other hand, the process leading to conversion may more frequently involve a sudden eruption of turmoil in people who have remained within the mainstream of their culture and who have managed a fairly successful adjustment to it.

But distinctions between converts who have stayed within the Judeo-Christian tradition and those who have abandoned it are not easy. The individual variations that exist in the dynamics and in the process leading to conversion do not seem to follow the obvious contours suggested by this distinction. The Jewish and Christian converts that I interviewed did not differ from the other converts in characterizing their childhood and adolescence as stressful. Indeed, a history of problem relationships with parents and of an unhappy childhood and adolescence was characteristic of religious converts irrespective of their religion of origin or the religious group that they joined. Despite the many sociological and theological differences among them, the different religious groups studied here seem to respond to similar psychological needs.

TURMOIL PRIOR TO THE RELIGIOUS CONVERSION

The emotional turmoil that characterized converts' descriptions of their childhood and adolescence was also apparent in the immediate antecedents to the conversion experience. About 80 percent of the religious converts in my study were judged as describing considerable distress during the two-year period prior to their conversion. They described their preconversion absorption in anxiety, anger, or desperation and cited the release from the upheavals of their emotional life as the most important consequence of their change of heart. The emotional states most frequently cited by converts while describing the two-year period prior to their conversion were distress/anguish (67 percent); anger/rage (25 percent); and fear/terror (22 percent). Guilt/remorse was explicitly mentioned by 15 percent of the converts. No comparison group is available that will allow an evaluation of these percentages, but the predominance of preconversion emotional upheaval becomes apparent when it is contrasted with the relative absence of other concerns during this two-year period preceding conversion. When describing the antecedents to their conversion, only 17 percent of the converts explicitly referred to a state of interest/excitement, and 15 percent mentioned this state in the description of the consequences of their change of heart. Less than a third (27 percent) of the converts I interviewed reported preoccupations which could be designated as "objective," "existential," or "other-oriented" as precursors of their conversion experience. When they were asked to recount their major concerns in the two-year period prior to the conversion, less than a third referred to concerns that reached beyond the immediate circumstances of their lives; that is, they spoke of having questioned the validity of religious dogma in their previous religious affiliations, of having an interest in political or social issues like class or racial injustice, or of a disappointment in nonreligious systems of truth. When questioned about the immediate consequences of their religious conversion, very few (less than 10 percent of the converts who took part in my research) pointed to specific resolutions of previously puzzling questions.

The two-year period preceding the conversion was, for the majority of converts, dominated by despair, doubts in their own self-worth, fears of rejection, unsuccessful attempts to handle rage, an emptiness, and an estrangement from others.

For Donald, a young Hare Krishna devotee, life outside the Temple was chaotic, competitive, and isolated:

> I could practically do anything I wanted but it seemed that the more I had the more unhappy I was becoming and the more distant in my relationships with people and it was pretty heavy. . . . I was disturbed by the way people acted. . . . [they] were nasty, big headed, very arrogant . . . engrossed in themselves and I became like that, too, very competitive and very nasty.

The desperation in the two-year period prior to the conversion was not confined to the reports of Hare Krishna devotees. For the following woman convert, a member of an Evangelical Christian community, life in the two-year period preceding the conversion was dominated by inexplicable fear:

> I had no peace . . . I'd wake up in the morning very upset. It was not depression as much as it was fear. I was terrified and I had no idea what I was terrified of. . . . There was a point where I could not stay alone in the house. I had to constantly be on the go, go to this meeting and that meeting, if I stayed in the house alone I would get terribly frightened but I did not know what I was frightened of.

The report of another woman, a convert to Catholicism, echoes the unhappiness and isolation described by the Hare Krishna devotee:

> I knew that I could not go on living the way I did, I was just too, in a very deep kind of way, unhappy, unsettled, dissatisfied. . . . I was a person that, before the Spirit released me, I was very scared of sharing any of my feelings. This was really my worst imprisonment.

For Mina, who converted to Judaism in her late 20s, life prior to the conversion was marred by her unsuccessful struggles to withdraw from a drug addiction and from an unhappy marriage. Others reported periods of sheer desperation, periods in which they were "vegetating in bed" or afraid of losing their minds. Yet others (about 25 percent of the entire sample) whose life seemed less chaotic reported specific traumatic events (e.g., rape, car accident, illness threatening loss of eyesight) in the two-year period preceding their conversion.

Similar portrayals of the events leading to conversion emerge in other studies that center on members of religious cults. The following Hare Krishna devotee, interviewed by Levine (1974), allows a glimpse into the process which had drawn him to the Temple in this poignant statement:

> A variety of sinful activities brought me here. Now when I'm on the street and someone says they're attracted to the Temple but they're uncertain and they mention doing things I've done . . . illicit sex which I've done . . . drinking which I've done . . . shooting heroin, which I've done, I don't know what to tell them. Why not? Because I don't know whether I'm sane. (p. 21)

In one of Cameron's (1973) interviews with devotees of the Guru Maharaj-ji, a female devotee of the young guru says that she had roamed India for four years prior to her conversion:

> weeping a lot, reading scriptures and mourning . . . [waiting] for the pit or whatever, I felt I had really had it and there was nothing else I wanted to try or any other place I wanted to go. (p. 111)

THE CONVERSION PROCESS AND THE PROMISE OF RELIEF

These data indicate that most religious conversions inside as well as outside the major religious denominations occur against a background of emotional turmoil and instability. That this background is relevant to the experience itself is revealed by converts' descriptions of their actual conversion process. When it emerges from this turbulent background, the process of conversion revolves around a search for stability and peace. At its core is the hope of psychological salvation promised by the protection of an omnipotent figure and loving peers. For most of the religious converts I interviewed, the actual conversion experience focused on newly found protection, attention, and acceptance by another or by a group of others, which rendered superfluous and unnecessary an examination of the beliefs or of the actions involved.

Ken, a Jewish convert to Christianity, reported experiencing God's presence like "a blanket of love." For Meir, a repentant Jew, the conversion experience consisted of a "falling in love with the Rabbi." A young woman who converted to Catholicism described her conversion as the consequence of her need to give up her life to one person and her need for more "direct experiences of love" lacking in her life. Another, similarly, talked of her need "to kneel" before a loving god. A convert to the Baha'i faith described the experience as a "falling in love at first sight." A Christian convert, whose case will be discussed in greater detail later on, explained his growing attachment to Christianity as based on the promise of an unconditionally loving relationship:

> [I] could start a relationship with someone [Christ] who would never cause me any pain, and this relationship was something that I always knew I wanted. . . . I would be getting everything I wanted and not having to do anything I did not want to do.

A Jewish convert to the Baha'i faith centered on the undemanding love and attention bestowed on him by the Baha'is: "I have never had as much fulfillment with a group of people as I had with this group." And another former Jew who converted to Christianity talked of envying the love and acceptance he witnessed among members of his new group.

Helen was a vivacious and attractive woman in her late 30s when I interviewed her. She had grown up in an upper-class Protestant family. Her parents had divorced when she was five; she hardly knew her mother, and her father, a high-ranking officer in the navy, was often absent. Religion was the only source of consolation in her early life. She saw God and the nuns at the convent school which she attended as her parents. She married at the young age of 18 and discovered gradually that her husband was "probably schizophrenic." Despite his inability to hold a stable job, his obsessive gambling, and his abuse of her and her two daughters, she could not separate from him, and their marriage lasted for 10 years. A separation was finally forced on her, following his attempt to assault her with a knife and his subsequent hospitalization. Instead of relieving her anguish, the separation left her more desperate and confused than ever. Unsuccessful in her attempts to support herself and her daughters, she moved to another part of the country where she was introduced to and was instantaneously attracted to Judaism. It was only her new Jewish acquaintances, she said, who had helped her at her greatest time of need. Like the convert son of Thomas, Milan Kundera's hero, she was "down and out" and the Jews took her in. She was immediately impressed by what had been so clearly lacking in her own life: the stability and closeness of the family ties she had observed among them.

Some reports of the Hare Krishna devotees center curiously on "the food" as an impetus and an incentive for their religious change. In addition to the atmosphere of love and bliss, they describe the "taking in" of food, literally, as influential in the process of their conversion. Consider the following conversion experience of Donald, who was studying music at the time of his conversion to the Hare Krishna movement:

> I was going to college. I was almost 19. I had a friend who had been to the Hare Krishna Temple and he invited me to his room and gave me some of his parsharam [the vegetarian, sanctified food Hare Krishna devotees eat]. It was nectar and he had a whole jar of it and we drank the whole thing and he told me that there was a feast every Sunday in the Temple and I thought that's nice, the food here [in college] was really bad, poor quality, and so I asked him to let me come with him to the feast and I went to the feast and I went through the program that they have every Sunday. I had the feast and I talked to the devotees and I was very happy there, it was so nice, it was different from anything else that I have done before. The whole atmosphere of love and trust between the devotees and everyone who was close to them, it was very nice, free from anxiety and peaceful.

Being fed is the central theme in the following conversion experience of another Hare Krishna member who had converted in his early 30s. This devotee was one of two PhDs who became members of the Hare Krishna temple I visited. Prior to his conversion, he had been a postdoctoral fellow engaged in biochemical research. When asked about the one factor that was most convincing in the process of his conversion, this well-educated convert did not refer to the truth value of his new beliefs. He talked, instead, of swallowing parsharam:

> When I first took parsharam, I could not eat hot food. It used to make me sick. I could not digest it properly, but anyhow, I took this bowl of hot

parsharam and I felt like I swallowed the sun. All of a sudden I felt like I
was raised out of my body, it was purifying, it was so nice. I remember
this feeling.

The "food" plays an important role in the religious beliefs of the
Krishna Consciousness movement. Their special macrobiotic diet is
part of their daily religious ceremonies, and the food offered to
Krishna is literally prayed to (cf. Braden-Johnson, 1977). The newcomers' emphasis on the quality of the food in part reflects this religious ideology. But, at the same time, it renders concrete a quality
that is apparent in the reports of converts in other religious groups.
Like the parsharam of the Hare Krishna devotees, new beliefs are
swallowed whole and never subjected to any scrutiny. Following the
conversion, all new beliefs and rituals are rigidly maintained. Indeed,
the newcomers who are closer to possible sources of disconfirming
information tend to hold on more rigidly to the new beliefs (cf. Festinger, Riecken, and Schacter, 1956; Batson, 1975) compared to religious people who are not converts and show an increased rigidity in
their religious views. In my study, converts and nonconverts did not
differ on global measures of tolerance of ambiguity, but they did
differ in their tolerance of ambiguity in their present religious beliefs.
Relative to nonconverts, converts were more adamant in their denunciation of other religious groups, less frequently engaged in contacts
with people of different religious persuasions, and were less likely to
acknowledge any doubts in their present beliefs. They were more
likely than most of us to attempt to maintain an impermeable belief
system, avoiding confrontations with beliefs different from their
own. This vehement religiosity is significantly correlated with the
degree of stress and unhappiness experienced throughout the preconversion life (Ullman, 1982). The greater the distress the convert
has experienced, the greater the impermeability of the beliefs he or
she now holds. The greater the emotional turmoil, it seems, the greater the necessity of guarding the beliefs professed by those who promise relief from this turmoil. In the urgency of their need, converts
cannot reflect or reevaluate.

The shallow, recordlike tone of many contemporary religious
testimonials and the vehement proselytizing which often follows the
conversion may be a manifestation of this urgency. The uniformity of

converts' claims of salvation does not always result from deliberate "programming" or "brain-washing" techniques, as bewildered relatives and friends of converts tend to believe. Notwithstanding the powerful attempts at total control practiced by some religious groups (Ofshe and Singer, 1986), the new "ready-made" self may reflect the inability of the convert to maintain any distance from the teachings advocated and may attest to his or her need to embrace instantly and without reservations the entire "package" which promises a psychological cure.

That their conversion had provided a matchless haven from incapacitating tensions and desperation was plainly and honestly recognized by some of the converts I interviewed. "I could never hack it out there," said a 25-year-old devotee. "I will never have doubts," said another, a young female convert, "because when you remember what kind of difficulties you were going through, if you ever try to go out there and live like that again you know you'd be very miserable." This convert did not hesitate when asked about the most important impetus for her religious conversion:

> What attracted me most was seeing that the devotees were very happy, like when everybody is dancing and chanting, the devotees are very blissful, everybody is free. They are just dancing and there are no anxieties. That's what attracted me most, this peacefulness, this happiness.

SUMMARY

The findings reported here are based primarily on a sample of young contemporary urban religious converts, who came from lower-middle- to upper-middle-class backgrounds and who actually changed their religious affiliation as a result of their conversion. The data presented here indicate that at least for this population of converts the religious quest is best understood in the context of a search for relief from emotional distress. First, relative to nonconverts, religious converts more often reported an unhappy and stressful childhood (47.4 percent vs. 13.3 percent in the control group) and adolescence (65 percent vs. 6.7 percent in the control group) and described specific psychiatric difficulties (35 percent vs. 6.6 percent in the control group). Second, a sizable majority of converts (80 percent) described

the two-year period preceding their conversion as fraught with negative emotions, and a similar percentage pointed to relief from this
turmoil as the primary consequence of their conversion. Thirdly, converts' accounts of the conversion process itself centered on new experiences of love and acceptance by real or imagined figures. Finally,
postconversion, converts tended to espouse their religious beliefs
more rigidly than nonconverts, and this rigidity was related to the
amount of stress experienced during their preconversion life, a finding suggesting that it served a defensive function.

These findings are particularly striking in light of the fact that the
people who participated in my study were relatively well educated
(16.1 was the mean number of years of schooling for converts) and
seemed relatively well functioning (50 percent of them were enrolled
at some academic institution at the time of the study). There are
indeed indications that rates of emotional instability are higher in
other samples of converts, especially those who belong to more extreme contemporary cults (e.g., Clark, 1979; Galanter, 1982; Simmonds, 1977; Singer, 1979). Furthermore, one would expect, for reasons of social desirability alone—that is, as a result of the natural
tendency to present oneself in the most socially acceptable light—that
reports of a search for meaning, clarity, or noble ideals would be
evoked more often, and reports of emotional instability would be less
frequent, in this relatively "academic" sample. Instead, for the majority of contemporary converts across religious groups, relief from anxiety was sufficient justification for any change of beliefs or practices.
For them, a pursuit of sanity and stability was more urgent than a
pursuit of a truth or a vision.

But a background of stress and turmoil in and of itself does not
elucidate the specific processes that lie behind the particular experience of religious conversion. A history of stress and an upsurge of
negative emotions may set the stage for a search for relief; yet they do
not account for the event of conversion as the particular means of this
change. In the following chapters I will examine more closely the
nature of the emotional upheaval pervasive in converts' lives, describing the recurrent themes that may be more specifically implicated in the religious experience.

2

The Relationship with Authority

Conversion and the Quest for the Perfect Father

The members of the People's Temple cult who committed collective murder/suicide in their agricultural haven in Guayana addressed Jim Jones, the cult's founder and destroyer, as "Daddy." "Dad knows best," "Just do as Dad tells you," and "Forgive me, Father" were frequently repeated in the letters and interviews they left behind. Indeed, the Temple members accepted Jim Jones as their only father, re-creating in this relationship the total dependence of a helpless infant on the perfect parent. Like a child eager for the protection and approval of a parent perceived as omnipotent, they totally submitted to Jones' authority and swallowed without reservation his increasingly deranged vision of the menacing outside forces out to destroy their haven. In his account of the rise and fall of the Guayana commune, Naipaul (1981) describes this relationship:

> Jim Jones was the axis about which the Temple revolved. The Temple was not devoted to abstract ideas and principles. It was not love as such or compassion as such that redeemed but Jim Jones' love, Jim Jones' compassion. (p. 229)

Unquestioning reliance on the invincible and tangible power of an authority figure, a leader and a prophet who sets the rules and who is the center of intense emotional bonds in the group, was extreme in the People's Temple cult; but it reflects a fundamental motif in the psychology of religious conversion in other groups as well. In many cases, conversion centers on an intense attachment to a figure perceived as a perfect father.

The father figure stood out in my interviews with converts. Close to 80 percent of the converts in my study were judged as experiencing an extremely stressful relationship with their fathers. In contrast, only 23 percent of the nonconverts I interviewed who were comparable in age and education were judged as having similar experiences with their fathers. From the childhood memories of this sizable majority of converts fathers emerged as either absent, extremely passive and therefore psychologically unavailable, or actively rejecting. About one-third of the converts had had very little or no contact with their biological fathers since the ages of four to five. This percentage of father absence is about three times higher than the norms reported for the entire white U.S. population (9 percent in 1970, as reported by Lynn, 1974). Other converts (45 percent) had fathers whom they perceived as weak, withdrawn, or hostile. Only 18 percent of the converts were judged as describing a positive relationship with their fathers, as compared to 47 percent of the nonconverts (see Table 3). The father problem appeared with equal frequency in men and women.

The following discrete emotional states clearly differentiated converts' and nonconverts' descriptions of their fathers: anger/rage (40 percent vs. 13 percent, respectively); indifference, that is, explicit claims of no emotional attachment to the father (32 percent vs. 6 percent); respect/admiration (10 percent vs. 23 percent); warmth/love (5 percent vs. 36 percent); and contempt/disgust (7 percent vs. 0 percent). On the other hand, one emotional state (anger/rage) differentiated converts and nonconverts with respect to their descriptions of their mothers. The two groups did not differ in explicit references to positive emotions (respect/admiration; warmth/love) while describing their mothers (see Table 4).

For a majority of religious converts this problem relationship seems to be the axis about which the conversion experience revolves. Consider the case of Meir.

TABLE 3. PERCEPTION OF PARENTS: CONVERTS VERSUS NONCONVERTS[a]

Category	Characteristics						
	Absent[b]	Passive	Hostile	Unstable	Overprotective	Neutral	Positive
Father							
Converts (n = 39)[c]	28.2 (11)	20.5 (8)	23.0 (9)	2.6 (1)	2.6 (1)	2.6 (1)	20.5 (8)
Nonconverts (n = 30)	3.3 (1)	6.7 (2)	13.3 (4)	0 (0)	0 (0)	23.3 (7)	53.4 (16)
Mother							
Converts (n = 30)	2.6 (1)	5.3 (2)	10.5 (4)	13.3 (5)	10.5 (4)	15.8 (6)	42.4 (16)
Nonconverts (n = 30)	0 (0)	3.3 (1)	0 (0)	3.3 (1)	0 (0)	23.3 (7)	70.0 (21)

[a]Reprinted from Ullman, C., 1982, Journal of Personality and Social Psychology, 42, p. 189.
[b]The first figure given is a percentage; the figure following in parentheses is the number of participants in the cell.
[c]One Hare Krishna devotee refused to discuss parents.

TABLE 4. DIFFERENT EMOTIONS TOWARD PARENTS[a]

	Mother			Father		
	Converts[b]	Nonconverts	Z	Converts[b]	Nonconverts	Z
Admiration/respect	17.9 (7)	13.0 (4)	0.56	10.2 (4)	23.0 (7)	1.85*
Love/like	17.9 (7)	26.0 (8)	0.81	5.1 (2)	36.0 (11)	3.22*
Indifference	10.2 (4)	3.0 (1)	1.45	33.0 (13)	6.6 (2)	3.37*
Anger/rage	23 (9)	0 (0)	3.4*	41.0 (16)	13.3 (4)	3.00*
Contempt/scorn	5.1 (2)	0 (0)	1.45	7.6 (3)	0 (0)	1.9*
Fear/terror	(0)	(0)	0	7.6 (3)	3.0 (1)	1.0

[a]The first figure given is a percentage; the figure in parentheses is the number of participants in the cell.
[b]$n = 39$; one Hare Krishna devotee refused to discuss parents.
*$p < .01$.

THE CASE OF MEIR

Meir was 31 years old and a graduate student at a prestigious university when interviewed. His middle-class parents were Jewish but antagonistic to anything religious. They made their children aware of their Judaism, but they did not expose them to any religious teachings: "To be Jewish meant concern for the world and a general humanistic attitude." Meir described his childhood relationship with his father as nonexistent. Perceived by all family members as passive and helpless, the father was despised by his wife and ignored by Meir and his siblings, an older sister and a younger brother. Meir's view of his father had changed somewhat since then:

> When I was in therapy, we talked about my father a lot, and now I think that he was not that passive actually, he was passive-aggressive. My perception of him as a child was always that he was very passive-deferent to my mother in everything. More recently, I am aware of the fact that he very quietly got what he wanted. You know, he would come home from work and turn on the TV and lie down on the couch and sleep—but if you'd turn the TV off he'd say why did you turn it off, I'm listening to it. But he had very little active role in bringing us up; actually, as far as I was concerned, he was not there.

In contrast to his father, Meir describes his mother as an active and emotionally intense woman who was domineering and over-protective towards her children. Meir was undoubtedly her favorite and she considered him a "genius," expecting him to be "the best in everything." Meir did well at school but was never good enough to satisfy his mother's expectations. Accepting her estimation of his "superior intelligence," he joined his mother in blaming teachers and school authorities for his occasional failures. At the same time, he resented her interference in his relationships with other adults and with his peers, as well as the constant pressure to excel. He recalls embarrassing scenes at school, his mother coming to his rescue, confronting teachers and classmates alike, dragging him home with her in the midst of a school day. Throughout his school years, Meir felt isolated and ridiculed, at once envious of and aloof from his peers, unable to maintain any friendships. Meir describes his childhood as:

> Very lonely, very tense, very unhappy, under constant pressure to produce. I remember being concerned at a very young age that maybe I

was crazy or maybe my mother was crazy. . . . I'd get very upset at the slightest failure and everything was my responsibility. My mother would never let me fight, you know, violence is bad, and in school, whenever I would get into a fight I was told rather than to learn to defend myself to immediately rush to somebody in authority and report it . . . this, of course, produced many more of the same [fights] and I had very few friends and I was, of course, picked on by other kids. . . . I am still very much concerned with violence, the avoidance of violence, but I believe in defending myself now.

Upon his graduation from high school, Meir decided to leave home and chose a college as far from his parents as possible. The move did not relieve his anguish. While fairly successful during his first year in college, he felt increasingly guilty about his failure to substantiate his inflated view of his abilities:

I was brought up in an environment that, as I said, I was told early that I was a genius and, you know, "A" is not enough and I have been near the top of my class, but here [in college] everybody was that, and the situation was such that I could not tolerate it and I started failing and I was very depressed.

He felt completely out of tune with his peers, inadequate and frightened in the face of what he saw as their preoccupation with sexual conquests. Meir himself avoided sexual contacts by carrying on a relationship with a girl by mail "which was basically an excuse, you know, I can't go out with anybody else." When this relationship came to an end, his depression intensified and he sought therapy. Following his therapist's suggestion, he underwent several psychological tests, which proved, his therapist told him, that he was certainly brighter than the average, but not a "genius." The test results convinced Meir to accept the therapist's second suggestion that he should take a leave of absence from college. Meir gave up his academic pursuits temporarily and found a nonchallenging job which allowed him financial independence. At his new job, he was "literally picked up by this girl who was in the process of becoming an Orthodox Jew." He was not ready to say much about this relationship, his first romantic involvement with a woman, except to comment that it was "tense" and that "it was not going anywhere." The two had frequent talks about religion, and in the course of one the girl managed to convince Meir to come with her to spend the Sabbath with her rabbi. In this visit, Meir was instantly converted:

> What convinced me [to become Orthodox] was very simple—I fell in
> love with the rabbi, that's the only expression that describes it. I just fell
> in love with him on the spot. He takes one look at you and you feel that
> he sees completely through you and that he totally accepts you. That was
> a very powerful experience, I was just taken by his dynamism, his
> authority.

Meir's relationship with the girl did not last long. Following his instant conversion, his relationship with the rabbi became the center of his life. He gradually adopted the Jewish Orthodox laws and rituals. Soon, with the rabbi's blessing, Meir moved in to live with the Orthodox Jewish community surrounding him, frequently visiting the rabbi's quarters. At present, Meir does not make any decision, large or small, without consulting the rabbi. He feels protected and accepted in his new life and believes that he is a happier person now. One of the major changes in his life, he feels, concerns his relationship to authority:

> Now I feel much less self-concerned. I am comfortably submissive to
> a higher authority in a way which I was never before. I was very resistant
> to any kind of outside authority, even minor meddling in my patterns.
> Now, I can accept the authority even about things I don't like.

Meir realizes that not all his problems are solved. He occasionally wonders whether his relationship to the rabbi is healthy. He still finds it difficult to maintain close friendships even within the Jewish Orthodox community, and his relatively recent marriage, arranged by the rabbi, is continuously in serious trouble.

Meir's conversion shocked and angered his family:

> My parents were very upset. Their reaction was out of proportion.
> They were really upset, both of them. My mother took it first of all as a
> personal affront, a rejection of their standards. . . . So at the time I was
> becoming religious I was not seeing my parents at all.

It was the rabbi's advice which convinced Meir to "make peace" with his parents: "I have to say, I used that. I said, look, I don't have to have anything to do with you, but the rabbi says I have to, so you'd better accept him because if you don't, then I don't have to accept you." At present, he sees his parents occasionally but complains about his father's inconsiderate attitude towards his religious practices.

Most striking in Meir's conversion is his passionate and irresistible infatuation with the rabbi. God was hardly mentioned in our interview, nor were the Jewish scriptures, the Torah, or the Talmud. Despite his intellectual abilities and academic background, Meir does not describe an intellectual conviction or a discovery of a moral vision, nor does he show interest in the truth value of his beliefs. His choice of Orthodox Judaism seems accidental. It is a by-product of his remarkable love at first sight. It is the powerful figure of the rabbi offering him guidance and acceptance, so clearly missing in his previous life, that transforms him.

The rabbi's tangible, dynamic, and protective authority stands in sharp contrast to Meir's description of his own father as a passive, humiliated figure. This description of an ineffectual father emerged repeatedly in my interviews with religious converts.

The Absent Father

Many converts report absent fathers who died or, more often, disappeared after stormy divorces. Vicki, a Baha'i convert, lost her father when she was six months old. She has no knowledge of the father's personality, background, or occupation. Max, an ex-Presbyterian who also became a Baha'i, lost his father when he was two years old. He, too, has no recollections of his father, but his account of his childhood plainly presents his need for his father:

> I had observed that my friends' families were very different from my own and decided that the thing that was different about them was that they had fathers. So, I asked my mother and she told me right out that my father had died of polio and it did not affect me because I was young, but it made me start to think in terms of searching for my father . . . . I suspect this happened when I was four or five; I began to think of God as my father. I had sought many times for a father figure.

Other converts had had sparse contacts with their fathers, contacts which seem merely to have accentuated the estrangement between them. Smirtana, a 26-year-old Hare Krishna devotee, was a typical case. He volunteered to be the first Hare Krishna devotee to be interviewed and was eager to cooperate with me. His report proved to be a prototype, containing all the principle themes which were to surface repeatedly in my interviews with other members of the Hare

Krishna movement. Smirtana joined the movement in 1970, one year after his graduation from college. His conversion ended a long period of depression which had been intensified by several crises. One of these crises had resulted in his discharge from military service and had eventually precipitated his religious conversion:

> I was going to join the air force. The Vietnam war was still on and that was a commitment that I made, it was a military commitment that I knew I had to face. It was the summer after college. I thought I'd go in the air force for four years and then to the army for three years. I signed up and was just ready to go in—I was at a training center—getting ready to fly to Texas for the training, and suddenly, it was not that I fainted but I was suddenly completely overwhelmed with a voice I heard, telling me, "You are not going, you are not going." I went over and I told the guy that I can't go because I am nuts. Actually, really, I was feeling those last weeks before I went in like I am starting to go crazy—my mind was just so completely divided about what I wanted to do. They were pretty good about it. They got me a meeting with a psychiatrist and I guess he became convinced that I was crazy and so I was officially discharged, declared mentally unfit for the service.

Smirtana characterizes his childhood as "not so bad," certainly happier than his teenage years. Although religion was not regularly practiced in his Methodist family, Smirtana describes his mother as a very pious woman who went through every organized religion in her youth, seeking, in vain, "spiritual satisfaction." Asked about his relationship with his father, he says:

> I can't tell you anything about my father because I did not know him. My parents divorced when I was five and I stayed with my mother and my sister; she is five years older than I am. There was no contact at all with him. Well, we met him last when I was thirteen for an hour and that was after I had not seen him since I was five. Actually, there was one other time, that was when I was in Junior High. He was dying in Canada, he wanted to see me and I went up there—but that was all. Practically, I did not know him.

When asked about his visit to his dying father, Smirtana's response was casual:

> It was not very painful or anything. I guess at the time there may have been some sentiments, but as I said, I practically did not know him and there was no attachment there. It affected my sister more strongly, I guess because she knew him more, but for me it was not much of a loss.

Smirtana's estrangement from his father stands in sharp contrast to his idealized perception of his mother:

> My mother is a very lovable person, people who know her love her. She has some very pious qualities, you know. She is very spiritual, she reads all the time. She is very, very dutiful in terms of her duty to her children and we had a very close relationship, more so than with my sister; my mother and I were very, very close, we could reveal our minds a lot to each other.

The memory of the absent father often provokes overt anger and resentment rather than indifference. Moses, a former Baptist seminarian who had become an Orthodox Jew, seemed suspicious and indignant when asked to describe his childhood relationship with his father:

> See, this is why I was not that enthusiastic about the interview. Why all these questions about my childhood? I'd rather not talk about this. Why is my father relevant? I don't really know him.

Like the parents of Smirtana, Moses's parents divorced when he was four or five years old. Moses stayed with his mother, whom he describes as a very special woman, and with his two older siblings. Thereafter, his contacts with his father were scarce. He had deliberately avoided the father's company:

> I have never liked or respected him. He did try to maintain contact with us and when I was young, I visited him and his new wife a few times. He would sent me money and birthday presents, tried to buy me with his money, but I never wanted to be close to him.

The Withdrawn Father

Passive and withdrawn fathers are also frequent figures in the childhood memories of religious converts. They are remembered by their sons and daughters as distant and ineffectual, too withdrawn to offer guidance or support. Bob is a 36-year-old student who converted to the Baha'i faith. Bob's parents were both physically present as he grew up, but in his perception, they were "pathologically withdrawn." Still, it is the father's withdrawal that appears to be felt more keenly, as is evidenced in Bob's description of his parents and of his childhood relationship with them:

> My father was very quiet, lacking a sense of humor, he would get angry and opinionated at times: I think he was sort of philosophical. I

remember, for example, once we were in a sort of Christian discussion group—that was before he stopped going to Church—and I was really surprised because he talked and brought up all sorts of questions about the nature and existence of God. But he never talked to me like that, never. So I think he had thoughts about things but just did not share them. Whenever we had a discussion or argument between us, it would always be this or that and that's it, he would not vary in his opinions very much, was inflexible, rigid, I would say . . . . Both my parents were very withdrawn, I don't know, I think it was pathological, it was quite a problem for me for a while, actually. My mother was more social, though, of the two, she tried to be more outgoing but she seemed social by force, I mean, she forced herself to be social. At home, she seemed timid and kind of scared all the time. But I had the strongest feelings towards my father, I used to get very angry at him, also feeling guilty or something. For a long time I felt as though he was inferior to me, that he could not take care of me. In fact, for a long time I treated both of them as though they were children, they seemed so helpless. It affected me a lot as I said, over the years I had problems. I was very withdrawn myself and I did not know how to reach my parents. I am not sure how withdrawn or sick my father was but it seemed that there was an element of pathology to it. I felt very unhappy. It was an agonizing time.

In his early adolescence, Bob had found a temporary father substitute in his paternal grandfather. The two had exchanged long and regular letters over a period of several years. This meaningful and influential, but short-lived, relationship underscored Bob's want of parental guidance and approval:

My grandfather was quite literate. He was a colonel in the army. He wrote long letters, wrote about religion quite a bit. He had an influence on me, I would say. Although we did not always agree, we always made up because it was important to me to keep it going, because my father was so quiet, it was difficult to get any kind of guidance from him, really, or even interest. So, with my grandfather, it was mostly the companionship, feeling that he cared, that he would help me. Well, that may be an exaggeration. There were certain things he wanted to get across to me, you might say, his own ideas he wanted to convey, but he took an interest in me and in what I was doing, in my plans.

A perhaps less "pathological" but nonetheless remarkably ineffectual father is portrayed in Sarah's description of her parents. Sarah, a young convert to Judaism, had been raised a Catholic. She described her childhood as "normal" but dominated by two women— her mother and grandmother:

My father is a very quiet, reserved person and my mother is the domineering one. She has very strong, set ideas and my father will go along with anything that my mother thinks is right. I would say I was closer to my mother because whenever there was any kind of decision to made it was up to her you know. If I asked him could I do this or that, he'd always say, "Go ask your mother." You know, anything is fine with him, I just would not get any kind of response from him.

A similar picture of an extremely withdrawn and ineffectual father emerged in my interview with Steve, at present a devout Catholic and a law school student who was raised in an agnostic Presbyterian family. Steve's conversion to Catholicism occurred during his fourth year in college, a few months after his agnostic father had experienced a dramatic religious conversion himself. The conversion, Steve claims, had transformed his father from a mentally ill patient who was "in and out of hospitals most of his life and the doctors were ready to give up on him," into a healthy and content person. A few months later, a similar miraculous cure affected Steve himself, pulling him out of an increasingly morose and suicidal depression:

> It was a very disturbing time. My father was getting worse. At home, life was pretty bad. I did not have any close friends at college and it got really lonely and I was exposed to a lot more ideas and philosophies, to existential philosophies, and I got very morose, I guess, and suicidal, I had many suicidal thoughts. Then, I guess after that year, my father had his religious conversion and I could see that he was changing, making an improvement . . . . So I began to think there may be something to this, and if there is, I have to know, I can't have this be real and not know about it. From my father's experience and from my reading I decided that the way other people found God was to accept him, just to make a leap of faith and say, "I believe." And I did that one night and immediately I felt that I was forgiven for all my sins, for everything, and that I was loved.

Of his childhood relationship with his parents, Steve says:

> My relationship with my parents was kind of distant; there were no hostilities but we were not what you would call intimate. I was certainly much closer to my mother [-Why?] Well, my father was very sick when I was growing up, you know, nervous breakdowns and that kind of thing, and he was very preoccupied with himself, so most of my relationship with him was to keep from antagonizing him and from causing any trouble . . . . I suppose I resented the lack of attention from him. My mother pretty much took care of the family and I was closer to her and my next oldest brother.

In this case, as in previous ones, the anguish associated with childhood emanates primarily from the relationship with the father. While he is depicted as absent, ineffectual, or rejecting, the mother often emerges as supportive, understanding, and capable. It seems likely that the lack of paternal guidance or support had enforced, in these cases, a reliance on the mother as the only source of security and had intensified the intimate bond with her.

This pattern of a weak father and a strong mother appeared more frequently in my interviews with male converts. However, the close bond with the mother and the estrangement from the father was also encountered, albeit less frequently, in women converts' descriptions of their parents. Consider the following, from an interview with a young housewife, a convert to the Baha'i faith:

> In raising us, I don't feel my parents gave me a lot of support emotionally, they don't really talk about feelings. Especially, my father, he deals with things only at an intellectual level, never considers feelings. It affected me strongly because through my teen years especially, I just became very angry. I did not know why, but I was very unhappy. Now I know that my anger was directed at him. I felt closer to my mother, definitely. My mother and I get along really well, most of my difficulties were with my father, my mother was more supportive and understanding.

THE AGGRESSIVE FATHER

A father–child relationship permeated by hostility, antagonism, and rejection also appears frequently in the childhood memories of religious converts. Dave, a Catholic convert, describes it: "My father never appreciated me as a son and I guess I never appreciated him as a father." Rebecca, a withdrawn and timid girl who drops in and out of the Hare Krishna movement, told me:

> My father had troubles as a kid and he did not understand us kids too much. He was not just strict, he did not understand anything you did. You could do nothing right. In fact, I got kind of confused because no matter what you did, it was wrong. My mother was just the opposite, but I was really scared of my father. I hated him. I mean, I knew I was wrong. He did not know what he was doing but he just did not understand and I started hating him.

Margaret, who seems better adjusted and more respected among the Hare Krishna women, describes her father in strikingly similar terms:

> My father was quite cold and hostile toward me, not very under-
> standing and very stern. I have never been very comfortable with him. I
> was always reprimanded for one thing or another.

In the following report of a woman convert who experienced
several intense religious revelations before finally becoming a Catholic, the daughter's response to her father's hostility is concealed by
her highly controlled style and by her eagerness to present the recent
amelioration of her relationship with her parents:

> My attitude in relation to my own faith and Jesus Christ having
> developed in the early 1970s, being transformed to the likeness of what
> Jesus wants it to be. I have come closer to my parents but I never had a
> real closeness to them when I was younger. . . . There was not as broad a
> respect and deeper love as there is now. I have been growing closer to
> them over the past, say, two and a half years, and the relationship is
> really coming to a fullness and depth and appreciation that led to this
> deeper love that, no, I did not have before. They were very strict, espe-
> cially my father. At least I felt so, they were very conservative and a lot of
> that I adhere to, not all, now, but there were times, many times, when he
> was overdoing it . . . . I felt closer to my mother but yet, there was a gap
> there too, really a gap, but, yeah, my father, his image in my mind was
> that of a harsh, authoritarian father who fulfilled his role of rewarding
> and punishing according to your behavior . . . . At times I felt, of course,
> that he was overdoing it.

Ruth Ben-David Blau was a convert from Catholicism to the most
extreme sect of Orthodox Judaism in Israel. As described previously
she became famous in the 1960s for her role in the kidnapping of
Yossele, whose parents were not sufficiently observant in their religion. She then captured public attention once again when she married the leader of the devout Orthodox community in Jerusalem,
many years her senior, despite the vehement objections of his many
zealous followers. In her autobiography (1979), she devotes only a
few paragraphs to her childhood, but the pattern that emerges is
unmistakably familiar:

> From her picture on the wall my mother smiles at me, as if sharing
> my thoughts. How beautiful she was! I really admired her and was proud
> of her when I was a little girl. She has always retained the grace of her
> youth even though her life was not at all easy. Her marriage to my father
> was unhappy. She was good and tolerant, and he impatient and often
> aggressive. Furthermore, he was domineering and I was not a very malle-
> able girl. And so I grew up in a joyless home . . . . It seems to me that her
> life was marred by the fear that one day her unstable husband would

desert her. When I grew up and realized that, I was determined to never depend on the whims of a husband. (p. 9; my translation)

The same pattern emerges in the autobiographical account of Dorothy Day (1952), another remarkable convert who shaped the map of Catholicism in America by founding the Catholic Worker movement. Her mother, Grace, appears often in Day's autobiographical writings. She is described with great admiration as a strong, protective, vivacious, and charming woman, who emerged triumphant from every challenge or hardship the family knew. To her father, on the other hand, Day devotes but one paragraph in her autobiography, *The Long Loneliness* (1952), in which she describes him with distance and detachment. He was often absent, Day tells us, and when he was present, he was impatient and stern with his children. He was a strict disciplinarian, rigid and set in his conservative views, which his daughter describes as an "impulse to protect innocence." He thought women and children should be at home and seldom allowed friends to visit. Throughout her life Dorothy had felt misunderstood by him:

> We children did not know him very well, so we stood in awe of him only learning to talk to him after we had left home. Then he began to treat us as friends, casual friends, since he was always impatient with our ideas and hated the radical movement in which both my sister and I were involved later on, probably his greatest unhappiness came from us. (p. 26)

Roger, a convert to the Baha'i faith, attributes the turmoil of his parents' marriage to his mother's relationship with her own stern and rejecting father:

> My parents' relationship with their own parents was really strange. My mother was not very attached to her own mother although she saw her occasionally. But she was very attached to her father, with whom she did not have a good relationship. She loved him very much and really cared about him, but he never gave her any feedback or love. She could get very upset by something he said even years later.

Of his own father Roger says:

> My father is very emotional and strongly committed to material goals. I have had much trouble relating to him. I was much closer to my mother. I never felt very attached to him and I would have liked to see more affection from him.

For some female converts, the father problem entailed overt sexual themes. While not necessarily bluntly rejecting their daughters, some of the fathers had kindled resentment by their sexually provocative conduct or by their extreme prohibitions of sexuality. Lisa, a convert to Judaism who had been raised a Catholic, describes a sexually provocative father. An infrequent visitor in the life of his four daughters—as his work required prolonged periods of travel—he was, according to Lisa, the "stronger personality" at home and a "relatively warm person." His visits were, nevertheless, a source of distress for Lisa and her three sisters:

> My father very much took to playing around with young girls, and so, especially in my teenage years, there was always the tension that Daddy paid more attention to the daughters than to the wife, which was a difficult position for all of us . . . . In one respect I have hated him because although it never culminated in an overt sexual act, he was always overly sexual with his daughters—fondling and that sort of thing, which made us want to fly out of home very early.

Extreme paternal prohibitions of any semblance of sexual interest are portrayed in the following excerpt from this interview with a young teacher, who became Catholic:

> My father did not get married until he was 50 and that had a lot of ramifications within the family. My mother was 30 at the time they married. This [age difference] was a major part of my life, I felt close to my mother but I guess I disliked my father . . . . My adolescence was really stormy, very difficult because that's where my father comes in—he really discouraged any social life whatsoever, he could not really relate to people. In his own family, his mother had died when he was 12 and his father shortly after. Any relationship that I or my sisters had, normal relationships, dating, could not occur within the family. He was supportive of female relationships, I think it was the sexual element that was really frightening for him. We certainly resented it, my sisters and I, and I think it drove us to maintain certain friends at home but do other kinds of exploring outside of the home.

WHY THE FATHER?

The findings reported here are correlational and one should be cautious in drawing causal inferences from them. The father problem was not the only variable on which converts and nonconverts differed. For example, more converts than nonconverts also tended to express anger towards their mothers. The obvious fact that there are many who have aggressive or ineffectual fathers and who do not become religious converts should also be noted. Hence, the father problem is certainly neither a single nor an entirely sufficient antecedent of religious conversions.

Nevertheless, the findings reported here require special attention: The father problem appears consistently and forcefully in these data, and it seems to loom large not only in childhood memories of converts but in their actual conversion experience, suggesting that this relationship often plays an important role in religious transformations of the kind examined here.

Other, more limited case studies of religious conversion report similar results. Allison (1968, 1969) studied male divinity school students and found that four out of the seven subjects who reported a dramatic religious experience had fathers who were "either adulterers, alcoholics or committed suicide" (1969, p. 31). Similarly, Salzman (1953), suggesting a distinction between "progressive" (adaptive) and "regressive" conversions, traces the "regressive" conversion to a hated father figure.

Examining the confessions of St. Augustine from a psychoanalytic perspective, Kliegerman (1957) traced Augustine's religious conversion to the Oedipal conflict, which was intensified by his apparently close relationship with a dominant and seductive mother and by an ineffectual father. Augustine's mother resented and undermined her pagan, unfaithful husband. Kliegerman observed that St. Augustine's persistent and intense religious doubts were shaped by the struggles aroused in him by this parental strife, and by his unusual involvement with his mother. Kliegerman maintained that Augustine's dramatic conversion experience was precipitated by a visit from his mother which rearoused and intensified the old conflicts of Augustine's youth. The conversion experience established a new equilibrium. It marked the mother's final victory over her husband: "It was her earnest care that Thou, my God, rather than he [natural father] shouldest be my father" (p. 476).

Deutsch (1975), who interviewed and observed 14 followers of the New York-based Meher Baba's cult, describes the majority of fathers as hostile and critical and all but a few of the parental marriages as unhappy. The data presented by Deutsch imply that for at least four of the converts fathers were absent.

The finding that a history of a seemingly nonexistent or turbulent relationship with the father is so frequently characteristic of religious converts raises the following questions: How is the want of fathering implicated in the actual conversion process? What is the chain of events through which ineffectual fathering may participate in bringing about a dramatic change of heart?

In the remainder of this chapter, I will attempt a speculative answer, describing the psychological dynamics that may link the two factors: the relationship to the father and the religious conversion. I shall start with Freud's interpretation of a religious experience, which assigns the father a central role. I will then discuss the role of the father in personality and moral development, delineating the ramifications of his absence or inadequacy. Finally I will describe conversions which center on an intense attachment to an authority figure, illustrating how the convert's relationship with his or her father may be involved in the conversion experience itself. This discussion will necessarily simplify the complexity and uniqueness of the parent–child relationship and of the life histories of the individual converts whose cases will be presented. It nevertheless captures, I believe, a pattern through which many instances of religious conversion evolve.

Freud's Interpretation of a Religious Experience

Freud believed than humans endow God with features that they have attributed to their own fathers in childhood. Our relationship to God, he argued, is always modeled after our relationship with our biological father, fluctuating and changing with it.

The psychoanalytic view holds that one source of the need for religious beliefs lies in children's inevitable disappointments in their parents. Once disappointed by the figures whom they have perceived as omnipotent and unconditionally protective, children transfer these perceptions and expectations to a new superior figure. Thus the child's wish for utter protection by an invincible power lives on in the religious beliefs of the adult. According to psychoanalytical theory, a second source of the need for religious beliefs lies in the Oedipal situation. Religious beliefs and the rituals which accompany them may be viewed as an expression of the boy's efforts to atone for his guilt over his desire to displace his actual father.

Freud thus assumed deep and universal roots for the belief in the perfect authority, in God, but he made no secret of his own atheism and of his view that people would be better off without what he viewed as a false umbrella. In *The Future of an Illusion* (1961/1927), he depicted religious belief as a fantasy wish fulfillment, as an illusion which distorts the reality of the human condition. The belief in an omnipotent God, he argued, provides people with an illusory father, sparing them the recognition of their own helplessness. Claiming that the path to human improvement cannot be found in the pursuit of an illusion, Freud concluded that people should seek truth and salvation on earth.

Freud's interpretation of a case of religious conversion is a logical extension of these ideas. In response to a letter he received from an American physician, Freud wrote "A Religious Experience" (1953/1928), his only paper dealing directly with the experience of religious conversion. The physician's letter protested psychoanalysis' disparaging views of religion and described his conversion experience: while at the morgue, the physician, then an intern, had seen the corpse of a "sweet-faced dear old woman" being carried into the dissecting room. This sight had aroused in him intense doubts about the existence of God: "There is no God; if there were a God, he would not have allowed this dear old woman to be brought into the dissecting room." That afternoon the intern determined to discontinue going to church. While meditating on this matter, he also heard a voice warning him: "I should consider the step I was about to take." Several days of unsettling religious doubts followed, culminating in a religious experience in which the intern accepted Christ again:

> God made it clear to me that the teachings about Jesus Christ were true and that Jesus was our only hope. After such a clear revelation I accepted the Bible as God's word and Jesus Christ as my personal saviour. (Freud, 1953/1928, p. 244)

The death of an old lady, sweet as she may be, is the way of the world. Freud reminds us: "God, as we know, allows horrors to take place of a kind very different from the removal to the dissecting room of the dead body of a pleasant-looking old woman" (p. 245). The intern's agitation seems unwarranted and puzzling. Why should a sight common enough to medical students impress him so intensely and trigger off such indignation against God? Freud's interpretation seeks to unmask the motives underlying the religious turnabout, which in his analysis becomes a repetition of the past rather than a transformation of it. The significance of the episode at the morgue, he suggests, lies in its symbolic tie to the Oedipal situation in which the male child perceives his father as the threatening rival for the mother's love. The intern's undue indignation is, according to Freud, the remnant of this archaic competition. The sight of a "sweet old woman" aroused in the young intern a longing for his mother. This longing, in turn, stirred the complementing emotion of anger toward his father for "taking her away" and a wish to dispose of him as a rival. This wish was expressed, consciously, as indignation and doubts in God's existence. Insofar as these religious sentiments are conscious manifestations of a rearoused Oedipal wish to "save" the mother from the father's possession, they are anxiety-laden and cannot persist. The intense anxiety stems from the young man's childish fears that his father will retaliate. This anxiety is manifested in the inner voices uttering warnings against resistance to God. In childhood, the original Oedipal struggle is resolved for the male child by a complete submission to the will of the father. The religious doubts in this case are met with a similar fate: They are quelled by inner voices warning against resistance to God, and the young man feels compelled to accept the religious teachings of his childhood and submit to the will of God. Freud points out that in the physician's letter there is no mention of arguments in justification of God's deeds, nor are we told what "clear revelations" removed the doubts in His existence. The reasons for the turnabout must therefore lie elsewhere.

In keeping with his views on religion as the pursuit of an illusion, Freud describes the conversion experience as a defensive process used to reduce anxiety. In this process an all-out surrender to an illusory father figure replaces and distorts the real but unconscious anger toward the natural father. The doubts and ensuing change of heart are epiphenomena, by-products of archaic needs. The religious conversion is an attempt to control anxiety over childhood conflicts between rearoused Oedipal rage towards the father and the fear of his retaliation that is stirred again prior to the conversion.

Freud concluded his paper with the statement "By no means can every case of conversion be understood as easily as this one" (p. 246). Indeed, not every case and not as easily. The Freudian interpretation is consistent with the findings associating the father figure with the experience of conversion (cf. also Rizzuto, 1981), but it does not fully explain them. It is concerned with the internal dynamics immediately preceding the experience and with the universal psychological themes thereby revealed. Emanating from universal Oedipal longings, the experience of the intern could have been the experience of any male, irrespective of his particular, unique relationship with his father. The analysis of this case does not elucidate, then, the various effects of fathers who were in actuality absent, withdrawn, or aggressive, as were the fathers of many converts in my sample. In addition, the Freudian interpretation of this case relies on the Oedipal urges of the male child. It is therefore less helpful in elucidating the experience of female converts, who are, according to my data, about as likely as males to report a history of inadequate fathering.

Why is the sudden infatuation and voluntary submission to a higher authority more likely to occur in the lives of individuals, men or women, whose fathers were absent, withdrawn, or rejecting? The answer is clarified when one examines the father's role in the normal course of personality and moral development.

THE FATHER'S ROLE IN DEVELOPMENT

The mother's primary role in the early years of childhood cannot be overestimated. Yet, as is increasingly becoming the consensus among psychologists (e.g., Abelin, 1975; Damon, 1983; Lamb, 1975, 1981; Ross, 1979), one should not assume that fathers function simply as occasional mother substitutes. Rather, they have an important and independent role to play in the child's socialization, and their absence or inadequacy often places their children at a disadvantage. Developmental research links father absence to subsequent problems in a number of areas such as sex role adaptation, inhibition of aggression, and ability to delay gratification. It indicates, in these cases, an increased probability of subsequent delinquency, depression, and suicide attempts (Biller and Meredith, 1974; Lynn, 1974). Domineering fathers were found to be associated with low achievement motivation in their sons, and conversely, high availability and warmth of the father seem to foster academic performance, social adjustment, identity formation, and sex role adaptation in both boys and girls (Enright, Lapsley, Drivas, and Fehr, 1980; Leonard, 1966; Lynn, 1974; Hetherington, 1972).

Three related functions can be identified as the special, though certainly not exclusive, arena of the father. First, insofar as he tends to be perceived by the child as the stronger adult figure, the father endows laws and constraints with authority, inhibiting impulses and imposing a meaningful structure on behavior. Second, as the traditional mediator between the family and the outside world, he promises protection from external dangers, assuring the child of her or his own eventual ability to cope with them. Third, as a different "significant other" within the family orbit, the father offers a necessary counterpart to the mother–infant relationship, aiding the differentiation of a separate sense of self.

Father as Inhibitor

The development of a conscience or, using the language of psychoanalysis, of a superego supplies the standards of right and wrong and the motivation to abide by them. Psychoanalytic writings on superego formation center on the superego development of the male child and point to the father as the primary motivating figure in this development. In Freud's view, the child's acceptance of the moral demands of his or her social environment is a derivative of the appearance of the father, in the child's eyes, as vindictive and powerful. This appearance is, in turn, dependent upon the Oedipal urges of the child and upon the male child's perception of the father as his sexual rival, that is, upon the male child's wishes to become the sole possessor of his mother and upon his simultaneous dread of the father's anticipated retaliation for these wishes, which is visualized in the male child's fantasy as the threat of castration. When these fears of the father are intense enough, and Freud thought that normally they are, the result is a complete renunciation of the Oedipal wishes and an identification with the invincible father, which alleviates the male child's feelings of powerlessness. He cannot beat his father; he therefore joins him. He defends against the retaliatory father not only by repressing the Oedipal wishes but by emulating the father's characteristics. This identification marks the victory, albeit shaky, of culture over nature. With it the male child establishes a set of internally imposed constraints, which Freud labeled the *superego*. Prior to the formation of the superego, morality consists of the dread of being discovered; there exists no internal set of rules and obligations. The resolution of the Oedipal conflict coincides with the generation of feelings of guilt and shame and of internal limits on gratification, which are stabilized into a structure of prohibitions and ideals.

In this formulation the superego is modeled upon an internal image of the father, not upon the father as he is. This internal image is bound to be vindictive and harsh, Freud argues, for it is based on the male child's own inevitable aggressive wishes.

The introjected father is likely to be more punitive than the real father for it is not only the father's real aggressiveness that defines the internal image. This image is also based on the strength of the male child's Oedipal wishes and the intensity of the aggression which arises in him, in response to the father's retaliation as anticipated in fantasy (Schafer, 1960).

The superego can be irrationally harsh and demanding. The harsher the introjected image of the father, the more arbitrarily punitive and irrational the superego. Thus, in the Freudian formulation of moral development it is the internal image of the father as vindictive and powerful, an image which is not necessarily reflective of the father's actual conduct, which is the principle generator of an uncompromising conscience in males.

Psychoanalysis models female development on the male child's development, attributing to girls similar desires and fears. As is well known, Freud's account of female development has attracted much criticism. For our purposes, suffice it to say that according to Freud the girl does not experience the boy's intense fear of the father's retaliation. Since she cannot fear castration, she lacks the motive to "identify with the aggressor," to introject the father's demands. Therefore, Freud (1953/1905) thought, women's superego is never as demanding, as impersonal, as independent of its emotional origin as the superego is in men.

The Freudian account of superego development thus rests on three arguments. First, it is the male child's fear of the father, resulting in an automatic, defensive submission to his authority, which lays the foundation for the superego. Second, the fear of the father is derived primarily from the father's appearance in the male child's eye as the sexual rival and from the child's own aggressive impulses. That is, the fearful image of the father is primarily a consequence of the Oedipal situation. It is these two stipulations which predict sex differences in moral development, placing the female at a disadvantage. Finally, there is the stipulation that this sequence of moral development is a universal one, predetermined by the child's own urges and fantasies.

But this formulation neglects the consequences of the father's actual conduct, his very real, not fantasized, presence or absence, acceptance or rejection.

In normal development, in the average acceptable environment, it is not necessarily the fear of the father that motivates an identification with him and his demands. Other powerful motives for identification with him, such as the fact that the father is perceived as exercising control over the environment, may invite emulation of his characteristics. In fact, there are indications that discipline encounters with parents that are based principally on the fear of parental power and the anticipation of parental sanctions result in learning hostility towards the self and towards others, rather than in guilt and ideals. Parental discipline that is based upon the daily experience of parental warmth and upon the information the parent provides about the consequences of the child's behavior seems to be more important in fostering the development of a reasonable moral code in both boys and girls (Block, 1971; Hoffman, 1983; Maccoby, 1980). Second, to the extent that fear of the father does play a role in the internalization of moral demands, this fear need not derive from the Oedipal drama alone. It may reflect the child's cognitive structure: at this stage of their cognitive development, children are particularly sensitive to physical dimensions and readily attach considerable significance to them. The sheer size and physical strength of the father undoubtedly enhance his appearance to children of both sexes as omnipotent and potentially frightening. The child's tendency to interpret rules literally, to ignore exceptions, and to perceive prohibitions as irreversible and awesome would reinforce further a harsh internal portrait of paternal authority. The cognitive peculiarities of the child may alone or in combination with the Oedipal wishes augment the harsher aspects of the father's internal image.

Finally, the internal image of the father is not untouched by the child's transactions with the real world: It is shaped to a great extent by the father's actual conduct.

In his discussion of "loving and beloved" aspects of the superego, Schafer (1960) describes the crucial role of an actual involvement with a benevolent father figure: "By imposing meaningful limits on behavior and by administering real punishment it corrects the terrifying archaic fantasies of punishment introduced by the child in his struggle with his own impulses" (p. 194). The father, if present and benevolent, tames the child's fantasies of his aggression. The daily encounters with him modify the harsh and omnipotent aspects of the internal image, and the ensuing conscience is less arbitrary and less irrational. When the father is in reality hostile and rejecting, the real transactions with him may tend to confirm the child's worst fantasies of retribution. When the father has suddenly left—especially if he has left at an age in which the child's egocentric thinking processes color events as reflecting his or her own faults or merits—there is no opportunity for testing the reality, and the child's fantasies of the omnipotent and vindictive father may be carried into adulthood.

FATHER AS PROTECTOR

In his traditional role as mediator between the family and the outer world, the father's presence promises protection from external dangers and assures the child's perception of her or his environment as safe. The father's competence may contribute to the perception of him as aggressor and intensify the fear and rage toward him, but at the same time, it is this very strength which also assures the child of the father's ability to protect and which arouses pride in this protection. Herein lies the inevitable ambivalence of the child's reaction to paternal authority: accompanying the child's fear and rage are his or her pride in the assurance and protection this authority provides.

The lack of paternal protection exacerbates the child's perception of reality outside the home as sinister and unreliable. Such perception prevails in the world view of many contemporary converts. My interviews with Hare Krishna devotees, especially, are filled with charged descriptions of the sinister, violent reality the devotees claim to have left behind. For example: "Women are not given ample protection, they are left to wander on their own . . . they become like prostitutes . . . elderly people are sent to homes to rot." And "What is there to the material world, only the forces of darkness, the forces of darkness come upon you and you don't even realize." Or "Everybody is messed up, you know, people that are not messed up don't go around killing other people and they [don't] use their time on all these temporary pleasures."

In the eyes of these religious converts the world "out there" is populated with hypocrites, vicious competitors and manipulators. The People's Temple cult is again an instructive, albeit extreme, example. Jones generated the megalomaniac accusations of persecution by hostile authorities but his accusations fell on fertile ground. The members of the People's Temple cult were ready to share his delusions, for in their experience the external world was indeed sinister and dangerous. The fact that converts—especially, although by no means exclusively, converts in cults—tend to portray the external environment in these dark hues does not only indicate a deliberate attempt to attract potential new converts and to prevent defection of present members; it also corresponds to the world view of individuals who did not experience the guidance and protection of benevolent parental figures.

We may conclude that the presence of a strong yet benevolent father figure provides protection from two dangers: As the benevolent inhibitor, the father may impose a meaningful structure on behavior, securing the child's ability to handle the internal danger posed by his or her own impulses. Insofar as he serves as a mediator between the family and the outside world, the father aids in securing the child's perception of reality outside the home as safe and malleable rather than sinister and manipulating. An absent father, a father who is ineffectual and withdrawn, or a father who is in actuality harsh and rejecting leaves the child wanting in these two consequential aspects of socialization, inducing a search for structure and protection.

Religious conversion may be an expression of as well as an attempted solution for these consequences of inadequate fathering. Religion provides imperative guidelines for behavior, inhibiting impulses and producing structure and stability, all with the promise of protection from an omnipotent authority. The infatuation with authority reflects the lingering effects of unmodified childhood fantasies of the father's omnipotence and ruthlessness and, at the same time, it provides the protection, acceptance, and guidelines he withheld.

Clearly, setting limits on impulses and promising protection are not solely the domain of the father. Many mothers take over these functions, and in the everyday life of relatively intact families, both parents may serve a variety of functions. But it is difficult for any woman or man to effectively serve as mother and father simultaneously. Furthermore, the mother's relationship with and her view of the absent father is an important predictor of the child's future adjustment (Damon, 1983). The mother, especially a mother who is angered or disillusioned by her husband's desertion or withdrawal, is unlikely to be able to act as a source of unconditional nurture and, at the same time, facilitate meaningful constraints over impulses and mastery of the environment. That this is indeed a difficult task becomes evident when one considers the father's third function, his role vis-à-vis the mother–child dyad.

THE FATHER AS ENHANCING DIFFERENTIATION

For both boys and girls, development begins with a close tie with the mother, from which the child eventually separates. The presence of the father as a different, significant other within the family orbit aids this process of separation from the secure, yet potentially restrictive bond with one caregiver. The father's typically less frequent but more exuberant and challenging interactions with the infant (Lamb, 1980; Clark-Stewart, 1978) enhance the infant's awareness of a separate body and the exploration of space, which may aid the consolidation of a sense of a differentiated self (Abelin, 1975; Lamb, 1980; Ross, 1979). In subsequent stages, the father becomes a crucial figure in the development of a gender identity for both boys and girls, although his presence is particularly important for boys, who need, in Greenson's (1968) words, to "dis-identify" from the mother—that is, to renounce the closeness with her—in order to develop both as individuals and as males.

When the father is unavailable or ineffectual the chances of an overdependence on the mother increase. Converts, especially male converts, whose fathers were absent, withdrawn or rejecting tended to report positive and close relationships with their mothers. The closeness often entailed special bonds: "My father preferred my sisters, my mother preferred me. I was the golden boy," says a convert to Catholicism who describes his father as extremely stern and rejecting. Smirtana, the Hare Krishna devotee who was abandoned by his father at the age of four, says:

> My mother and I were really, really close. We could reveal our minds a lot to each other as I was growing up. We discussed everything, spending hours at the dinner table . . . again, we were very close, we could talk for hours, there was a real friendship there, too.

Another convert to Catholicism describes his mother as an intense, emotional, and dramatic woman who "clearly had special ambitions for me as her only son."

Similarly, a Jewish convert to Catholicism explains his mother's dismay and anger at his conversion: "She had a lot at stake . . . . I was going to be her success story."

Two Hare Krishna women who had described their fathers as relentlessly hostile and their mothers as the counterpole had this to say: "My mother and I were really close, she was a very kind and loving person," and "My mother is a saint, everybody loves her." For some, the mother emerges as extremely overprotective and possessive, and her demands for special intimacy provoke resentment:

> My mother is very sensitive and concerned. I am not sure sometimes why she is so concerned about us, always seems to want the best for us but it is always what she feels is best. I know she is not selfish although she may appear that way, but . . . I would rather have my mother to have more of a life of her own than be so involved with me.

Dick, a lawyer in his early 40s who defines himself as a Hebrew Christian, tells how, when he was 8 or 9 years old, he became seriously ill and, at about the same time, his father disappeared. For a while, he stayed with his Jewish maternal grandparents, but it was his mother who had "nursed him back to life." Dick goes on to relate the special bond with his mother but he is aware of the distress it has caused:

> I had a great deal of guilt and I just did not know how to get rid of it. I knew, for example, that my mother relied on me much more than she should have because she had such great difficulties with my father, who eventually ran off with her best friend . . . and I realized she was asking me to fill in the gap. Even when I was in the service I had to call her, see her on vacations, make up for what was missing in her life, and I did not know how to get rid of the guilt.

In other reports the intense bond with the mother is manifested in less obvious ways. The mother of one Hare Krishna devotee experienced a dramatic conversion herself shortly after her son's conversion, and the mother of a Baha'i convert had joined the same group the same night her daughter converted.

When the father is absent, ineffectual, or rejecting and the mother is the only source of security, as seems to be the case for many of the converts, the process of separation and individuation becomes at once more urgent and more arduous. The father's unavailability or animosity intensifies the need for the mother's protection. At the same time, it may blur the boundaries of the relationship with her. In his study of conversion experiences in male divinity school students, Allison (1969) claims that the conversion experience, in providing a substitute father, may also provide "a protector against the regressive nostalgia for the undifferentiated union with the mother and serves thereby in aiding the process of individuation and differentiation" (p. 36). Through the conversion, the convert finds not only an inhibitor and protector to replace a father who is deficient in these respects but also a shield from the seductive unity with the mother. By filling these two roles the relationship with a benevolent authority provided by the conversion experience helps consolidate the convert's previously shaky sense of identity. But conversion may also allow partial fulfillment of the "wish to unite with the mother." Indeed, as we shall see later, in lieu of or in addition to providing authority and structure, the conversion often promises renewal of the blissful, nondemanding, and totally protective relationship usually associated with early maternal care. The following excerpts exemplify such "maternal" features in the religious conversion. They reveal the converts' need to cling to a love object that is totally protective and nondemanding. Describing his conversion from Judaism to Christianity, Ben, who finally became a convert to the Baha'i faith, says:

> I could start a relationship with someone [Christ] who would never really cause me pain and this relationship was something I always knew I wanted all along . . . this relationship seemed to me perfect because I would be getting everything I wanted and not having to do anything I did not want to do.

Another male convert describes the "baptism of the Holy Spirit" which he had experienced in the process of converting from Judaism to Christianity:

> It was like being drunk . . . I was lying in bed and it was like a blanket of love . . . you become like a baby, like a helpless child, like getting food. I just cannot function and He [Christ] takes care of me.

In a discussion of "father-god, mother-goddess" concepts in religions, Grollman (1963) characterizes Judaism as primarily a father religion, which emphasizes superego demands, and Christianity as a mother religion, which emphasizes love and forgiveness. It is interesting to note that the above quotations, in which the "maternal" components of the conversion are particularly clear, describe conversions from Judaism to Christianity.

Indeed, a number of the converts who had turned away from Judaism portrayed the God they had left as harsh and demanding. This is most clearly articulated by Barbara, a new Christian. In her perception, she has turned away from demands and discipline into unconditional acceptance. She has found enthusiasm and approval without effort and without sacrifice. Asked why she did not look for the comfort she was seeking in Judaism, the religion of her upbringing, she replies:

> If you read the Bible and realize how much law you would have to live under, that would be very overwhelming to me, I don't think I could

live under that law, I choose to live under Grace. It would be too harsh a thing for me to live under all these rules, I would not make it.

THE FATHER FIGURE IN THE CONVERSION PROCESS

The absence, withdrawal, or hostility of the father places specific obstacles in the individual's development. It may affect children's perspective on moral prohibitions and may hamper their perception of the environment as safe and masterable. It renders difficult, especially for boys, the process of separating from maternal care. A religious conversion, whereby an inhibitory structure is imposed and the protection of an omnipotent authority figure is supplied, offers ways of bypassing these obstacles while simultaneously reflecting them. If this is truly the case, we would expect to find the father figure and the remnants of the conflicts generated by paternal unavailability or animosity in the accounts of the process of religious conversion itself. The father figure is indeed implicated not only in the converts' memories of childhood but in the very process of conversion. Consider the case of Meir presented earlier.

The ramifications of the ineffectual fathering that Meir described are revealed in his life prior to his conversion, when Meir was guided by arbitrary and perfectionistic demands to be a "genius"—demands which he inevitably failed to meet. He seemed to be fearful of his own impulses, avoiding at all costs contacts with women and any opportunities to express aggression.

Two important changes in Meir's life preceded his conversion experience. First, as a result of his therapy he tried to give up his inflated self-image and to relax the harsh demands imposed by it. He attempted to adopt a lifestyle less inhibiting and less pressured. All of this served to increase his awareness of "internal dangers"—those sexual and aggressive impulses which, until now, he had managed to avoid. Second, he became intimately involved with a woman. These two changes are likely to have intensified Meir's need for a protective father figure. One may speculate that the prospect of an intimate relationship was extremely threatening for him. In his experience, intimacy with a woman entails suffocating overprotectiveness. He may fear the prospect of losing his separate identity, of becoming, like his father, passive and despised. Submission to the rabbi provides him with the strong paternal model which will prevent repetition of his engulfment by his mother. It postpones the dangers of intimacy and offers him a new set of values through which to define himself as separate and independent from his parents. The conversion has also offered him clear and manageable prohibitions of his impulses. It allows partial expression of his anger towards his parents. Like his father, he is now behaving in a passive-aggressive fashion, using the rabbi's authority to confront them. An expression of his sexual impulses through his subsequent marriage now becomes possible as well, since it is sanctioned by the authority of a father figure.

Meir's case is compatible with Freud's interpretation of the conversion experience. Prior to his conversion, Meir had started his first relationship with a woman, a girl who had, in his own words "practically picked me up." The girl's attention to Meir may have rearoused the pleasures as well as the threats interwoven in his uninterrupted entanglement with his mother, whom he had described as overprotecting and possessive. From a psychoanalytic point of view, being the mother's uncontested favorite, in essence victorious over his father, may have intensified Meir's fears and his fantasies of retribution. Prior to the conversion these fears were manifested, perhaps, in his exaggerated response to the "meddling in his affairs" of any authority figure and in his concern with violence. The new relationship may have rearoused Oedipal longings. These, in turn, would have rearoused the fears of retribution, activating a defensive process of submission to a powerful new father figure: the rabbi.

Certainly, Meir's conversion may have served several functions. But in terms of his childhood relationship with his parents, the submission to the rabbi compensates both for his anger and for his "victory" over his passive father. The rabbi's acceptance relieves him from his guilt and from fears of retribution.

In Meir's case, the conversion was initiated by a timely encounter with a powerful benevolent authority. Though Meir did not directly refer to his own father when recounting his crucial meeting with the rabbi, his sudden conversion seems to make better sense when we consider this relationship. Other similar cases show direct references to the real father. Consider the following from a woman converted from Christianity to Hare Krishna:

> When I started chanting, there was this picture of the Spiritual Master in the room and I was looking at it and when I started chanting it was, I suddenly felt, that the Spiritual Master is my father. I felt so much love for him, I wanted to satisfy him. There was so much joy, it was something I never felt with my own father.

A Jewish woman, who describes a stressful childhood and a stormy, angry relationship with both her parents, became an Evangelical Christian a few months after her father had a heart attack and after he had stopped talking to her. She describes, thus, her final conversion experience:

> One day I was doing the dishes and I never read the gospel of John but it was clear in my heart that the Lord told me to go read John 14. I went up to the bedroom and I opened the book and saw "Let not your heart be troubled nor let it be afraid, I am with you," and then it said, "If you have known me you would have known the father," and I thought, wow, that's what I wanted to know, that's what I really wanted to know.

The following cases will illustrate the various guises in which the father figure appears in the conversion experience. In the first, the consequences of the father's absence are particularly apparent in the account of the events precipitating conversion. In the second, the imprint of the father is prominent in the preconversion and postconversion relationship with God, a relationship that seems to reflect and perpetuate the convert's attitudes towards her father. In the third, the conversion is a by-product of a total surrender to a much older lover.

THE CASE OF DONALD

Donald is the 30-year-old president of a local Hare Krishna temple. When I asked for his permission to interview the Hare Krishna devotees, he gave his consent with the provision that he be interviewed first "to see what kind of questions you are going to ask." Like other temple presidents in the Hare Krishna movement, Donald is the unchallenged authority. With me, Donald was cooperative but indirectly hostile. On the one hand, he often put down his fellow devotees as if joining me in an outsider's attitude, claiming his superiority over them. On the other hand, he repeatedly announced his contempt for and distrust of all psychologists and his disdain toward those in the outside world who are busy in the "stupid" pursuit of "fame and PhD."

Donald grew up in a nonpracticing Presbyterian family. When he was four years old, his parents divorced and his father left the family, never to be seen again by his son. Donald does not remember the circumstances of his parents' divorce. He does not know whether his father is still alive and does not care to find out. He describes his mother as "very simple, not very spiritually inclined, but I had a good relationship with her, not unusually close, you know, normal, close enough." Although his recollections of his early childhood are very vague, Donald remembers his maternal grandmother and her frequent visits as a source of strife and distress for both his mother and himself. He also concedes that through his childhood and adolescence he felt lonely and rejected, but he hastens to add that "everybody feels lonely, we are all alone in this material world." His peers in high school were "disgusting, just getting drunk, trying to make it with some woman," and Donald disliked their company: "I was trying to become a real person, more authentic. I was dissatisfied with relationships; I thought they were superficial." Despite his contemptuous attitude toward his peers, Donald adopted what he perceived as their impulsive and exploitative lifestyle. These were the stormy days of the early 1960s and Donald took part in his friends' political activities and in their experimentation with drugs. He began to take LSD and other drugs regularly. He became infatuated with an older sports instructor, formed a musical group with him, and began touring the country. But Donald soon began to feel betrayed by his friend: "I don't remember the details now, it is not important, but I have discovered that he really exploited me." The musical partnership fell apart and Donald looked for other occupations. He tried college for a while but dropped out after a quarrel with the school authorities, whom he describes as "hypocrites" and "ignorants." Again, he joined a musical group and became dependent on its members. But he still felt a pawn in a game directed by others:

> I was really dissatisfied with myself as a person. I realized that I was a very superficial person, I was not really sure of who I was, that I was putting on a show for others. I was bewildered by it, I didn't understand

how to become authentic . . . . It was like what Shakespeare said that all the world is a stage and people are the players. We are all players in this game and I felt I was putting on a show for others for different reasons.

After several months, Donald joined a commune:

> I wanted to get away from all that, to live on a farm, to relax. At this period I wanted to devote myself to music. I was not interested in working because I wanted to do music and this was just not possible—so we decided to make our money by dealing with drugs.

He was picked by the commune leader to smuggle drugs across the Mexican border. He resented being chosen but could not resist: "That was pretty heavy. I went up there [across the border] just by associating with these filthy people, this man who was dealing with cocaine, etc. I myself did not take drugs any more and I didn't want to be there; it was not a good influence on me." When the supply of drugs and money dwindled, his struggle with the commune leader intensified: "Again he was on me to get more—get more [drugs]— and I did not want to go again, I was feeling like I was pushed into the situation but I did not want to go and I didn't know how to stop this process of being forced into this position I didn't want to be in." It was at this point, as he tried to fight back the demands of his commune peers, that Donald experienced a dramatic religious conversion:

> I just suddenly got this realization that God was there. It was a feeling of tremendous love through him, that he was always there, that he was with me on the farm. I looked back at my life and saw how insignificant all the material achievements were . . . . I understood that God the Father, that God was a person who loved me and I was rejecting him. It was very overwhelming.

Donald was already familiar with the Hare Krishna movement and interpreted his experience as a "glimpse of Krishna." Instead of supplying the drugs, he drove to the nearest Hare Krishna temple:

> The [realization] experience did not last long, as usually these experiences don't last long on this bodily platform. It was dark again . . . the forces of the material world were coming back upon me, I had to get the money, had to go on another trip but because of the revelation I decided to drive to the temple instead and it was a very rewarding experience, just to go there and see the purity of the lifestyle.

One of the principle unifying themes in Donald's life is his response of contemptuous anger and simultaneous submission to authority figures. He volunteers only a vague description of his childhood, and his account of his life is somewhat obscured by the Hare Krishna jargon. It is clear, however, that throughout his life he has been attached to and, in his perception, betrayed by a number of authority figures: the sports instructor, the school authorities, the commune leader. It would be an oversimplification to trace Donald's erratic and alienated life and his sense of himself as unauthentic and superficial to the absence of his father alone, but it is likely that his ambivalent attitude towards authority is related to this fact. His relationship with authority is permeated by rage and simultaneous fear. These emotions may have been intensified by Donald's clash with the authority figure in the commune, precipitating his conversion experience. Donald felt helpless and enraged by the demands for more drugs and by the "filthy person" who made them. And yet he could not resist these demands. The leader's authority was too powerful and the dangers of directly challenging him too threatening, perhaps not only in Donald's fantasy. It was only through an attachment to a new, benevolent, omnipotent, and protective authority that Donald was able to rebel. By accepting the love of this eternal father, and aligning himself with an omnipotent God, he is now able to withstand the real and fantasized retribution of the "material" authority.

As in Meir's case, the qualities Donald found in his "new father" seem antithetical to those of his biological father. In the religious experience, the father becomes an all-encompassing presence, a loving but rejected father. By attributing these qualities to the newly found authority, Donald is guaranteed the consistent paternal love he found lacking in his childhood. No longer is the love of the authority figure given by whim. No longer does Donald feel that he is being manipulated by alien powers. This perception of God reduces, at least temporarily, Donald's vulnerability to external powers and enables him to resist the commune leader's manipulations.

Meir's and Donald's conversion experiences exemplify the replacement of an unavailable father by an accepting and powerful authority figure. In the following case, the conversion did not replace the actual father with a perfect loving one. Rather, it may be seen as accentuating and perpetuating the convert's childhood perception of a ruthless, punitive father.

THE CASE OF JANET

Janet became an Orthodox Jew at the age of 17. At the time of the interview, she was 24 years old, a shy and soft-spoken woman. She needed continuous encouragement throughout our interview. Janet was currently working as a salesperson in an optometrist's shop and claimed that she was "not smart enough" for higher education. Her responses to my questions conveyed, however, a sharp intelligence and a moving sincerity.

Janet grew up as an only child. Her three, much older siblings left home when she was an infant: "The closest to me in age is already 10 years older, so there is such a big difference, they were grown up and gone by the time I even have childhood memories." Janet's parents had been brought up in practicing Jewish homes but her father had rejected his religion, so Judaism was not practiced throughout Janet's childhood.

Janet's mother was a believer and would have liked to "keep a religious home" but was not strong enough to oppose the father's atheism. When she was five, Janet's parents divorced after 25 years of marriage. Janet recalls the experience as extremely traumatic: "It was a very violent divorce, lots of hostility and bitterness between the two, lots of fights." The father left and Janet stayed with her mother, becoming the mother's only source of comfort as the other siblings sided with the father. Janet seems to have internalized the mother's anger and bitterness towards her husband:

> She [the mother] remained bitter for a long time and would talk to me a lot about her anger . . . . I don't really know my father even though I know where he lives and everything, I just prefer not to see him . . . . When I was little he would come to visit regularly once or twice a week for a long time, and I tried to be out, over at a friend's house, every time I knew he was coming.

And yet Janet seems also to admire her father, describing him as "very smart, very successful in his work and in his new marriage." Her childhood was not happy:

> I was very lonely and very unhappy. I was not close to my sisters and brothers. Because of the divorce, I was not very successful in school or in making friends, I would not play at all with the other children. I'm really not sure why, whether I did not want them or they did not want me . . . . I was characterized as very withdrawn and very introverted.

Although she did not have any formal religious education, Janet recalls being interested in God throughout her childhood, an interest that was sustained by the mother's Bible stories and her frequent references to her own disillusionment in God. Janet thinks that her mother's religious disillusionment was related to her feelings for her husband: "I think that the divorce also has to do with why my mother was not religious. She was so disillusioned in the marriage that she also got disillusioned with God, even though I think she still believed in Him." In high school, Janet learned about the Holocaust: "I became very angry too [like the mother]. I guess I thought that if He could forget us like that, then I am going to forget Him—and for a few years I did just that." This intense anger and disillusionment sparked a period of rebellion: "I called myself an atheist, I was involved in radical politics, I was very vehement about the women's movement, I wanted to fight the world. I still want to do that sometimes, but now, it is not so desperate." The rebellion did not relieve her feelings of isolation and worthlessness, and she remained withdrawn and intro-verted, unwilling or unable to share her peer's preoccupations: "I was dissatisfied with my friends, my peer groups at home. A lot of them were beginning to take drugs and I didn't want to do that, and the other group was also very high-school-oriented, football and things like that and I didn't want to go that way either."

A few months before her 17th birthday, Janet was involved in a car accident. This further deepened her depression and led, eventually, to her religious conversion:

> I was driving and there was a friend of mine in there and he was injured, I was injured too. We were both all right, you know, objectively speaking, it was not as bad as it affected me emotionally. I very much overreacted to it . . . . I started spending a lot of time by myself, even more than I did before, thinking . . . mostly I felt very guilty about the car accident.

Her religious conversion occurred shortly after this traumatic event. One Friday night, "out of the blue," Janet decided to go to the

Orthodox services at the neighborhood synagogue. After the services, she asked the rabbi if she could join his study group. She had decided that she wanted to learn the Halacha, the strict Jewish Orthodox Law, and gradually began practicing it. She sees her conversion not as a dramatic transformation, but as a gradual change which she cannot explain. Her only explanation for her conversion is curious: "I started keeping the commandments, not for God but in a spite of God kind of thing. I wanted to prove something, I wanted to show Him, I guess, that we exist even though He deserted us."

Despite her perception of her conversion as gradual, Janet realizes that others in her immediate environment saw it as a sudden and intense transformation, related to her accident. The only one who was not surprised, Janet claims, was her mother, who by her own account had expected and waited all along for her daughter's religious conversion.

Janet's current adherence to the Halacha is absolute and demanding. As a member of several Bible study groups, she attends at least one every night. Recently, she has embarked upon a lifetime mission of memorizing several volumes of elaborate interpretations of the Old Testament. She feels she is competing with those who have known and practiced the Halacha since their childhood, those who were brought up in a religious environment. She feels that she has to "make up" for all the years she has lost. Janet recognizes that this overload of religious chores may serve a defensive function:

> I know I'm a lot happier now, I just don't get as depressed as I used to. It may just be because I have other things to think about. I have always had this very bad self-image, like if I made a mistake I would overreact to it. Now it is much better because the Orthodox way of life is so structured. You can learn the rules of how to do things and I have learned all these rules so I don't make so many mistakes, though, if I do, I still get very depressed about it. I don't know, maybe there is something still there, just covered up, although once it does not bother me, I prefer not to think about it.

Janet's conversion differs in some important respects from the conversion experiences described earlier. It did not involve a sudden realization and instant relief, nor a "falling in love." She did not feel absolved and unconditionally accepted by a religious authority. But her experience still reflects an intense, albeit ambivalent, attachment to God's authority. Rather than willingly surrendering to the authority's love and protection, she chose to fight it. She converted "in spite of God," not for Him. Through her conversion she claimed to declare her defiance and anger toward the authority for "deserting us." Her perception of God's desertion produced an unexpected, contradictory consequence: She attempted to punish Him, to call attention to her own existence by accepting His laws. The contradiction is settled when one considers her attitude toward God in light of her attitude toward her biological father.

Janet's perception that God deserted His followers reflects her acute awareness of injustice in the real world. It was her response to the inexplicable horror of the Holocaust, as well as to her own near brush with death in the car accident. At the same time, this perception and her need to "prove" something to God, to declare her existence, constitutes a remarkable parallel to her childhood attitude toward her father. He, too, had deserted her, and in retaliation she bluntly rejected his visits by going to visit friends whenever she knew he would be coming. She was envious of her siblings, who, in her perception, enjoyed the father's acceptance and was tormented by guilt and by a conviction of her worthlessness, as manifested in intense depressions and what she described as "a very bad self-image." In her childhood fantasies, Janet may have interpreted her father's violent departure as her own fault, a result of her own mistakes: Her parents had been together for 25 years, caring for their other children until she came along and "ruined" their "happiness."

Janet described her adolescence as a period of rebellion. She had rejected God's existence and had attempted to "fight the world." The car accident, occurring as it did in the midst of this period of rebellion, may have been interpreted by Janet, again, as a well-deserved reprisal. The accident may have thus intensified her conviction of her guilt as well as her conviction of God's power. In this manner the car accident aborted her attempt to directly rebel and defy authority. Through her conversion, she attempted once again to express her defiance and anger. But her rebellion this time was intended as a reminder of her own existence. It was also a "safe" rebellion. Recognizing the power of God, she sought the means of appeasing Him, of winning His protection, and of perhaps magically undoing His desertion and atoning for her guilt. She was also competing with those who had been born into an Orthodox way of life. If she could only memorize all the rules, if she could make no more mistakes, she would join those who were lucky enough to be born into the father's protection, like her own siblings.

In many respects, Janet blurs the distinction between her father and God in much the same manner that her mother did. The mother traced her own disillusionment with God to her own disillusionment with her husband. For Janet the mother's religious views are juxtaposed to her father's atheism. The strife between the parents and the father's desertion are amalgamated with religious beliefs. Janet's conversion is, then, not so clearly a defiance of God as it is a defiance of her father, for through it, she sides with her mother against the father's values. Through her conversion Janet wins her mother's fight with the father's atheism. At the same time, she defends herself against anticipated reprisal by holding on to the strict rules which will prevent mistakes.

The overlap between parental disputes and religious sentiments is not unusual in the reports of religious converts. When religious disputes between parents occur, it is invariably the mother who is described as religious or "spiritually inclined" while the father is actively opposed or indifferent to the religion.

Ruth, a convert to Catholicism, is an extreme example of this pattern. Asked about her parents' religious affiliation, Ruth says:

> That's a long story. My mother is Baptist now, she was Methodist until my father told her that he did not want her to be Methodist and then she became Baptist. My father was originally Methodist and then became Unitarian for a short while and now he is a pretty well-set atheist. My mother was very religious, my father was antireligious. See, I never dared make a commitment because it was always strong battles between my parents, always arguing about it. It was not that much of an open fight, it was more like a cold war. There was just this tension in the house, you never dared mention it . . . . I never dared making a religious commitment because it would have meant siding with one parent against the other.

In college, after a series of traumatic events, Ruth did make a religious commitment and became Catholic. She describes her father's reaction:

> The thing that kept me from doing it [converting] sooner was that I discussed it with my father and he had told me that if I did he would

disown me—which, in fact, he did . . . . We wrote a long series of letters. He wrote very bitter, very terrible letters . . . . He still did not change his mind; he speaks with me now but he is still very angry about it . . . . He has finally realized that it is his problem, not mine. He is very disappointed in me but he realizes that I am still his daughter. I suppose he does not love me any less but he does not respect me.

THE CASE OF CATHLEEN

Cathleen, a 30-year-old teacher, converted to Catholicism in her early 20s. She is the eldest of three daughters born to middle-class Methodist parents. Cathleen reports that her parents attempted to bring their daughters up within the church but that faith was not an important facet of family life. Her father, a bank clerk, was 50 years old when he married her mother—herself a 30-year-old schoolteacher at the time. The marriage had been prearranged and was a "very stable one," although, as Cathleen perceives it, her parents were ill-suited to each other. She describes her mother as an intellectual, "a real explorer," impelled to ask questions and to share ideas, and her father as the opposite—rigid, silent, and narrow-minded. She felt close to her mother, who was more dominant at home, and admired the mother's aspirations and intellectual curiosity. She felt distant from and resentful of her father, who "did not know how to relate to people" and could not tolerate any of his daughters' relationships. Cathleen remembers her early childhood as stable and happy, her adolescence as stormy and painful:

> My teens were really stormy . . . I was trying to find an outlet, I was feeling very frustrated, other kids were dating and going to parties, etc. Because of my father, that kind of thing did not come naturally to me or to my sisters; they ultimately went "off the deep end," as the saying goes, socially, [they] got involved with the black community, and with drugs and drug dealings, they got involved with the "wrong people," so to speak.

Cathleen herself stayed away from drugs until much later in her life; but she, too, got involved, early in her teens, with the "wrong people"—in her case a man in her neighborhood, married and 20 years her senior, with whom she carried on a prolonged love affair. She knew that the knowledge of this relationship would horrify her parents. She now views this affair as a necessary battle for independence:

> I was dating him secretly for two years and that split me away from my family and introduced me to a whole realm of experience which was against the norm. I think, ultimately, it was the only way that I could break away from my family and get into a relationship with a man that was meaningful. When I look back at it, it all seems bizarre. I guess in some way I always felt part of a counterculture because of that.

The clandestine liaison continued throughout her years in college and contributed to another split between Cathleen and her home environment:

> I was programmed in one direction—I was very academic and my whole goal in life was to get a PhD; that's what my mother wanted for me and that's what I wanted for myself. I went to college, still going out with that married man, which meant that I did not get the usual college experience. All of a sudden I was getting B's and C's instead of my usual A's, and I lost interest in math, which was my major.

A year after she had graduated from college and was still stumbling toward her goal of a PhD, she felt empty and lonely. The relationship with her married lover ended, and she joined a small commune run by an ex-professor, who had been fired for his radical politics, and by the anarchist-communist woman he was living with. Cathleen did not share their political views. Politics, she says, had never been of any interest to her, but she had been intrigued and attracted by the dominant presence of the commune leaders. Throughout a long and difficult year, she became immersed in the group and let its leaders run her life. At the end of that year, she met William, the man who was to become the "master" of her life for several years. Once again, she chose to devote herself to a man 25 years her senior. In her view, this relationship became the cause for her religious conversion:

> What happened there was really my conversion, in the sense that I met a man. He was about 45 to 50. He was the strongest influence on my life for the next seven years, so strong that I finally had to go to a psychiatrist for what I consider literally exorcising him from my life. He had been raised a Catholic, left the church, divorced three times, and lived an amazingly dissolute life, starting a period of real poverty. But he had the ability to talk, he could talk for 24 hours straight, and I would just sit there and listen. He was interested in my ideas, he really had charisma and he

gave me a sense of identity and meaning. He had not been a practicing Catholic but, within the first two years that I knew him, he was getting back into the church and I, at the end of the two years, I was baptized as Catholic. Needless to say, I lost all interest in biology. I left the commune—that was also his suggestion—and I did not know where I was going. I was intrigued by his talk about Catholicism. I decided that Catholicism was the genuine true religion. It had the mystery and the wisdom of the ages attached to it. Those were years when I was not close to my family. They did not like him, everybody who knew me did not like him, he had such power over me that I think everybody was upset because he was totally dominating my mind, my thoughts, ultimately I lent him incredible amounts of money, my car, he just had total power over me.

Becoming Catholic strengthened Cathleen's involvement with William, but it did not change her lifestyle "one iota." Although she started to go to Mass every Sunday, her conversion, she recalls, felt unreal, isolated from the rest of her life. She did not feel emotionally moved or transformed by it. But the conversion won her the approval of her mentor and severed her last ties with all other influences in her life. Her parents, appalled by her relationship with William, were alienated further by her conversion to a church which they disliked and by Cathleen's infuriating attempts to convert them. The more she tried to proselytize, the angrier they—and she—became.

Although she did not abandon her desire to get a PhD, she felt unable to pursue her goal in any constructive way. About a year after her conversion, she followed William's urging and moved from her hometown to another city, expecting to get a doctorate there. She started dating William's son, a man of her age, all the while maintaining her attachment to his father through letters and endless phone conversations. This triangular arrangement lasted for two years, during which time Cathleen felt increasingly confused and listless. She had serious difficulties functioning at her job and experienced a severe writing block which made it impossible for her to continue working towards her PhD. Realizing that "something was not right at all," she began therapy with a Jesuit psychiatrist. In the process of therapy she finally managed to "exorcise" William out of her life: "This, to me, was like regaining my identity: I got back my identity and my self-respect." In the process she also realized that " I had no desire for a PhD." Convinced that she had been pursuing a goal her mother had set for her, she turned to a career in teaching.

With these changes came a new affirmation of her religious faith. She began attending Mass every day, looking for a support group; she developed "a secret bond with people to whom believing was important" and describes being "moved to tears" by the beauty of the religious ritual. She refers to these experiences as her "true" religious conversion.

Cathleen's story repeats the by now familiar pattern: she, too, describes a close relationship with an idealized mother and a resentment of her father. Her attachments to men so much older than she may reflect her difficulties with her father and yet her longing for him. Indeed, her initial religious conversion began with an infatuation with and total devotion to a paternal figure.

But Cathleen's conversion to Catholicism also reveals the fragility and instability of her own sense of self. Her conversion was a part of assuming an identity designed for her by her lover. Throughout her adolescence and early adulthood, she experienced great difficulties maintaining her independence. In all her relationships her autonomy was easily thwarted. She turned away from her parents early in her adolescence only to submit to the authority of her first lover, who further alienated her from family and friends. She describes her political involvement and counterculture lifestyle not as the product of convictions but as reactions to the dicta of commune members whose personalities she had found intriguing. At the same time she had struggled, for a long time unsuccessfully, to separate her own wishes from the goals her mother had set for her. Cathleen's story provides an extreme example of Carol Gilligan's (1982) and others' (e.g., Baker-Miller, 1985) arguments that place relationships and empathy at the center of women's development of a sense of self. Contrary to what seems to be the typical developmental process for men, who proceed from a premise of separation and autonomy and for whom identity precedes intimacy, Cathleen's adult life began with a total fusion with another, and her coming of age consisted of gaining some measure of autonomy.

Her initial conversion shows how difficult it was for her to differentiate from an idealized companion. Her conversion was part of a process of assuming aspirations, commitments, and goals set for her by another. As she herself realizes, in her religious conversion she "borrowed" the religious beliefs of the "master" of her life. Consequently, for several years her religious life remained inauthentic and fragmented. For several years she felt like an impostor.

Notwithstanding other themes prominent in Cathleen's story, the vicissitudes of her religious life are related to her struggle to separate from her parents, and, subsequently, to "regain" her identity. These themes, most often associated with the psychological tasks of adolescence, are described in more detail in the following chapters.

3

The Infatuation with the Group
Conversion and Social Influence

Linda is a Jewish woman who became a devout Christian at the age of 20. Her religious turnabout occurred in the midst of a typical, though unusually intense adolescent struggle. When she left home for the first time to go to college, she felt overwhelmed and bewildered by the lack of structure in her life and by the perils of impending sexual involvements:

> There was increasing confusion, maybe about what my place in the world was, the alternatives in college were so broad, drugs and lots of men. You know, all of a sudden going out with lots of guys and the choices of sexual involvement and being easily influenced . . . all that presented a lot of confusing choices and I was not very happy with the choices I made.

During this period in which Linda's confusion and loss of direction "got to a frenzy," she learned that some of her peers had become Christians. Initially, she was skeptical, even scornful, but was finally persuaded to visit one of her born-again friends who had moved to the West Coast. She traveled to visit him accompanied by another skeptical but hopeful friend and discovered that the stories she had heard were true: the person whom she remembered as a desperate drug addict seemed to have become a peaceful young man, serene and confident and exuding a clear sense of direction. She felt envious of him and of his new group of peers: "I wanted what they had, I wanted this vitality." In the presence of this group of young, zealous Christians, she had her conversion experience. It was in a group meeting that she followed the exhortations of her reformed peers to surrender to God. Following their suggestions to let go of her doubts and to surrender rather than struggle, she had prayed for the Spirit to take over her life. As they had promised, she immediately felt a sense of peace and love, a confidence that her prayer had been heard. Her conversion did not revolve around an authority figure. Instead, it seems to have occurred through the attachment to a new group of peers.

About half (47 percent) of the converts in my sample either experienced their conversion in the presence of a group of peers or were initially introduced to their new faith by zealous converted peers.

The infatuation with a group may be the consequence of the efforts of groups to recruit new members. Indeed, powerful group dynamics often play a role in the religious conversion. The processes that incite the change of heart may include direct pressure and persuasion techniques known by the often misused terms *brainwashing* and *thought control*. In other religious gatherings, the convert may be drawn by the less menacing and less direct, but no less powerful, techniques by which all groups can exert their influence on an individual. This chapter will delineate the power as well as the limitations of group process in inducing a transformation of the self.

CONVERSION AND PROCESSES OF SOCIAL INFLUENCE

The thoughts, feelings, and behavior of individuals are influenced by others in their social environment. Social influence is transmitted not only through the interpersonal, subjective dialogue between the person and those specific others who are important to him or her, as stressed in the psychoanalytic tradition, but also through the relatively impersonal context provided by social structure. The various groups into which we are born, which we join or which we value become important sources of validation of our feelings and beliefs. They take part in shaping our identity and may therefore participate in its transformation.

Three concepts typically describe the transmission of social influence and its effect upon the individual. These are social roles, which are the parts we are called upon to play as members in a social structure; social norms, which provide the prescriptions and the scripts that define a given social role; and reference groups, which are the particular audience whose judgment the person values and to whom he or she looks for direction and approval.

That subtle social pressures exerted by roles, norms, and reference groups influence religious stance is evident by the long list of social background variables that predict religious experience. Sex, race, age, socioeconomic status, parents' religion, and marital status all bear a relationship to the religious belief and practices of the individual (Argyle and Beit Halahmi, 1975). In the USA, for example, blacks are more likely than whites to attend religious services and to consider religion as important in their lives. Religion has traditionally served more social functions in the black community, and holding or at least reporting religious experiences receives greater social support in this community. Socioeconomic status typically influences how religion is practiced. Lower socioeconomic status is associated with more religious Fundamentalism and with a more frequent report of mystical experiences (Bateson and Ventis, 1982). Strong norms and the subtle pressures of reference groups apparently play a part in maintaining the religious affiliation and the religious behavior which are consistent with one's race or socioeconomic status.

The influence that reference groups exert over the individual stems not only from the goals of the group but from persons' needs to compare their feelings and beliefs to those of others and to evaluate themselves relative to others. The more ambiguous or nonobjective the belief, the greater the tendency to rely on social comparison for its validation (Festinger, 1954). Norms provided by reference groups direct our behavior because we are motivated to abide by them in order to avoid the psychological consequences of deviation and nonconformity. The more cohesive the group—that is, the greater the forces operating to maintain membership in the group—the greater the influence of the group's norms.

The subtle pressure exerted by groups effects long-term changes to the extent that the pressure is internalized, namely, to the extent that it is felt as the individual's choice to promote beliefs and goals that she or he values, to remain in the social setting that feels comfortable, and to engage in behavior that she or he deems appropriate.

Roles, norms, and reference groups thus typically explain the continuity and the similarity of beliefs and behavior between parents and children, within communities of similar backgrounds, and within different cultures. They help describe the relatively smooth process through which presumably separate individuals become members in a stable and continuous social structure and perpetuate the core beliefs, values, and prescriptions of their social setting. But the religious conversion experiences studied here typically entail a radical departure from the links that tie most of us to the small (e.g., family) as well as large (e.g., socioeconomic-status) groups of which we are a part. For Linda, for example, encountering the group of zealous Christian peers erased quite suddenly and unexpectedly her previous bonds to the religion of her upbringing as well as to the areligious, permissive, and politically active college environment of which she was a part. In this and similar cases a new group, often far removed in beliefs and practices from groups which were previously important, becomes the sole source of guidance and approval.

What are the processes of social influence that may account for a sudden discovery, internalization, and maintenance of a new set of beliefs that require a total commitment of the self?

A gradual shift of beliefs may be the result of a change in social environment which introduces the person to new reference groups. The subtle influence of reference groups on a change in beliefs was first demonstrated by Newcomb's (1943) classic study of political attitudes at Bennington College. At the time of the study the women students at the college came mostly from wealthy and conservative families affiliated with the Republican Party, but the college community was liberal. Newcomb's main finding was that with each year in the college environment the students moved farther away from the conservative political attitudes of their parents and closer to the more liberal attitudes prevailing at the college. The political shift reflected for most women a deliberate choice between the two reference groups. Newcomb's findings were repeated in scores of investigations which demonstrate the subtle and mostly unintentional influence of reference groups (Bem, 1979).

Indeed, social influence is most clearly at work in those functions of the conversion experience that draw the individual into an intense interaction with a new group. It is most evident in the conversion experiences that occur in the midst of a group meeting and in the future adherence to the new beliefs among those who have joined a tight religious community.

The influence of others may also become evident at the final stages of exploring the new faith. For example, increased contact with devout followers of the new group increases the likelihood of conversion.

Hierich (1977) studied a large sample of Catholic Pentecostals at the time this movement held a controversial status within the Catholic church. He compared a control sample of professed Catholics to a sample of Catholic Pentecostal converts, namely, those who reported receiving the baptism of the Holy Spirit. At the time these data were collected (1969) the Pentecostal movement within the Catholic church involved a radical redefinition of Christianity and Catholicism and a reaffirmation of past commitment to "Christ and His Church." These conversion experiences seem to fall in the middle of the range of definition of religious conversions. They involve less radical a shift of world view and practices than most of the conversions I examined but are a more dramatic shift of position than is experienced by "converts" among Protestant Evangelists or members of Protestant Pentecostal sects who continuously seek and hope for conversion.

Hierich examined the relative impact of stress, of previous socialization, and of immediate social influence on the process of conversion. Indicators of stress included self-report of stressful events and/or presence of major role shifts (widowhood, divorce, change of occupational plans, entering university) in the two-year period preceding conversion. But Hierich did not distinguish the severe from the mild forms of stress (e.g., divorce vs. entering university) and did not examine stress during childhood and adolescence. Indicators of previous socialization included attending parochial schools and being the eldest child of devout parents. Immediate social influence was measured by frequency of attendance at Mass (assuming it represents accessibility to proselytizers), by previous friendships with Catholic Pentecostals, and by positive reactions from close friends or relatives during the period of exploration. Hierich concluded from a careful analysis of these data that stress as measured in the study had little impact on conversion: 83 percent of the Catholic converts reported exposure to stress but 66 percent of the controls also reported personal stress as measured by Hierich. Previous socialization also proved unrelated to conversion. Indicators of social influence proved, on the other hand, to be more powerful predictors of conversion. An "encapsulation" process whereby potential converts were not exposed to discordant information and increasingly spent more time with persons who had received the baptism seemed to be at work for many of the converts. For example, a fifth of the converts reported that they spent less time with regular companions during the time they were exploring the movement, and 56 percent reported spending noticeably more time during the exploration period with others who had received the Pentecostal signs. However, there was a high proportion of converts (70 percent) for whom full encapsulation did not occur, a finding indicating that encapsulation is not a necessary condition for conversion. Furthermore, examining the circumstances under which social influences have most impact, Hierich (1977) concludes that "the impact of social networks is striking indeed—*for those already oriented towards a religious quest*" (p. 673; italics in the original). The route that conversion takes for those who are already religious seekers is clearly influenced by social contacts. In the process of conversion the seeker makes use of the available social networks, but if one is not already a religious seeker such contact is insufficient. It thus seems likely that when it occurs, the process of encapsulation reflects the prospective convert's choice of social contacts that are meaningful in the context of a growing attraction to the group rather than his or her unintentional surrender to social influence.

Social influence is more noticeable once the potential convert has become a frequent participant in the group's functions. Several group processes then shape the religious quest among those orientated towards it. In the following I will describe the major processes through which groups increase the likelihood of religious conversion.

Religious groups often require of prospective members a public denunciation of their previous ties. The new group then becomes the sole source of social comparison and the only significant reference group. In another study of commitment to a Pentecostal church, Virginia Hine (1970) points to "an observable act of bridge burning," an act in which former affiliations are explicitly denounced, as essential in inducing commitment to the new group. In this act the convert announces his or her rejection of former groups. Once the old connections are severed, the convert is compelled to hold on to the new ties and to justify the denunciation of the old ones. Both purposes are met by an increased emotional commitment to the group, by abiding by its rules, and by adopting the new world view it proclaims. Hine also reports that converts' conviction and emotional commitment to the new community intensify with an increase in actual participation in the group's activities. She argues that it is the actions per se, and the frequent contact with veteran members of the group which these actions involve that account for the increased commitment. Once again, these processes affect those who are already frequent visitors of the church.

The potential convert who is present on the scene in which a group engages in a uniform performance is exposed to powerful expectations that influence participation in beliefs and rituals that may seem bizarre to the outsider.

Glossolalia is a trancelike state, also known as *speaking in tongues*, in which foreign-sounding syllables uttered without conscious control are interpreted by the believer as a visitation of the Holy Spirit. Felicitas Goodman (1972), who studied this religious experience in a cross-cultural anthropological investigation, reports that the practicing glossolalists she studied in different churches appeared normal and well adjusted to their social environment. She argues that the trancelike state is learned by explicit "explanations" given by the pastor, and by imitating others who have experienced it, and is induced in the individual by the sheer force of the cultural expectation that it will occur. Noting that while studying glossolalia, and frequently observing the rituals during which visitations occurred, she had been herself on the verge of experiencing this phenomenon, Goodman argues that the religious trance can be activated in anyone who happens to be in the right place at the right time.

The setting of religious revival meetings, or of similar religious gatherings for purposes of proselytizing, is likely to induce experiences of physiological arousal in the participants, for example, by demanding repeated chanting. The likelihood of conversion increases in these settings. Experiencing physiological arousal, the participant looks for a label, for an interpretation of the arousal, in the immediate environment. The potential convert is then likely to interpret the experience in the terms provided by the group, namely, as a religious revelation of a particular kind (Proudfoot and Shaver, 1975). Similarly, religious groups often demand of newcomers demonstrative acts of commitment and sacrifice prior to the teaching of the new faith. Linda's peers suggested that she put aside her doubts and arguments and pray first. Asking potential recruits to "do" first with the promise that the understanding will follow is a practice that promotes conversion, for having engaged in these elaborate and sometimes taxing acts or rituals without sufficient prior reason, the person is bound to look for a way of justifying his or her actions, and the most accessible justification is the new beliefs. The religious group then offers the solution for a dilemma which it has itself produced.

Direct or indirect suggestions generated by the group and by the situation in which the conversion occurs do shape the form that the religious experience takes. As Jerome Frank (1974) observed, no one in a Billy Graham crusade has converted to Buddhism. Indeed, in many conversion stories, the particular interpretation of the experience and the religious beliefs and lifestyle which are thereby adopted are clearly provided by the cues, the information, or the models available in the immediate context in which the experience occurred. Consider Donald, a convert who described a typical revelation experience that seemed no different from many others centering on a realization of God's love and personal interest. The realization, which could have been interpreted in numerous ways, happened to precipitate his joining the nearest Hare Krishna temple. He interpreted the experience not as a message from Christ, nor from the God of Israel, but as a "glimpse of Krishna" for he had recently learned about the Hare Krishna movement from his peers. In a similar case, a religious experience resulted in a conversion to Catholicism because the Catholic church had been "the most visible on campus."

Group process is most influential in determining the future maintenance of the new beliefs. The presence of continued group support is important in cementing the new commitments. Festinger, Riecken, and Schachter's (1956) classic work on a prophecy that failed provides a dramatic illustration of this process.

A back-page headline of the *Lake City Herald* drew the attention of these investigators. The newspaper reported the claims of a suburban "clairvoyant" that visitors from outer space had "contacted" her to warn the city dwellers of a flood which would destroy the city on December 21 of that year. The three social psychologists and most of the believers in the prophet's mission, some of whom had given up jobs and possessions and had publicly declared their devotion to the prophet, gathered together at her house on the eve of doom's day. The prophet announced that a special messenger would arrive at midnight to lead the believers to safety in outer space. When midnight passed and the prophecy failed, believers became depressed and apprehensive. Toward morning, however, a new message was received which changed the group's mood. The prophet now declared that the true belief and prayers of the small group had canceled the impending disaster and saved the world. Those believers who had stayed with the prophet awaiting their savior on the eve of doom's day became more intensely convinced of the prophet's extraordinary powers and engaged in fervent proselytizing. Others who had not been able to join the group that night for various reasons left the faith following the failure of the prophecy. Continued group support was then, necessary for the future maintenance of the new beliefs.

Continued group support helps maintain the new beliefs by creating environments in which either new information can be avoided or other persons support one's own beliefs, by soliciting active participation in actions and sacrifices that enhance the commitment to the ideology that justifies them. Finally, group support creates solidarity and a commitment to the group that prevents "relapsing" which will let the group down. It should be noted, however, that these determinants of the persistence of the change of heart may not be identical with the determinants of its cause.

CONVERSION AND THOUGHT REFORM

The making of converts in the religious groups new to this culture has been compared to the coercive thought-reform programs employed in China and in the Soviet Union to modify a political world view (Bromley and Richardson, 1983; Glock and Bellah, 1976; Ofshe and Singer, 1986). Several techniques are described in the literature as effective in producing and maintaining these conversions.

During the revolution led by Mao-Tse-tung, the Chinese undertook a vast project of "reeducation," "thought reform," and "political study" which critically examined individual lives and thoughts in relationship to revolutionary doctrine. Lifton (1961) described the methods used by the Chinese to transform dissidents and intellectuals into believers and loyal members of the new communist society. The thought reform process was aimed, according to Lifton, at transforming the "filial son" or "filial daughter" into the "filial communist," that is, at replacing the traditional Chinese emphasis on family life by a devotion to the all-encompassing and ever-present "revolutionary family." The great and programmatic shift of emphasis included an imagined messianic utopia that resembled the very religious mode that the revolution condemned (Lifton, 1979, p. 288).

Based on his study of Chinese communist thought reform or "brainwashing" techniques, Lifton identified several criteria for ideological totalism which clearly apply to extremist religious cults that have recently flourished in America and elsewhere.

Ideological totalism, according to Lifton, takes the form of an all-or-none subjugation of the self to an idea system. Claiming exclusive possession of truth, the totalistic environment attempts to control all communication within it. Claiming that it contains the key to absolute virtue, the totalistic environment mobilizes shame and guilt in order to eliminate "poisons" or "impurity." It imposes a demand for total exposure of the individual member or "a cult of confessions" and public denunciation of sins. Claiming a monopoly on immortalizing ideas, it presents them as a "sacred science" that combines the authority of a scientific method with the sacredness of a Divine Word. On the basis of that "sacred science," the totalistic environment institutes a jargon, a "loading of the language" in a way that eliminates ambiguity and presents definitive-sounding answers even to the most complex human problems. The totalistic environment imposes a principle of "doctrine over person" which presses the individual to reshape direct experience and past history in ways that fit the doctrinal mold. Finally, totalistic environments assume that there is only one valid mode of being and hence draw a sharp distinction between those who possess the right to exist and those who do not.

Lifton's work on Chinese thought-reform provided a preliminary description of the techniques that may be effective in producing and maintaining a subjugation of the self to an ideological system.

In the Chinese form, these techniques relied less on physical torture and more on psychological means, especially on the manipulations of group processes in an attempt to secure a transformed self (Frank, 1974). Physical maltreatment, especially in the form of loss of sleep, was sometimes present but it was not essential for the process of "reeducation." Psychological harassment was always present. In fact, the more dramatic "conversions" occurred in violence-free settings, in which participants were coerced not by physical torture but by peer pressures (Ofshe and Singer, 1986).

The initial stage of the indoctrination invariably involves intense emotional arousal. The targets were already in a state of extreme emotional arousal when brought into the camp, prison, or revolutionary university. The disorganizing emotional state was enhanced by their progressive isolation from other prisoners who might have shared their world views, by creating uncertainty and anxiety about the future, by personal humiliation, and by unpredictable shifts from leniency to harsh treatment. Secondly, total milieu control was used to cut prisoners off from all previous social ties and to immerse them completely in the new milieu. Ties among prisoners who might have shared the same world view were prevented, and authorities broke off group cohesiveness among prisoners, for example, by transferring leaders. Every prisoner was emotionally isolated from every other prisoner, and his or her privacy was manipulated, forcing prisoners to appeal only to the system for guidance. The prisoners were immersed completely in a communist communication system in which information input from the outside world was reduced and systematically manipulated, while "output" which conformed to the communist world view was rewarded. This communication system also created a linguistic polarization between "God categories" used to embody the revolutionary vision versus "devil terms" (e.g., *demons, devils, monsters, freaks*) used to describe political enemies. In the thought reform procedure, the devils were "capitalists," "imperialists," and "members of the exploiting classes," whereas the Party, the people, and communism were "on the side of history," promising progress and immortality (Lifton, 1979, p. 323).

Finally, and especially in the thought reform process used in the Soviet Union, the process of reeducation culminated in a confession produced in the context of an intense relationship between the prisoner and a powerful interrogator. The thought reform process forced a participation of the prisoner in the confession. The prisoner was responsible for "building up" the confession, providing the details of the previous, misguided life. He or she was required to participate in and initiate criticism of others and to demonstrate enthusiasm in the process. The completion of the "confession" guaranteed relief and joy. In return for complete self-submission, the prisoner was offered release from suffering and apprehension and warm acceptance by the group (Frank, 1974).

There are differences between the process of thought reform and the process of conversion in religious groups.

Firstly, the potential convert arrives voluntarily at the set on which a religious group stages its persuasive drama.

Secondly, at least in the initial stages of the process, the capacity to exert total control over the milieu of the potential convert is more limited even in the more extremely isolated, sectarian religious groups.

Finally, the new religious groups cannot back their demands for compliance by the use of force.

Nevertheless, the process of induction into present-day cults bears a resemblance to the thought-reform or manipulative-influence techniques used in the totalistic environments described by Lifton (1961) and others (e.g., Segal, 1957; Schein, 1961).

The process of recruitment into the Unification Church (the Moonies) involves such programmatic and deliberate use of techniques of social influence. According to Lofland (1977), the initial step in the recruitment process is the "pickup"—a random contact with a "seeker" through front organizations not identified with the church. The "seeker" is invited to dinner, a lecture, or both, and the hosts typically deny the religious aspects of the gathering. Throughout this initial contact the place exudes friendliness and solicitude. Newcomers are assigned a "buddy," and veteran members are instructed to show personal interest in newcomers, to treat them as special and important. During this initial gathering, there is usually a general noncontroversial lecture on "principles" which again fails to identify the church, and newcomers are invited to a weekend retreat. Those who are "hooked" and who return for the retreat find themselves in a totalistic environment. The day is tightly scheduled. From 7:30 in the morning to 11:00 at night the newcomer does not have a moment of privacy; even trips to the bathroom are escorted by a "buddy." The planned activities all occur in groups. There is no physical restraint of participants but leaving is strongly discouraged. Information input is controlled by the organizers. Newspapers, radios, TVs are not allowed. The activities are planned to induce physical exhaustion: there are lectures a few hours each day, food is Spartan, sleep is controlled, and "fun" activities are physical and intense (e.g., gardening, contest dancing). As we shall see later, emotions play a major role in this process. For now, suffice it to say that throughout the weekend retreat the prospective members are drenched by love and approval and made to feel special and wanted, but their fear of the outside world is also manipulated by pointing out the dire consequences of returning to the "demonic" world.

Another thorough and well-controlled investigation of membership in the Unification Church reports induction procedures that center on shifting the social ties of the potential convert to committed members of the organization and on continuous monitoring by peers (Galanter, 1980). In the 21-day workshop designed by the church to introduce potential new members to its teachings, Unification Church affiliates constitute half of the membership. During the workshop, guests are constantly in contact with the hosts who originally invited them and with other committed members of the church. The workshops are tightly scheduled in planned group activities: religious discussions, sharing experiences, singing, sports. Participants spend virtually all their time in small or large groups where more than half of the people present are active members in the church. This technique of mixing "successful" veterans and initiates in joint group experiences is often used by contemporary "self-help" groups (e.g., Alcoholics Anonymous). By offering many opportunities for imitating and identifying with successful members this technique promotes within the newcomer a strong sense of solidarity with the group.

In a study of the Christian community ("Jesus People"), the induction of new members to this group is also described as primarily dependent on peer pressure similar to the reeducation methods used by the Chinese during the cultural revolution. At the first stage of the induction, the newcomer is awarded a special status and is engulfed by lavish waves of warm interpersonal contacts. The group soon "closes in," however, setting clear demands, expectations, rigid time tables, rewards, and threats, which shape behavior in the new direction desired by the group (Harder, Richardson, and Simmonds, 1972).

Hustlers of Orthodox Judaism in Israel organize weekend retreats and marathon sessions that resemble those organized by EST, in which ties with the outside world are prevented, in which the audience is alternately praised and humiliated, and in which public confession is encouraged. In the course of these sessions, the few who remain skeptical are subjected to increasing pressures from the group to halt their belligerent questioning or else to voice their doubts elsewhere.

Once the seeker becomes a member of a "totalistic" community, which requires communal residence and near isolation from previous nongroup relationships and interests, and which allow close surveillance of members, devotion and commitment to the new group are likely to increase. First, with decreasing contacts, previous ties are likely to wane, especially if the new group proclaims beliefs that seem bizarre and foreign in the converts' previous world. The new group then increasingly becomes the only source of social and emotional support, and leaving the group presents the threat of total isolation. Secondly, the convert now becomes immersed in a world in which external as well as internal pressures to conform are exceedingly high. Conformity means approval and esteem; any opposition to community rules means criticism and rejection. The group's standards become the only standards for self-evaluation. Faced with a constant demand to inhibit doubts and disagreements and lacking external supports for private judgments, the individual is likely to relinquish or at least suppress old standards and values and conform to the community's viewpoint (Ofshe and Singer, 1986).

The group process that influences converts in totalistic environments thus operates simultaneously at several levels. To the extent that the new group demands relinquishing and denunciating previous ties, interests, and beliefs, it attacks central aspects of the member's previous self. To the extent that it curtails members' privacy, allowing surveillance, encouraging public confessions, and discouraging any expression of doubts and disagreements, it inhibits the experience of a private self that may observe and judge its surroundings. To the extent that it demands constant participation in group activities and subservience to the goals of the group or its leader, it promotes a redefinition of the self in the terms provided by the new ideology.

This process creates a new group identity, an identity that has no meaning outside the context provided by the group. Converts in totalistic environments may indeed face a "reentry" problem: a sense of disorientation, confusion, and unrealness upon attempting a return to the external world (Lofland, 1977; Ofshe and Singer, 1986; Singer, 1979)

GROUP PROCESS AND INDIVIDUAL IDENTITY

Religious groups vary greatly in the nature and extent of social influence exerted on new as well as veteran members. As described above, some, although by no means all, of the new religious groups which flourished during the 1970s employ "compliance-gaining strategies," deliberate deception, misinformation, and physical deprivation to recruit and keep new members (see Anderson and Zimbardo, 1984; Langone, 1986; Ofshe and Singer, 1986). But all groups exploit to some extent the tendency in all of us to imitate behaviors that are perceived as successful in peers, to conform to the group's expectations, to interpret inexplicable arousal experiences in terms of the immediate context in which they occur, and to attempt to minimize discrepancies between beliefs and actions. These tendencies may sway the person who participates in an Evangelical Christian revival meeting, a Baha'i fireside, a Divine Light mission set-song, or a Hassidic Sabbath.

But do religious groups transform anyone who happens to be present at their gatherings? Do the powerful processes of group influence automatically affect those who are exposed to them? There is little evidence that this is the case.

Based on their study of the initial process of recruitment into cults among high school students Zimbardo and Hartley (1985) reject the portrait of the "cult seeker" as the passive, "innocent" bystander deceptively manipulated into a conversion, and the description of recruitment as a random process. Rather, their data point to a complex interactive process in which the recruiter attempts to identify potential "catches" and in which the potential affiliate expressed openness and interest in the cult prior to the contact. Furthermore, the direct and often elaborate induction procedures practiced by some groups affect only a few. For example, the large majority of the potential converts who participate in the introductory workshops sponsored by the Unification Church do not become members: 71 percent of the guests do not stay beyond the initial weekend workshop. Of the 29 percent remaining for the subsequent, more rigorous workshops, only 9 percent choose to join the church, and a mere 6 percent are still members four months later (Galanter et al., 1979). Mere exposure to extensive persuasion techniques and to "successful" models in the Unification Church workshops is not enough to make a convert.

The intense group dynamics and the clear expectations generated in these gatherings seduce only a few. The more subtle influences at work in the gatherings of mainstream religious communities and of the less aggressive new religious groups are even less likely to "produce" converts indiscriminately. The rate of backsliding following conversions among those who have experienced dramatic conversions in fervent group settings is also remarkably high.

At Billy Graham's revival during the 1950s, an average of 2.5 percent made a "decision for Christ" and only 50 percent of them remained active converts a year later; about 15 percent of those become permanently converted. Similar proportions were reported for Billy Graham's crusades in 1970 (cited in Frank, 1974, p. 82). Levine (1984) reports that over 90 percent of those who join religious cults return home within two years.

Describing the effects of religious revivalism and of thought reform as used in China and the Soviet Union, Frank (1974) concludes that for both movements, the failures to produce permanent changes in personality and ideology are more impressive than the successes. The extreme pressures of thought reform techniques are unable to produce long-lasting changes. In fact, changes produced under circumstances of extreme physical and psychological pressures tend to "snap back" once these are removed, as for example, in Patty Hearst's short-lived conversion to the Symbionese Liberation Army, experienced under the duress of kidnapping and isolation. Circumstances of extreme social pressures are likely to produce conformity and a suppression of aspects of the previous identity, but these tend to reappear once the environmental pressures are removed. It is, in fact, questionable whether, for the majority of people, such circumstances result in a long-term transformation of the self.

Adult identity is very resistant to change. The mere presence of direct or indirect forms of social influence is hardly enough to make a convert. In the conversion experiences that involve group process, it is not merely the presence of the group that transforms observers into avid converts. The potential convert is hardly a passive recipient of social manipulation. The effects of deliberate or inadvertent social pressures are not automatic.

In 1969 Lofland and Stark presented an influential model of conversion to deviant perspectives. Based on their study of a "Doomsday Cult" (their pseudonym for the Unification Church) they described seven conditions emanating from the immediate circumstances of the person's life and from the group process as determining conversion to deviant perspectives. A few years later, Lofland (1977) revisited this model of becoming a "world saver." Although he observed that the recruitment techniques of the church had become more sophisticated and possibly, therefore, more effective than the techniques used a decade earlier, Lofland's criticism of his "world saver" model rested on different grounds. The world saver model, he argued, assumed a thoroughly "passive" process of conversion. It implied "a conception of humans as a neutral medium through which social forces operate" (p. 817).

Indeed, drawing on a model of conversion provided by the work on "brainwashing" and coercive thought reform of POWs or other captives of totalitarian regimes, our view of group process and persuasion techniques is enriched, but our understanding of conversion is somewhat distorted. This model necessarily neglects the part that the convert plays in the drama of transformation. The conversion depends not merely on the presence of group process but on the willingness—in fact, the desire—on the part of the potential convert to engage in an emotional relationship with the group. Those who are effected by group process are those who are desperate for a miracle transformation and those who actively maintain an emotional involvement with the new group. The convert's previous history and his or her experiences of some distinct emotions during the process of conversion are the vehicles which enable the group's success.

The Role of Emotions in the Group Process

The potential convert arrives at the group function full of apprehension, discouragement, and doubts in her or his own self-worth and full of hope for relief. The group process heightens the emotional intensity, but the state of emotional arousal experienced by the potential convert is not merely the result of the immediate situation as manipulated by the group but often the consequence of prolonged emotional distress. The majority of those who convert are more akin to hopeful psychotherapy patients than to the prisoners or captives of totalitarian regimes in that they typically arrive at the group function eager and hopeful for a personal cure. Furthermore, as we have seen in previous chapters, the transformation is at least initially the consequence of the experience of unconditional acceptance, lavish love, and boosts to their self-esteem generated in the midst of a new relationship. These emotional experiences may occur in a private, solitary setting as well as in the intensity of a group function. They may be enhanced by the convert's own wishes and fantasies as well as by the group's deliberate or inherent means of influence.

Describing the processes that are common to religious healing in primitive societies and religious healing in the Western world, Frank (1974) posited the previous emotional state of the "sufferer," the heightened emotional intensity of the healing process, and the bolstering of the seeker's self-esteem and emotional ties with a supportive group as the essential components of religious healing. In primitive societies, the ceremonies of religious healing are not undertaken lightly. They are reserved for those who are in acute distress and who are also hopeful for relief. The shaman heightens emotional intensity, for example, by dramatizing his or her own risks in encountering evil forces, by acting out a life-and-death struggle, and by the rhythmical music, chanting and dancing to physical exhaustion. The patient's sense of self-worth is heightened by becoming the focus of the group's attention, and he or she gains merit by public rituals of atonement and forgiveness.

Describing the religious healing at Lourdes, Frank notes that Lourdes has failed to heal those who live in the vicinity. The emotional excitement connected with the preparatory period and the journey to the shrine (cf. Linda's pilgrimage to the West Coast) seems essential for the success of the healing. There is no evidence of cure of gross organic illness at Lourdes, but those who report relief share a common characteristic. They are not detached or critical of the elaborate religious proceedings at the shrine. People who remain unmoved by the healing ceremonies do not experience cure. Furthermore, Frank notes that cases of "cured skeptics" also involve an intense emotional investment. Those skeptics who were cured, he argues, typically have had a devout parent or a devout spouse suggesting that their skepticism was a "reaction formation" or at least, that their pilgrimage involved conflict.

A bright young woman, a PhD candidate at the time I interviewed her, was one of the few converts in my sample who described an intellectual conversion as preceding her decision to join a new faith. Her account of her conversion to the Baha'i faith centered on her initial skepticism and on a gradual intellectual discovery of the "logical consistency" of the Baha'i writings. Her story supports, however, Frank's argument. It reveals a curious mixture of resistance and attraction, of persuasion attempts and active quest, and of intellectual efforts and an intense conflict.

This convert described her parents, especially her mother, as unstable and hateful. As a child, she dreamed of "going in and chopping my parents to little pieces." As an adolescent, she was "very unhappy," preoccupied with trying to get away from her family "as soon as possible." During her senior year in college she took a trip to Europe "just to be far away." While in Europe she learned that her boyfriend of several years and the only person she had been close to throughout her adolescence had become a Baha'i: "I never heard the word before so I asked people around me what it was and they told me that Baha'is were people who shaved their heads and put orange robes on, so I got really upset and I could not understand how someone so intelligent and rational could do something like that, so my first reaction was to break up with him. Essentially, I considered not coming back home." She did come home to a period of arguments with her boyfriend who refused to sleep with her and who kept trying to explain the faith to her and have her "investigate" it. She was finally persuaded: "Just to get him off my back, I decided to show him how the faith was illogical and inconsistent and wrong. To do that I was going to go through all the books and point out to him all the wrong things so that he would wake up and see the light." In this process of intense scrutiny of the Baha'i faith, which took about a year, she converted herself, coming to the conclusion that "the Baha'i faith must be true because I could not find anything wrong with it."

But this, she claims, was only an intellectual conviction which intensified her conflict. She now could not decide whether there was a God and whether she actually wanted to join the faith. Two "miraculous events" which occurred at the time her fiancé was in Latin America on a Baha'i teaching mission brought about her final conversion. In one, her mother, who was furious and horrified that her daughter was considering the Baha'i faith, converted herself. The daughter interpreted this event as an answer to her own prayer:

> I decided to pray and that was really the first time in my life I prayed. During that time that I was investigating, both of my parents were horrified that I was considering something other than Judaism even though they were not religious, just for traditional reasons . . . my father . . . took my Baha'i books away and tore them and threatened to throw me out of the house. Both my parents were furious. So in my prayer I asked that even if I could never know if the Baha'i faith was true or not because I seemed to be at a wall and it seemed I could never go beyond that, so I

prayed that my mother would know, that God would let her know, if there was a God. So right at that moment, when I finished saying my prayer, my mother came running into my room with a giant smile on her face and she goes, "I can't explain it but I just had the most wonderful experience while I was sleeping and I decided to become a Baha'i." She [the mother] became a Baha'i and has been a Baha'i ever since, she has changed quite a bit from the way I described her before.

The second miracle involved again the conversion of a second party:

I was very shaken by this [the mother's conversion] and I thought maybe there is a God, maybe he does answer prayers, so I decided to go to a fireside and I went there with the idea that maybe I will become a Baha'i, maybe I would not, I just was not sure and there was a man at the fireside, he was questioning and putting the speaker down and yelling at him, "You're so stupid," etc. . . . and it went back and forth like that, so I decided to give God one final test and if he answered this prayer I was going to become a Baha'i and I said if this man becomes a Baha'i tonight then I will become a Baha'i too. Well, the main said, "Oh I've had it with you Baha'is, I can't fight you and so I might as well join you," and he became a Baha'i right then, so I became a Baha'i too.

At first glance this story of conversion suggests a major role played by the group and by the active attempts at persuasion on the part of the girl's boyfriend. Upon further examination, however, this story of conversion seems remarkable, not for the various attempts at social influence to which this woman was undoubtedly exposed, but for the purposeful, active efforts she invested in converting herself and for the intense emotional conflict thereby revealed. Joining the Baha'i faith clearly held great rewards for this young woman, who might have otherwise lost the only stable relationship she had. She felt resistance but she also threw herself into an intense effort of investigating the new faith. She doubted God's existence but she prayed for signs that would convince her. Her skepticism, possibly like the opposition of her mother and that of the opponent of the speaker at the fireside meeting, did not lead to a detachment and a distancing from the group. On the contrary, her resistance was coupled with a desperate effort to prove herself wrong.

Susceptibility to group process depends on the emotional state of the prospective convert. As is well recognized, religious groups may attempt to intensify and manipulate emotional arousal (e.g., Frank, 1974; Harder, Richardson, and Simmonds, 1972; Lifton, 1979; Proudfoot and Shaver, 1975). But a distinct emotional state seems to be common to the majority of religious conversion experiences whether or not they occur in a group setting, whether or not they entail membership in a totalistic environment. It is the experience of being loved and the hope of future emotional care which is most likely to attract the convert.

This experience is the core element in conversions to "totalistic groups" as well as conversions in traditional groups. Reviewing the recruitment process of the Unification Church Lofland (1977) described "love" as the "most coercive and cruel power of all" (p. 812). Consider the following account of a convert who had left the Moonies: "Whatever I wanted, except privacy or any deviation from the schedule would be gotten for me immediately and with great concern. I was continuously smiled at, hugged, patted. I was made to feel very special and very much wanted" (cited in Lofland, 1977, p. 812). The feeling of being loved, the desire to "melt together," and the experience of feeling special and wanted are central in the transformation of recruits in cults as they are in the transformation of a Jew who "falls in love" with the rabbi or of a Christian who experiences a visitation of the Holy Spirit.

The suggestions and the setting alone do not produce the intense infatuation with the group that makes a convert. When present, the group's direct or indirect suggestions and the cues provided by the particular setting fall on fertile ground. They seem to furnish the final touches on a process that had started independently of them. In the majority of cases, it is the group's promise of unconditional acceptance that is most impressive for the potential convert. Consider the following story of a young convert to the Baha'i faith, whose conversion consisted of a love affair with a new group of peers.

THE CASE OF ED

Ed, a meticulously dressed 22-year-old convert to the Baha'i faith, is the second child in a family of four. His upper-middle-class Jewish parents were not religious, albeit cognizant and reverent of their Jewish heritage.

Ed had little to say about his childhood relationship with his parents. His mother, whom he describes as the dominant figure at home, was a "nice-looking woman," adamant and opinionated, a champion of civil rights and humanitarian causes. His father was described as "about 57 years of age, Jewish background, his parents, particularly his father, were very strongly brought up in the Jewish faith, Orthodox, yet he was estranged from the Temple . . . . He is not religious in the sense of practicing but in the sense of identification. He has worked most of his life. Physically, he spent many hours at his job . . . and does not take much time off, so we didn't see him that much." Ed's description of his father's relationship to his children curiously centers on the father's avoidance of physical punishment:

> He is, something which I respect very much, he is very much against physical punishment and even would get to the point of faking that he was hitting us; . . . he would just yell and would not do anything, so there was just very limited physical coercion, very little.

Ed's disclosures about his relationship with his parents were sparse and vague throughout the interview. He was clearer about the general mood of his childhood:

> I would not say it was necessarily happy, because I had some phobias, I had like a dog phobia, I had obsessional thoughts. No, I could not say it was particularly happy. I did not excel in school, although I feel, of course, I had the potential to, I really can't say I had the desired position for myself.

He does not recall specific traumatic events during his childhood but describes people whom he "disliked quite a bit." As in his description of his father, they are remembered for various "physical confrontations." Most vivid in his memory are peers who would ridicule and threaten him with physical abuse, threats which had him paralyzed with fear. Ed remembers his adolescence as no less distressing than his childhood, marked by two major preoccupations: First, aspiring to achieve the "desired position" for himself, he was in a continuous search for status and approval. Like many adolescents, he attempted to attach himself to peers who seemed to possess the power he lacked. His aspirations, once again, centered on "physical things":

I was strongly influenced by peers at certain points, in terms of my own behavior. I would say people who were popular; it was very important to be in a clan with people who looked nice, dressed nice, who were athletic; I looked very much into athletics, in terms of body image type of things, that was a very important thing for me . . . . This relates back to childhood, too, to the fact that I did not excel athletically, I just did not, I always wanted to, I wanted to be a sports hero. Also parties and clothes were important, too.

Ed's preoccupation with status and his expectations to excel and be admired are also evident in his reported attitudes towards his Jewish background:

It is obvious that the Jews academically and otherwise excel tremendously. They are a very intelligent people, so I had a very strong identification with that, but that was confined to cultural things or to the people that were Jews and accomplished.

But more disturbing than his unfulfilled aspirations for the desired position was a dread of death and eternity which he describes as a major source of anxiety. Throughout this period he suffered neurotic symptoms which he labels as anxiety neurosis and obsessional thoughts, and for which he occasionally sought psychiatric help.

The symptoms and preoccupations continued into Ed's first year in college and were intensified after a short involvement with "a young lady." This involvement, Ed says, resulted in "some messy things psychologically." But during his second and culminating in his third year of college, when he became a Baha'i, Ed started what he describes as an "upward trend," an "upswing." He started to do better academically; he became more involved in athletics, which "did wonders for me ego-wise"; and he was associated with a group which he deemed powerful and successful. But the comforting association with power did not last long. Following a heavy drinking episode during which he had been "saying and doing things for which afterwards I felt very disappointed with myself," he decided "to change the group of people" that he had been associating with. His description of this change in his life and of the conversion which accompanied it centers on the recognition and approval of peers. Describing his previous affiliations Ed says: "I decided that this was not the most edifying thing that you could do . . . . Although I was very funny and I could be the center of attention, I was very entertaining, etc., it was not something that could keep me going." He describes himself here as the "center of attention," but in his account of his introduction to the Baha'i faith he discloses simultaneous fears of exposure and ridicule. His attraction to the Baha'i faith was based on the group's prohibition of gossip:

> So I did meet my roommate and I was very interested, immediately, in him and in his group of friends. I never had found any time of fulfillment with a group of people as I had with this group because they were different, they were nice, accepting, and one of the principles of the faith was that people should not gossip and that this should be eliminated from society. This is a very comforting thought to me, because this was something that I always was really worried about, what people thought of me, to the point that I am sure that it was paranoid thinking, even earlier on, just in the overly vain sense. Whereas with these people it was not like that; they were people who were trying to rid themselves of gossip and all the junk that goes with it.

Similar themes permeate Ed's description of his actual conversion. He elaborates on becoming the "center of attention." Although, he says, he had in fact "joined them right away," he decided to wait a few weeks before declaring his faith. He had chosen to actually join the group at a festive gathering:

> It was after some festive activities, I went to a party that afternoon . . . it was a very diverse group and I met some people and there was something very nice about the gathering, it was a unified although diverse group. So there was this older woman there, reading something that she wrote . . . it was, I had to laugh [at her] so I left the place and there outside I met this other person who left for the same reason and he was a Baha'i and a nice person, just very humane . . . so that night I just decided, I was thinking mundane things, you know, last things before I became a Baha'i, which was a very serious thing, like jumping into sainthood, not that you immediately become a saint but you are starting on the process, so I was thinking to myself, you can't fool around. Chastity, you know, which I really agreed with, this type of thing but then I decided to go ahead, I very formally called them [the Baha'is at the gathering] and I came up and I gave a little talk and the reaction was tremendous . . . . I felt good, very good. I loved the people I was with and now I became a member, although they showed me much respect and love even before, this was the qualitative difference between them and other people.

Ed's conversion supplied him with a lifestyle and a mission which he believes will set him on the road to "sainthood." It will provide recognition and, as he believes, a guaranteed impact upon the entire world: "I am really excited. I'd say perhaps that's the thing that provides me with the most enjoyment, being able to appear, give talks, teach about those things because I feel that its impact would indeed prove in the future to be the most significant thing that has come along for our civilization."

Although the group provides the center of Ed's story of conversion, there are in this story no direct indications of any of the "brainwashing" or thought control techniques described earlier in this chapter; nor are there indications of other forms of deliberate induction of the change. Less menacing forms of social influence and group dynamics may have contributed to Ed's conversion. But the conversion was also clearly a manifestation of Ed's prolonged search for the "desired position" for himself.

As will be elaborated in Chapter 5, this case of a conversion to the Baha'i faith allows a glimpse into a self that is precariously lacking in cohesion and esteem. There seems to have been no authority figure that played a major role in Ed's conversion experience. Instead, the promise of recognition and admiration of chosen peers and the promise of future "sainthood" were seized upon by this young man, who reported fears of being exposed and ridiculed, coupled with a desire to excel. Ed's conversion was the occasion of an attachment to a new group, a group different from previous ones, not, as far as we can tell, by its use of deliberate persuasion techniques, but by its promise of acceptance and the promise of a new powerful vocation. A hunger for recognition and for the opportunity to have an impact has been at least temporarily fulfilled in his religious conversion. By allowing an attachment to loving and admiring peers, his religious experience has mitigated his fears of inferiority, at the same time enabling him to express grandiose expectations of success in a manner more acceptable to himself and to others.

The account of Ed's conversion begins with the curious, seemingly unrelated incident of his walking out, ridiculing the speech of another convert, and concludes with the audience's "tremendous" reaction to his own performance. In lieu of the ridicule which he had perhaps anticipated, for he had felt it towards another convert, he was applauded by his peers. His new beliefs were reaffirmed by the "tremendous" reaction he received. Impressed by his declaration speech, the new peer group offered him love and respect.

Ed's description of the process of his conversion hardly touches on the meaning or the truth revealed in his new faith. The principles of the Baha'i faith which he does mention are the ban on gossip and the vow of chastity, rules that are most directly relevant to regulating his own fears and desires. He does not claim that he converted because he had found "the truth." He became a Baha'i because he found a context in which he finally felt admired and approved.

CONVERSION AND THE "LOOKING-GLASS" SELF

The data on religious conversion indicate that group process often participates in shaping the particular form that the conversion experience takes and in the future maintenance of the new beliefs. The effect of the group process on those who are exposed to it, is however neither automatic nor uniform. When groups apply forceful manipulative pressures, their failures to produce long-lasting transformations are more impressive than their successes. The subtle or direct attempts of religious groups to gain new members transform those who are willing to engage in an emotional exchange with the group, those who "work" at an attachment that will relieve them of past and present anguish. The vehicle for the group's influence is primarily the convert's emotional state, which may be intensified, although not necessarily produced, in the midst of fervent group process. The experience in a group setting that transforms some religious converts is similar to the experience that moves the solitary private conversion. The core element in both cases is the experience of being special, loved, and unconditionally accepted by a particular figure or figures and the hope for future care.

This view of conversion raises some questions with regard to a long tradition of understanding the self that has influenced much of the social-psychological research on the self-concept. In this tradition, the self is primarily a cognitive and a social construction. In the symbolic interactionism tradition of Mead, Baldwin, and Cooley, the self develops in a process of social interactions at the symbolic or ideational level.

Cooley (1902) described the self as a "looking glass." Awareness of the self, he argued, evolves indirectly by taking the perspective of others. The self is identical to a social self-concept, namely, to the individual subjective construction of others' judgments of the person which arises out of his or her social interactions with primary groups. Mead (1934) approaches the problem of the self, which may be at once an experiencing subject and an object of that experience, by assuming that the individual "experiences himself as such not directly but indirectly, from the particular standpoint of other individual members of the same social group or from the generalized stand-points of the social groups as a whole to which he belongs" (p. 202). In this formulation, the self has a social function, connecting the person to a social order. Self-reflection becomes identical to role taking, involving reflecting on the self from the perspective of other persons. Following James (1908/1892), Mead suggests a distinction between an impulsive, unorganized, fluctuating "I" and a "me" which adopts the standpoint of the "generalized other," but in his formulation the "I" remains undeveloped and unpredictable, and the social "me's" provide the direction and structure to the developing self. The socialized "me" emerges in three stages of social activity, each associated with a distinct form of self-reflection. At the "play" stage, the child interacts with particular others. At the "game" stage, the child participates in organized, rule-bound activity which requires internalizing the coordinated perspectives of several others. From this activity emerges the internalized perspective of the "generalized other," which provides the only structure and stability to the self and which reflects the social structure in which the self is embedded. Mead argued, then, that the development of a self carried the child from a point of isolation and instability to the developmental achieve-ment of submersion in an organized social structure.

In other sociological accounts of the self, personality is reduced to its various social roles. Possibly the most extreme example of this reduction is embodied in Goffman's (1959) theory of the presentation of the self. For Goffman, the self is a series of false facades or masks, presented semideliberately in order to predict and control the reac-tion of the other.

From this perspective, a socialized self is the endpoint of devel-opment. The self and the social order are inseparable as the self reflects numerous elements of the social structure (e.g., roles) and becomes embedded in the multiple social views of the self. Moreover, the self is primarily a cognitive construction, an interpretation and an idea based not on direct experience but on a collection of inferred roles or attributions by others. Similarly, the other is a product of the ideas that the self has of the other.

Several writers have recently reviewed the advantages as well as the difficulties raised by this theoretical perspective on the self and have outlined its influence on the psychological study of the self (Blasi, 1983; Broughton and Riegel, 1977; Hart and Damon, 1985; Leahy and Shirk, 1985; Mischel, 1977). At the risk of simplifying this complex paradigm of understanding the self, I will outline here some of the limitations of the "looking-glass" view of the self that become apparent in the data on religious conversion.

Symbolic interactionism has in common with the self-concept approach in psychology the view of the self as a concept, a theory, an interpretation. In both, the self is a cognitive rather than an emotional phenomenon. In both, the difficult question of the accuracy of the self-concept, the possibility of a false vs. true self, and the questions of self-deception and self-protection are deemphasized. The approaches that emphasize the social nature of human beings through the structure of the self-concept also tend to underscore the basic similarity between understanding the self and understanding the other. But empirical evidence points to some important differences in these two processes (see Hart and Damon, 1985) that derive from the fact that understanding the self is emotionally involving in ways that are not present in our attempts to understand others. Finally, there are theoretical as well as empirical grounds (see Leahy and Shirk, 1985; Mischel, 1977) to question the equation of the self with its social components, whether those are described as roles, masks, or social self-image (i.e., one's perception of others' judgments of the self). The significance of these may vary from one individual to the other and with developmental level. Social self-image, for example, is probably most important during adolescence but its significance decreases at higher developmental levels (Elkind and Bowen, 1979; Leahy and Shirk, 1985; Ullman, 1987).

The nature of conversion as an infatuation with the group has some implications with regard to these issues. First, as Lofland (1977) argued, it indicates that persons are not mediums through which impersonal social forces operate. To transform a self, the group's influence must be integrated with the person's subjective experience and cultivated by an attachment to particular figures. In most cases of religious conversion as studied here, rather than being "coerced," "brainwashed," or "reformed" by a group, it is the person who takes advantage of a group process and enters a relationship with the group that resonates with his or her desires and emotions.

Secondly, it is precisely in those cases where the group process is particularly forceful and manipulative and clearly unintegrated with elements of the person's previous self, as in the attempts at political thought reform reviewed here, that one may question whether a transformation of the self has indeed occurred. When groups attempt to abolish private self-reflection and require a total subjugation to the group not only of ideology and deeds but also of the "internal" space that we think of as the self, their members appear to us as lifeless robots. When identity becomes merely a reflection of its social environment it seems to have lost the essence of a self.

In the normative developmental process, then, the self cannot be simply a "looking glass" which reflects the beliefs, roles, or prescriptions delineated by groups.

Finally, to the extent that conversion affects a transformation of the self, what seems to be transformed in the exchange with the group is not an idea, an interpretation, nor a "self-concept," but a basic emotional experience of the self in relation to others. The role of this immediate and directly known experience of emotions in the formation of the self cannot be ignored.

4

Adolescent Conversion and the Search for Identity

Dramatic religious experiences may occur at any age. Leo Tolstoy experienced his at the age of 50, by which time he was already well known and admired for his masterpiece *War and Peace*. Thomas Merton, who converted to Catholicism, experienced his first profoundly moving religious experience at the age of 19. At the time he was vacationing in Italy, still mourning the death of his father a year earlier (Furlong, 1980). In the intense religious fervor of some revival meetings of the early 19th century, children as young as seven were reported to have undergone conversions:

> Services were held for seven days and sometimes all night. A girl of seven preached from a man's shoulders till she fell exhausted, a lad of twelve exhorted till he fell and was then held up and continued till the power of speech was lost. (Hall, 1905, p. 286)

Studies indicate that the average age of people experiencing conversions does indeed span a wide range: from 46 in one study (Fren, 1959) to 16.4 in another (Coe, 1900). There is evidence, however, that religious conversions are most likely to occur during adolescence. At the turn of the century, G. Stanley Hall (1905) was the first to describe adolescence as a developmental stage worthy of psychologists' attention, and he devoted a chapter in his book on adolescence to religious conversions, identifying the experience as primarily an adolescent phenomenon. In the first large-scale empirical investigation of conversions, Starbuck (1899) reported that conversion occurred most frequently among his Christian subjects at age 16 for boys and age 13 for girls. Other studies of the same period show that religious conversions were most likely to occur between the ages of 12 and 20.

Although exact statistics are difficult to obtain, this trend seems to continue today. Argyle (1959) and Levine (1984) indicate that conversion occurs most frequently during the teenage years, and a recent textbook on adolescence (Adams and Gullotta, 1983) again devotes a chapter to religious conversions. The average age of conversion for the religious converts in my study was 21. About 50 percent of the converts I interviewed had had their change of heart during their first or second years in college, while away from home for the first time. Most members of contemporary religious cults are between the ages of 18 and 35 and experienced their conversions during their late teens or early 20s (Braden-Johnson, 1977; Deutsch 1975; Galanter, 1982; Levine, 1984). They are thus older than the Christian converts cited in the early studies, but by the standards of modern middle-class expectations, they are still in the process of becoming adults. Indeed, whether or not they fall in the appropriate age group, potential converts are often troubled by the issues that are typical of adolescent experience.

This chapter describes the psychological characteristics of adolescence that seem particularly relevant to understanding the frequency of conversions at this developmental stage. I will examine the normative changes of adolescence and the parallel developments that appear to shape the new identity of the adolescent convert.

ERIKSON'S CONCEPT OF IDENTITY

Since Erikson introduced the concept of identity in psychology (1950), it has become widely accepted that the formation of a coherent personal identity is the major task of the adolescent years. Although the process of identity construction does not begin in adolescence, and does not end there, adolescence is a period particularly sensitive to this process. The pubertal changes, the cognitive developments, the new demands, and the new options for independent functioning

111

combine to render the search for identity during the adolescent years particularly intense and the stakes of failure particularly high.

There have been several attempts to organize Erikson's various writings on identity (e.g., 1950, 1956, 1968) along a number of defining characteristics (e.g., Bourne, 1978; Waterman, 1985). The following discussion owes much to Blasi's recent attempt (1988) to articulate the various components of this notion and to assess the empirical work that derived from it.

Erikson's complex notion of identity may be grouped along the following components: (1) the content of identity; (2) the processes through which identity is established; and (3) the consequences of success or failure in identity formation.

The content of identity refers, on the one hand, to the specific answers the person discovers to the question "Who am I?", particularly the answers that arise in the fundamental domains of ideology, occupation, and sexuality. At the same time, identity refers to the more illusive but nonetheless fundamental subjective sense of sameness and continuity and to the emergence of a new unity among elements of one's past and future.

The processes through which identity is established include a "silent" process of selection and unification of past identifications, a realistic appraisal of oneself and one's past, and a reflection on and a comparison of one's own self-evaluation and other people's judgments in an attempt to discover what it is that is significant about the self in the eyes of those who are important. These processes occur at all levels of the personality. At the same time that one appraises other people's judgments and expectations of oneself against one's own evaluation, a more general questioning of the appropriateness of society's ideology, prescriptions, and values should occur.

The adolescent questions the validity of solutions readily available in her or his immediate social environment and explores alternative routes. The exploration often involves a "trying out" of new opinions and behaviors. These processes culminate in the sense of a crisis that may be experienced as intensely disturbing by some adolescents.

The consequences of identity formation include personal and subjective qualities as well as societal manifestations. The identity-achieved person experiences a basic sense of well-being, of being at home in one's body, a deep feeling of rootedness, self-esteem, confidence, and a sense of purpose. The crisis should lead to basic commitments in the areas of ideology, occupation, and intimacy which provide future directions and which guarantee the person's productive integration into society. A failure to establish an identity leads to role diffusion, which Erikson viewed as a developmental disorder, experienced partially or briefly by many essentially "normal" adolescents. Identity diffusion is manifested by some of the following symptoms, or in the more pathological cases by all of them: a diffusion of one's perspective on time, self-consciousness, fixation on self-defeating roles, work paralysis, a sense of inadequacy and futility, and bisexual confusion.

The various components of this notion of identity thus combine subjective experiences of unity, continuity, and autonomy that arise in the search for one's "true" nature, with objective behavioral manifestations at the personal as well as societal level.

Despite the attempts to conceptualize identity as an "existential position" (Marcia, 1980), the empirical work that attempted to examine Erikson's notion centered primarily on the "objective" manifestations of identity.

Marcia's work (1966) generated the most systematic and influential attempts to examine identity formation empirically. Marcia attempted to operationalize Erikson's concept by centering on the processes of crisis and commitment in the domain of ideology and occupation. Identity was defined by the presence or absence of a period of questioning (crisis) and the formation of a commitment in these domains. Marcia's initial study of adolescent boys (1966) resulted in the description of four identity statuses that presumably refer to different points in the developmental progress towards a consolidated identity. Individuals classified as "identity-achieved" have experienced a period of questioning and exploration in the areas of occupation and ideology and have arrived at their own clear-cut decisions concerning these two areas. Individuals classified as "moratorium" seem to be in the midst of exploring alternative directions in these two areas and have not yet arrived at definite commitments. Individuals who hold clear occupational and ideological commitments, but who have never experienced a crisis in these domains are classified at the third status, "foreclosure." Finally, individuals classified as "identity-diffused" seem to have made little progress towards commitments in these domains. Some have never experienced a crisis, others have been unable to resolve it.

Most of the research on identity has derived from this clear conceptualization of Erikson's theory. By and large, the data support the theoretical predictions. For example, reviews of the research (Damon, 1983; Marcia 1980; Waterman, 1982) indicate that those classified as foreclosed and identity-diffused are lowest in self-esteem and most likely to shift their self-evaluation as a consequence of external feedback. Foreclosed individuals are also low in anxiety whereas individuals classified as moratorium experience high levels of anxiety. Individuals in the "higher" status of identity achievement and moratorium have, on the other hand, the highest levels of self-esteem. The research also indicates that most adolescents change in their identity status between the ages of 18 and 22, shifting from foreclosure or identity diffusion to identity achievement. But the reviews of the developmental findings also suggest that shifts from identity achievement to lower statuses are possible and that identity, as defined by the presence or absence of exploration and commitment, cannot be viewed as a unified stage and is achieved independently in different specific domains. Another set of findings that seem incongruent with Erikson's theory concerns sex differences in the psychological significance of the statuses. In contrast to men, women in the foreclosed status seem better adjusted than women in the moratorium or even identity-achieved categories. They are high in self-esteem, low in anxiety, and low in fear of success and have warm and close ties with their families. They thus seem to manifest the psychological consequences of identity achievement.

Marcia (1980) interprets the findings on sex differences as reflecting the greater cultural support for "foreclosure" in women relative to men. While this is undoubtedly plausible, one may still question whether the Eriksonian tie between an autonomous identity on the one hand and confidence and self-esteem on the other holds unconditionally. Under some conditions, achieving an autonomous identity may incur psychological costs that may affect one's self-esteem (Blasi, 1988). On the other hand, one may question the validity of a procedure that measures identity merely by choices and decisions in a fixed set of domains and neglects the relations between the crisis and commitment in these domains and the experience of oneself as a distinct and unified whole. Similarly, one may question the relevance of a conceptualization of identity as a series of interrelated but separate decisions in various domains, to the Eriksonian concept that emphasizes unity and synthesis.

Reviewing the various interview formats and measures used to assess identity statuses, Blasi (1988) observes that these measures focus attention on objects outside the self and do not orient the subject nor the coder to the experience of the self or to the way one's basic "truth" is grasped.

For many, the chosen occupation and political or religious beliefs may indeed be intimately tied to the way the self is experienced. But the instruments that define identity status are not aimed at discovering when, for whom, and how there is a connection between the various domains and the sense of identity. Blasi concludes that "most of the identity measures, by neglecting the way identity is subjectively experienced and the relations that crisis and commitment, as well as certain important issues have with the construction of identity, have lost the meaning of the Eriksonian concept" (p. 19).

As we shall see next, similar questions are raised when one examines "identity statuses" in light of adolescent conversions.

Conversion and Identity Formation

Erikson's concept of identity is clearly relevant to the understanding of the phenomenon of adolescent conversions.

Adolescents may find in the religious conversion a remedy for the identity crisis. Exploring new expectations, ideologies, and values, the adolescent may temporarily "try out" the identity supplied by membership in a new group. In other cases, conversion may provide the final resolution to the identity question, unifying a previously divided self and allowing an investment of the self in new commitments and goals. By placing the adolescent in the context of a group or a tradition which spells out clear commitments and clear guidelines for behavior, a religious conversion supplies the important ingredients of a self-definition. It may facilitate the pursuit of independent goals and ties, or, for the troubled adolescent, it may offer an extended moratorium from them. According to Erikson, identity formation also involves a process of unifying and synthesizing some of the previous past identifications with significant figures, while suppressing others. As we shall see, adolescent conversion may offer a resolution when this process is arduous: by divorcing the adolescent from influences that have hitherto dominated his or her life, by amplifying the inclinations of one parent and rejecting those of the other, or by supplying new figures for emulation, the religious conversion allows a separation from parental authority, although not necessarily an autonomous identity.

The empirical work on identity statuses, however, raises some dilemmas when examined in the light of adolescent conversions.

Parker (1985) studied the relationship between identity development as defined by Marcia and the conversion experience. His subjects were 49 men and women ranging in age from 15 to 26 who belonged to various denominations. As expected, the gradual converts in this sample tended to have higher overall identity statuses, although they did not differ from sudden converts in their specific scores of identity statuses in the ideological domains of religion and politics. The second finding of Parker's study was counterintuitive and surprising: Converts in sectarian organizations achieved higher identity statuses than members of liberal or conservative churches. Parker interprets this finding by arguing that the level reached by the sectarian converts is "pseudo achievement," more closely akin to foreclosure. This form of "as if" identity achievement, he argued, reflects a submission to authority rather than an internalization of the dicta of the faith. Although the decision to surrender is freely made by the convert, the adherence to the new faith in these cases reflects the fear or love of the authority figure and therefore cannot be considered a "true" commitment.

Parker suggests that this group represents a fifth status that lies "somewhere between foreclosure and achievement" and concludes that these sectarian converts do not fit easily into the "Eriksonian structure." The present study indicates that conversions motivated by "fear or love of the authority figure" are indeed frequent, not only among sectarian converts. Regardless of their frequency, however, these adolescent conversions do not seem particularly problematic in terms of the Eriksonian structure as reviewed here, only in terms of the empirical paradigm suggested by Marcia's work. Erikson did not view the presence of a firm ideological decision, which these adolescents undoubtedly possess, nor the rejection of parental values per se, as indicative of ego identity. He in fact emphasized the often paradoxical and emotionally conflicted nature of adolescent commitments: "Young people offer devotion to individual teachers and to teams, to strenuous activities and to difficult techniques; at the same time they show a sharp and intolerant readiness to discard and disavow people. This repudiation is often snobbish, fitfully perverted or simply thoughtless" (Erikson, 1958, p. 42).

Rather than suggesting a fifth status, Parker's results, as well as other data that seem incongruent with the theory (e.g., the high level of adjustment of women in the "foreclosure" category, the unclarity with respect to the developmental sequence of the statuses), may point to the difficulty of capturing the sense of identity via the processes of crisis and commitment in specific domains. These processes may be important components of identity formation, but as defined in most of the measures for identity statuses it is not clear how they are related to the experiences of uniqueness, autonomy, unity, and continuity that seem central to this notion.

The measures used to classify identity statuses are likely to identify adolescent converts as identity-achieved at least in the fundamental domain of religious ideology. By definition, adolescent converts have formed clear-cut commitments in this domain. To the extent that their religious affiliation prescribes political views and regulates future choices, as is particularly true for the converts Parker classified as "sectarian," they may be committed in other domains as well. By definition, adolescent converts who have abandoned the religion of their upbringing are not "foreclosed" on their parents' views. In the criteria for identity achievement, this simple difference between one's view and the beliefs of one's parents is taken as an indicator of autonomy. But one may still question whether they have achieved an identity. The data presented here suggest that most converts, while perhaps meeting the objective criteria for the presence of crisis and commitment in the ideological domains and often in the domain of occupation as well, did not experience the deliberate process of distancing themselves from societal demands in order to evaluate ideological issues that Erikson seems to describe, and that their rejection of parental views does not necessarily indicate autonomous choices.

Parker noted that sectarian converts portray their parents' religious views as highly dissonant and attribute to their fathers more negative religious attitudes than do other subjects. In these cases of conversion, separation from parents is attempted by adopting a world view that is opposed to theirs. Technically speaking, these adolescents may be classified as identity-achieved; they have questioned parental values and have formed a new commitment. One may still question, however, whether and how these developments are related to their experience of a unified and distinct self. As we shall see next, the crisis and commitment involved in adolescents' conversions often reflect adolescents' difficulties in experiencing themselves as autonomous.

THE STRUGGLE FOR AUTONOMY

Attempts to separate from persons who have been important and influential to oneself do not begin in adolescence. Psychological development throughout life may be seen as a dialectical process of increasing socialization as well as increasing individuation (Damon, 1983). Just as children become more aware of and more knowledgeable about the social world that surrounds them, they also gradually sort out self-representations from the initial subjective experience in which the self and the world are not clearly differentiated. As normal development proceeds, self-representations become more stable and more sharply delineated.

The process of securing an autonomous identity is, then, a continuous one. But this continuous process of increased behavioral independence and internal representational differentiation reaches a peak in adolescence. It may then be manifested in a particularly bitter struggle for detachment from parental influence. Describing the resurgence of Oedipal fantasies during adolescence, Freud (1953/1905) wrote:

> At the same time as these plainly incestuous phantasies are overcome and repudiated, one of the most significant but also one of the most

painful psychical achievements of the pubertal period is completed: detachment from parental authority, a process that alone makes possible the opposition, which is so important for the progress of civilization, between the new generation and the old." (p. 227)

Josselson (1980) describes the process of adolescent individualization in terms of Mahler's sequence of infants' individuation which unfolds in four subphases: differentiation, practice and experimentation, rapprochement, and consolidation. The attempts to detach oneself from parental authority and the search for other sources for the adolescent's psychological needs begin in the differentiation phase. During this phase, the adolescent questions parental behavior and values and realizes that parents have their own attributes and flaws and that their advice may not be relevant to one's own life. The childhood assumption of parental omnipotence is replaced by an adolescent readiness to question and devalue parental wisdom altogether. During the "practicing" subphase, adolescents exercise this new spirit of rebelliousness. Like the two-year-old infant, they delight in contradicting, opposing, and provoking their parents, practicing and demonstrating their separateness. They then turn to peers, seeking in them the approval they formerly received from their elders.

Simultaneously, however, the majority of adolescents remain strongly and positively attached to their parents, continuing to trust and respect them and to desire their support (e.g., Offer, 1969; Bengtson, 1970; Douvan and Adelson, 1966). The new sense of distinctness achieved and practiced at the previous phases generates fears of losing the parents' love and leads to the realization that independence can be a burden. During the third phase of the individuation process, therefore, the adolescent attempts to reestablish the bond with the parents. His or her behavior towards them is more conciliatory and he or she is ready to reaccept their guidance. This rapprochement does not abolish previous autonomy but establishes a new balance in which independence and attachment are not experienced as contradictory. The relationship of the adolescent with parents, as well as other adults, now involves a new mutuality, cooperation, and selective acceptance, rather than outright rebellion.

The final substage of the individuation process leads to identity formation. It involves the consolidation of a sense of personal identity that incorporates independent choices with a selective acceptance of past identifications.

Adolescent conversions are often indicative of intense struggles at the first two substages of this process.

For some adolescents, achieving a separation requires drastic means. The new commitment of adolescent converts may reflect totalistic efforts to "stamp out" parental influence altogether, to reject all signs of parental authority and importance. In a discussion of the development of adolescent boys, Schafer (1976) views the totalistic struggle against parental authority as the most outstanding manifestation of adolescent difficulties. Rather than reflecting autonomy, a totalistic rejection of parental influences may reflect its opposite. An unrelenting fight to break away, Schafer argues, reflects the adolescent's fear of that which he wishes for most: the dependence on the omnipotent, omniscient parent of his childhood fantasies. In his ambivalence (that is, his fear of and simultaneous wish for dependency), the adolescent is alert, sensitive, and overreactive to any signs of parental influence. His view of emancipation is then uncompromising. When the "fight or flight" devices are the adolescent's only means in the struggle for personal autonomy, then his predicament is perpetuated and his independence thwarted. For true autonomy requires more than the rejection of all previous influences. Schafer here echoes Erikson's notion that the achievement of identity requires selection and a new synthesis. True emancipation is built on revision and selective acceptance, on flexible mastery and on complex substitutions, as well as a rejection. The troubled adolescent cannot fight so flexibly. Indeed, in his totalistic struggle to obliterate previous identifications and attachments to people who have remained both emotionally and practically important to him, the troubled adolescent ends up expelling himself: "He comes to think of himself as empty and dead and of the world as desolate and to feel and behave accordingly, that is, he adopts the dropping-out, rock-bottom, nonnegotiable mode of action" (Schafer, 1976, p. 187).

The religious conversion experienced by some adolescents reflects the two sides of the ambivalence Schafer describes. In these cases the conversion is a step in a totalistic rejection of the real parents, at the same time allowing an emotional and often practical dependence on the peer group or on a parental figure that is omnipotent and forever available.

The infatuation with the new religious group or with one of its members offers totalistic emancipation, "stamping out" the contemporary parents by turning away from their values and practices. At the same time, it promises the adolescent what he or she may wish for most—to be constantly protected by the parent of childhood fantasies: an ever-present, all-powerful, infallible figure. It is the adolescent who has to resort to drastic measures in order to separate from his or her parents who is more likely to adopt radically different new beliefs or a new lifestyle. Ironically, this may be achieved by a nonselective emulation of others: peers or substitute parents.

The increasing preoccupation with and allegiance to the peer group is a well-recognized characteristic of adolescence. The group life with peers may become for the adolescent a single-minded pursuit. Contrary to common stereotypes, this pursuit is often useful and adaptive. Peter Blos (1976) regards the adolescent involvement with peers as a vehicle for attaining better inner unity. Others point out that for the majority of adolescents, parental and peer influences are generally concordant (Brittain, 1969) and that interaction with peers facilitates the transition to heterosexual intimacy (Coleman, 1980) and the learning of reciprocity and equality (Damon, 1983). In the normal course of adolescent development the peer group aids individuation. On the other hand, the precarious sense of self of the troubled adolescent may result in an overidentification with the peer group. In this unselective and exclusive acceptance of ideas, roles, and modes of behavior dictated by the peer group, personal identity is negated rather than consolidated.

It should be noted again that these themes are not confined to the lives of adolescents; but their heightened urgency at this time of life may partly account for the higher frequency of adolescent conversions.

CONVERSION AND ADOLESCENT COGNITION

The "totalistic," uncompromising mode of action describes not only the battle waged by troubled adolescents against their parents; it is often described as the adolescent-preferred mode of ordering the world and of people in it (Blos, 1976; Erikson, 1968; A. Freud, 1958). Adolescents tend to view the world in black and white. They order things in absolutes and polarities. Everybody, including themselves, is either brilliant or dumb, exciting or deadly boring, very friendly or hostile. This new boastfulness and commitment to the extremes may indeed reflect a new and remarkable achievement, namely, the emergence of formal operations in which reasoning becomes more abstract and less tied to the concrete (Inhelder and Piaget, 1958). Those who reach formal operations are less tied to the here and now and can distinguish the real and the concrete from the abstract and the possible. They can generate and test hypotheses, they can think about the future, and they are capable of thinking about thoughts. During adolescence, ideas and systems of ideas become intriguing in their own right. For the first time, the young person is cognitively ready to become actively engaged in the world of ideas rather than in the world of objects.

The onset of formal operations may render the adolescent easily seduced by ideologies. With the emerging but still tentative ability to image the possible, adolescents are more likely to become enthralled by all-encompassing, uncompromising ideologies, to reject what is in favor of a possible world, and to view the acceptance of compromises or exceptions as weakness or insincerity. The young person may then reject shared conventions as arbitrary and unnecessary rules. The new cognitive abilities may also be characterized by a special brand of cognitive egocentrism (Elkind, 1967). Although emerging formal operations enable the adolescent to conceptualize his or her own thoughts and the thoughts of others, the adolescent fails to differentiate the objects of his or her own preoccupations from the objects that are the focus of the preoccupations of others. He or she then feels exposed to an imaginary audience, believing that others are continuously concerned with him or her. As a consequence, adolescents demand greater privacy for their feelings and thoughts and tend to construct a "personal fable" of their uniqueness and importance. They believe that their ideas and concerns, their plight and their view of a just world are unique and special.

With the emerging ability to think about thoughts, introspection and self-reflection become central in the adolescent experience. Self-understanding undergoes well-documented developmental changes with the onset of adolescence and continues to develop throughout the adolescent years (Damon and Hart, 1982). The physicalistic and peripheral attributes of the self that children tend to stress are replaced by an emphasis on the self as a mental and psychological entity (Broughton, 1978; Montemayor and Eisen, 1977; Rosenberg, 1979; Selman, 1980). More specifically, adolescence begins with an emphasis on the self as an active controller of one's experience, as having unlimited and private access to its own inner processes. This new respect for the self's volitional powers is accompanied by minimizing the limits of self-control and self-awareness. Later in adolescence there is a tendency to view the self as divided between a "false" or "phony" public self-presentation and a real or authentic "me" (Broughton, 1981; Ullman, 1987).

The onset of formal operations, the cognitive egocentrism associated with it, and the changes of self-conceptions increase the attractions that the religious group holds for the adolescent. Adolescents are fascinated by utopias and totalistic ideologies. Their interest in the "ideal world" and disdain for compromises and conventions result in an increased attraction to the absolute, unambiguous core beliefs that the new religion may offer. The religious peer group that points the way to "sainthood" reinforces the young person's view of his or her inner world as unique and special.

The religious emphasis on the spiritual nature of humankind and on the power of faith resonates with the adolescent's new tendency to distinguish the mental and the physical and to endow the former with unlimited powers. The young person who is attempting to identify a "real" me is more likely to reject the self that is continuous with the beliefs and demands of his or her social environment as phony and false and to cultivate a juxtaposition of a disdainful "material self" with an authentic "spiritual self."

The normative changes of adolescence described here contribute to an increasing fascination with ideologies. However, as already suggested by the data presented in previous chapters, it is not the "typical" but the emotionally troubled adolescent who is likely to become a religious convert of the type studied here.

CONVERSION AND ADOLESCENT TURMOIL

Of the converts in my study, 65 percent characterized their adolescence as extremely unhappy (versus 6.7 percent of the nonconverts in this category). A turbulent adolescence is thus associated with the experience of religious conversion. However, 64 percent of these same converts also characterized their childhood as extremely unhappy and only two of them (8 percent) described their childhood as happy and free of turmoil. For the majority of converts, then, adolescent difficulties continued a pattern of previous psychological upheaval.

This finding is consistent with the research reported by Offer and Offer (1975), who empirically challenged the assumption that "storm and stress" is inevitable during adolescence. In Offer and Offer's study of adolescent boys, those who were viewed as in a state of turmoil had a common background of family crisis (divorce, overt marital conflicts, mental illness). On the other hand, those adolescents who were classified as exhibiting a continuous and smooth growth pattern came predominantly from stable and intact families in which the parents encouraged independence. The developmental tasks of adolescence and the upsurge of changes during this stage are, then, not necessarily experienced as tumultuous. Those already at risk for psychological maladjustment are more affected by the demands of this age.

The normative changes of adolescence described here contribute to an interest in and an openness to examine the message of various religious groups. Zimbardo and Hartley (1985), for example, report that over 50 percent of the West Coast high school students they studied were open to considering or accepting an invitation to attend a cult meeting. Interestingly, however, the receptiveness to a cult invitation was greater among those who had no prior contact with cults than among those students who reported previous contacts with cult recruiters. This finding may indicate that initial contacts with cults are often motivated by curiosity, which is then diminished by the actual contact.

Clearly, only very few of those youth who are open to considering a cult invitation would actually become a member of a cult or would ever experience a religious conversion. The normative changes of adolescence may contribute to a curious "shopping" for various ideologies and lifestyles, but religious conversion is likely to occur when this fascination combines with the experience of disturbing emotions toward the self and others, which in most cases began prior to adolescence.

Several psychological investigations of religious conversions conducted at the turn of the century described the experience as a typical adolescent phenomenon connected with the normative changes of this age and with a tendency to succumb to the power of groups. In his study of Christian conversions, Starbuck (1899) claimed that abrupt, dramatic conversion experiences are predominant in adolescence since the physiological changes at puberty "condition" the individual for conversions. By some unspecified maturational process, these physiological changes cause a greater amenability to suggestion and imitation and thus cause a "neurological potential" to experience abrupt conversions in a group setting. Religious conversion, Starbuck concluded, is built upon inherent adolescent tendencies that merely condense normal experiences. They shorten the period of stress and crisis inevitably experienced by all adolescents. The conversion experience prepares the adolescent for entry into adulthood. Starbuck emphasized the adaptive potential of the experience in helping the adolescent achieve "greater harmony" and "unity with larger life."

During Starbuck's time, this positive view of adolescent conversion was shared by others. The experience was regarded as a necessary change at a stage when self-centeredness gives way to an interest and a participation in the life of the community. Conversions were described in this early psychological research as a part of the process of becoming an adult, of achieving a "unified self," and of securing "a better life" (e.g., Hall, 1905; Pratt, 1907). The early studies emphasized the role of group pressures and social expectations in precipitating the adolescent conversion. Daniels (1893), for example, compared religious conversions to the adolescent initiation rites of tribal societies. He argued that both experiences introduce younger members to the norms and rituals of their social environment. Another study, centering on adolescent conversions at Christian revival meetings, concluded that the experience could be best understood as a group phenomenon. In the religious revival experience, temperamentally passive, suggestible individuals dealt with typically adolescent pressures through a "gang instinct;" they were carried away by the group's expectations (Coe, 1900).

Although it was recognized that individual variations exist and that the sense of guilt and sin in some individuals may be "morbid," the general consensus in these early studies was that conversions, in most cases, were a part of the inevitably intense social and psychological changes of adolescence and that they represented a condensed and essentially normal form of adolescent development.

There are some important differences between the religious conversions studied at the turn of the century and the experiences of the typical contemporary convert, studied here. First, the early studies centered on abrupt conversions experienced within the convert's own Christian denomination. The characteristic subjects in these early studies reaffirmed through their conversion experience an already well-established religious faith. They embraced with increased enthusiasm beliefs and rituals well entrenched in the life and culture of the people around them. This kind of experience, however keenly felt, involved little change of core beliefs or lifestyle. Secondly, in most cases, the conversions studied at the turn of the century had occurred in some large group setting, such as a religious revival meeting, often attended by the converts' entire community. In this setting, group pressure to undergo a conversion had been intense. Young participants were expected, almost required, to accept Christ and be saved. The conversion was often considered by parents and teachers an essential part of the youngsters' education (Hall, 1905).

Since the religious experience which occurred under these circumstances involved little cognitive change and promised great social rewards, it is not surprising that the experience was characterized as an expected ritual, similar to initiation rites, and as a common enough occurrence within the range of prevalent adolescent experience. The conclusions that were reached in the early studies, which stressed the importance of suggestibility to group pressures and the developmental value of the experience, may thus reflect primarily the particular context in which the religious conversion was studied.

Aware of these limitations, William James (1902) suggested that future empirical investigations focus on "sporadic adult cases" which did not occur in the midst of revival meetings. He maintained that such adult cases constituted "purer" examples of the phenomenon. In contrast to the Evangelical converts who were studied at the turn of the century, the contemporary converts I interviewed, even those who had stayed within the major religious denominations, had adopted beliefs and a lifestyle that were, at least at the time of their conversion, remote from the mainstream of their culture. They had moved away from the religion of their parents to embrace new views, often severing their ties with their former social milieu and drastically changing their lifestyle. In the majority of cases these changes were hardly welcomed by parents and relatives. Rather, they were judged as bizarre and disconcerting.

Clearly, converts who completely abandoned their former social milieu existed at the turn of the century, and conversely, religious revival experiences similar to those studied at the turn of the century are rising in frequency today. The present study focused on converts who had actually changed their religious affiliation and therefore cannot be seen as representative of conversions in which a personal religious experience is an entrance requirement and an expected ritual in a community of which the potential convert is already a member. But the present-day phenomenon is striking and distinct in the number of youth (e.g., recent estimates of five million members in cults, Paloutzian, 1983) who have abandoned the expectations of their social milieu through their religious conversion. Joining groups new to this culture or changing their religious denomination, they have rejected the lives prescribed by their parents, often turning their backs on the rights and responsibilities of adulthood as defined by their former environment. In particular, conversion experiences of youth in the new groups (e.g., Unification Church, Divine Light Mission, Hare Krishna, Rajanish, to name but a few) offer little by way of initiation into the adult world and allow a retreat into a protective, homogeneous community of peers instead. When the religious experience takes this form, it does not comprise the typical, expected course of adolescent development, as turbulent as that course may be. It usually occurs on a background of struggles that are of longer duration and are more disturbing in scope and effects. Nevertheless, even these extreme retreats into the haven of well-structured, protected group life may ultimately result in psychological gains.

THE FRUITS OF ADOLESCENT CONVERSION: ACHIEVING SEPARATION

In his book on young members in religious cults, Levine (1984) argues that the leave adolescents take of their families to join religious communes is a necessary step in the adolescent attempt to separate from powerful parental influences. The majority of the contemporary converts in cults (90 percent), Levine claims, return to their families within two years. Many of them seem better able to deal with the demands of autonomous living. There are also indications that a temporary separation from parents, resulting from a conversion experience and an involvement with a new group, may indeed start a process of achieving a stable self-definition and a gradual, selective acceptance of parents.

In the following excerpt from my interview with Ruth, the fruits of the conversion experience are described in terms reminiscent of Eriksonian criteria of ego identity. Ruth converted to the Baha'i faith at the age of 21. As described in the previous chapter, her conversion occurred in the midst of a fireside meeting, in the presence of peers. She decided to join the group despite her father's vehement objections. Her mother, on the other hand, had unexpectedly, miraculously joined the Baha'i faith herself. The conversion helped this young woman consolidate realistic long-term commitments and goals and enabled her to develop an intimate relationship:

> It changed my whole outlook on life, my career aspirations, my view about my role as a woman, and about having children. I never wanted to get married or have children because of my experiences in my own family, and I would not have, had I not become Baha'i. Before, I did not know what I wanted to do, I did not have any ambitions . . . now I have gotten interested in education and I have very defined goals . . . . Everything has opened up and my whole life is organized around goals and ways to get there.

For the following convert, the religious experience seems to have been a necessary step in "stamping out" parental influences, a drastic declaration of independence which ultimately enabled an affinity and increased closeness with the family.

Stanley, a Jew who converted to Catholicism, describes his conversion as the occasion of a "push–pull" struggle to separate from his parents:

> My mother had a lot externally and internally at stake because I was going to be her success story. So it was heavy for me too, because I depended a lot on my parents' approval . . . so this [his conversion] was tearing the family apart. I was being a traitor to one's heritage and she was also angry with me for being a religious fanatic, more so because I removed myself totally from the Jewish milieu . . . . I could be very forceful and stubborn in my attitudes, I insisted on my views. I tried to talk to them, but they were interested in why I did it to them rather than in why I was doing it . . . . I would stay in my room, praying, and somebody would be at my door, demanding to know what I was doing. So I would have, first with my father, then with my mother, then with each of my brothers and sisters, and then with the whole family, these conferences that would drag on for months, because every time I'd mention something about my religious views it would flare up again.

The struggle subsided when Stanley decided to move out of his parents' home. For a while, there was little contact. Finally, Stanley says, the separation started a "healing process":

> We can sit down and discuss it with each other now and I think there is a real atmosphere of acceptance. I probably have been more loyal to the family than some of the other children, and I think that my parents sense that . . . so they seem to say, "We cannot agree with you, but it seems to be working in your life, so we'll accept it" . . . and I came more to accept them as persons.

Similarly, Linda, who converted from Judaism to Christianity in the presence of loving peers, returned home to an ambivalent and prolonged struggle of emancipation from her parents, whom she described as loving but overprotective and intrusive. At first she tried persistently and enthusiastically to convert them. In her zeal, she could not understand their dismay over her embrace of a world they considered alien, threatening and even persecutory. Later on she retreated into a passive resistance of their countless efforts to influence her. Finally, she felt compelled to leave home, despite her love for her parents:

> I felt it was God over my parents, which was very hard for me. My mother: she so much as said that she might, you know, ask me to please never come home again, but at that time my commitment to God was so strong that I felt in my heart that they [the parents] would not do that. Our relationship was such that I knew that they could not live without me and I could not live without them, so they'd never do that, but there were

times when it got pretty close. So I decided to leave and let it cool for a while . . . . I left to stay with born-again friends because I could not take the heat, but then I left for school and we did not communicate much after that, but things have gotten better over the years.

Unlike the majority of converts in my sample, Linda described her childhood as quite stable and secure and cited her adolescence as the first period in her life characterized by confusion, alienation, and "frenzy." The themes that emerge in her conversion story are indeed not too far removed from typical adolescent struggles, and her conversion may have contributed to a resolution of this turmoil.

5

Merger with the Perfect Object
Conversion and the Narcissistic Condition

Previous chapters described conversions that centered on an attraction to tangible human figures, powerful authorities, or loving peers. This chapter centers on conversions in which the object of infatuation is primarily a transcendental object. As one would expect, in some conversion stories the love relationship is between the convert and the Divine, but in these stories the Divine becomes a personalized, concrete object responsive to the convert's needs. The conversion is the occasion for a nondemanding love relationship that offers unconditional salvation through a union in which the convert's wishes are promptly recognized and cared for. In the religious revelation the object of infatuation is experienced as merged with the self, thereby endowing the convert with new powers. A wish to unite with a perfect, idealized object, a sense of being a pawn in a struggle of giants and yet of being chosen or called for a special mission, and the perception of personalized miracles—special messages to the self that the convert decodes in common, everyday events—these themes are examined in this chapter and are discussed in light of the development of narcissism and self-worth.

THE CASE OF PETER

Peter is a 32-year-old "born-again" charismatic Christian who had also been at one time a follower of Meher Baba's religious cult.

Peter's account of his childhood replicates the pattern of early losses and inconsistent parenting we have encountered in other cases. His father died when he was three years old, leaving Peter and his baby sister in the care of their maternal grandparents while their mother continued to go to school. A few years later the mother remarried "a very authoritarian kind of a guy," who was hated and feared by Peter and his sister.

Although he had been brought up in a clan of Evangelical, born-again Christians and had "turned onto the Lord" himself when seven years old, Peter pulled away from religion early in adolescence. He then felt reborn through his discovery of a life without God:

> I came into my teens and felt a lot of peer pressure and in that respect I left God further and further behind. I went to church because it was expected of me. I came out of that [religious life] and felt like a snake shedding its skin or a butterfly coming out of a cocoon. I felt that God and my new understanding of the richness and joy of life were antithetical.

Throughout his adolescence Peter describes feeling lonely and lost, confused about his goals, and isolated from parents as well as peers. During his first year in college his confusion had intensified, culminating in visions which were terrifying and deeply unsettling for him. He recalls two of them most vividly:

> I was lying in bed in the early hours of morning and was fully rationally awake and could see everything and so forth and all of a sudden when the tower clock struck a certain hour I had a vision, in my mind's eye. I saw a figure of Christ standing before me in silence as he is described by Bernard Berenson in a painting by Botticelli, wearing a brown and blue robe, and Berenson said beholding this painting is enough to make a convert. I saw it, I felt no emotion, I could not speak to him, I felt myself to be totally an observer. Two weeks later I had fallen into a deep sleep and awoke at the last stroke of the clock in the tower, again at the very same hour, but as I came into consciousness I realized with the same kind of mind's-eye vision that lying next to me in bed was a charred corpse. And as I came awake this charred corpse lightly and airily rolled off the bed and bounced on the floor and disintegrated into ashes, and immediately the whole room seemed to be filled with the presence of evil. Just as I beheld the reality of Christ as calm and peaceful, I felt that far from a take-it-or-leave-it situation, I was overwhelmed with evil and again the room was filled from floor to ceiling with snakes writhing. I was so petrified that all I could do was lie there and repeat over and over again things I learned from childhood, like the Lord's Prayer and 23rd Psalm and so forth.

In this frightening religious vision Peter also experienced a fear of beholding his own reflection in the mirror: "After about 20 minutes I managed to creep in to the living room, all the while being very careful not to look in a mirror because I was convinced that if I looked in a mirror I would see something in my eyes so terrible that it would drive me crazy." During the following two years he became increasingly withdrawn and desperate, obsessed with fears and ideas he could not control, tormented by indecisiveness and emptiness:

> I didn't feel I was crazy but I did think I was neurotic and plagued with terrible indecisiveness and depression. I would lie in my bed for hours and hours and have no appetite whatsoever and at the same time be obsessed with music I could not turn off in my head.

Fearing hospitalization, he succeeded in concealing his psychological disintegration from his parents. Without their knowledge, he dropped out of college in his freshman year and tried night school in a different college, remaining isolated throughout this period: "Much of the time was spent in a tremendous stupor and vegetating on my bed in tremendous depression." After moving to another school, he met a former drug dealer who had become a follower of Meher Baba. He converted to Meher Baba's cult overnight, rented a house with other devotees of the loving and silent guru, and immersed himself in the occult, astrology, and Eastern religions.

Basking in Baba's "infinite love," he felt "as happy as a clam," experiencing "supernatural beings" with whom Baba was "supernaturally in contact" and waiting for his master to set the world free by breaking a self-imposed silence in "one cosmic syllable."

Though he does not wish to put down "these people," (Baba's followers,) at present, Peter views his involvement in the cult as a "psychological trip," a way of avoiding responsibility:

> I felt I found reality in the context of people who were happy and loving. I did not see I was fulfilling a psychological need, I had gone into debased Christianity in oriental dress . . . . Here I was believing in Karma, and no responsibility, there was always another trip around it.

In Karma, a concept central to the complex system of accountability held by most cults with Eastern roots, God alone can give a new direction to the various reincarnations of oneself. Believing in this view, Peter thinks, absolved him of personal responsibility and freed him from participating in the lives of others: "It set me free from people around me who had needs because they were going through their Karma and I could even, if I approached them, impede their progress in getting off the wheel of life."

As a faithful Baba follower, he patiently awaited the promised reward of ultimate realization, of a transformation which would set him free of all desires and all painful strivings. He recalls occasional "supernatural experiences" meditating or drifting off to sleep, which would convince him that he was "just close to that realization." But the more he searched for the promised metamorphosis, the more fearful he became of being deceived. He began to harbor growing doubts in the powers of his master. On his way home from a rare visit with his parents, he asked God for a sign which would resolve his doubts, which would prove to him whether or not he had been deceived. This became the occasion of his second conversion—back to the Evangelical Christianity of his childhood. This second conversion was the outcome of a prearranged meeting with a "hard-shell" Baptist minister, a friend of his parents. Peter had anticipated that he would be able to convince the minister about Baba's divine powers. Instead he was himself persuaded that he had been deceived, that he had been "working with the forces of evil," and that Jesus Christ alone is the real God. The meeting with the minister, Peter decided, was the unequivocal divine sign he had been praying for. As in his conversion to Meher Baba's cult, he felt again instantly converted.

It was a promise of transformation and a guarantee of perfection which gave the impetus for Peter's second religious conversion:

> Other religions give things you have to do to get close to God, renunciations you must make by your own efforts. Jesus is the only God that is utter holiness, utter righteousness, utter perfection, and utter love; you in no way out of your own strength and out of your own effort can attain that standard of perfection or maintain it with any consistency, and what you need is a new life source.

Peter believes that his conversion to Christianity offered him a new life source, furnishing him with ultimate perfection through a simple gesture of acceptance. The depth of his need and of his desperation and the conviction of his own insignificance, which underlay this wish for perfection without effort, are clearly expressed in Peter's description of the religious yearnings and doubts that dominated his adolescence:

> Deep in my teens I think I'd decided there was not a God that could love me as I understood love. He would have to love me so much. He would want me out of this impossible situation, where no matter how much I tried I was not making any progress. I could never get away from just feeling like a chip on the tide of the universe. Here's this vast complex thing and I somehow have to find my way in it and I somehow have to grab a chunk and hang on.

Relationships with other people were never satisfying to Peter for they could never supply the unconditional love that he needed. Others have their own needs: "I sensed that they could only give it to me conditionally, when they felt up. When they felt down, they could not. When they felt up and had some insight it was great, otherwise it would be a disaster."

Peter's second conversion did not immediately produce a sense of peace and joy. For several months following his dinner with the Baptist minister, he was still plagued with doubts and depression. Convinced that he had not yet fully accepted Christ, he was sure that he was in constant danger. This aftermath of his rebirth as a Christian had imparted to him again the "reality of evil," reviving images like the "writhing snakes" from his adolescence:

> The man I had dinner with told me, "Peter, if you ever try to break away from the forces of evil that you are working with it might kill you," and I thought, "How romantic," but that's exactly what happened. I had some narrow scrapes with near accidents, people phoning me and attempting to lay a curse on me. One person tried to attack me physically.

Peter interpreted these events as indications that he had been "keeping God out and just hurting myself." Once again, he accepted God in prayer, subsequently experiencing profound peace, a sense of certainty and release. He knew then that God had taken his hand:

> God had just in huge leaps lifted me out of one problem after another. I'd had incipient colitis and ulcers and asthma and migraine headaches . . . . I'd been tempted with thoughts of suicide. God pulled me out from under the worst of it in an astoundingly short time.

Peter believes that God's miraculous guidance also inspired his vocation in the Evangelical Christian community where he now re-

138

CHAPTER 5

sides and works as a motivational consultant for Christian corporations. About a year after his conversion, he experienced the "Lord's word," revealing to him that within 13 months he would be taken "to a different context and a different ministry." Indeed, Peter claims that 13 months later, to the very day, a friend invited him to join her community, an invitation which he accepted as the fulfillment of the Lord's word.

Peter describes his childhood as lacking in parental love and protection: His mother was unavailable, his father was dead, and he hated and feared his stepfather. During his adolescence, his desperate attempts to "grab a chunk and hang on" prevented him from engaging in any meaningful tasks or relationships.

In this affecting story of a dual conversion, the religious experiences seem to have prevented severe psychological decompensation. Desperation, a sense of futility, and frightening visions became less arbitrary and less disintegrating through a religious interpretation. Peter's eloquent description of his life is replete with imagery and ideas that reveal a fragile self. He experiences himself as a shell only tenuously covering insignificance. He is a snake shedding his skin, a "butterfly out of a cocoon," "a clam," "a chip on the tide of the universe." He is afraid of his own reflection in the mirror. He experiences himself as powerless in the midst of a struggle of giants—the forces of good and the forces of evil. His world is split between the powerful and frightening writhing snakes and charred corpses—the forces of evil—and the no less powerful but unattainable utter perfection and utter holiness. In the midst of this struggle he is tossed about like an insignificant chip.

The message Peter heard from the Baptist minister, that he had aligned himself with the forces of evil and that his life would be endangered while trying to break away from these forces, was easy for him to accept for it supported Peter's experience of himself as inauthentic and insignificant and as the playground for the powerful forces of good and evil. His religious conversion offered the means to avoid this fate. The conversion promised constant caretaking by an unconditionally loving, perfect object. Throughout his life, Peter had avoided relationships. Others, like those who had failed him in his childhood, could not be relied upon to satisfy his enormous needs. They could not be trusted, for they had their own needs: "They could only give it to me conditionally." For this young man, "conditionally" had not been enough. He rejects the religions which require some effort on his part: "things you have to do to get close to God . . . renunciations you must make by your own efforts." He seeks unconditional salvation and he finds it in his second conversion. By means of his conversion, he attaches himself to an object that is unconditionally giving, that has no needs and wants nothing of him. He seems to become one with this perfect object, incorporating a "new life source."

CONVERSION AND NARCISSISM

The language of Peter's conversion testimonial and the preoccupations thereby revealed suggest the themes that the psychological literature describes as narcissistic. In many contemporary conversion testimonials, the traditional sense of sin and burden of guilt seem absent. Instead, these testimonials reveal the experience of the self as inauthentic and empty. The themes that permeate these testimonials—namely, extreme vacillations of self-esteem, a basic uncertainty in a sense of self that most of us seem to take for granted, and a wish for an undemanding merger with an idol—have become the focus of a new school of psychoanalysis, in which psychopathology is described primarily as a consequence of developmental deficits in the self and as a manifestation of misguided narcissistic activity.

The myth of Narcissus is the story of a charming youth who pines away as a result of his infatuation with himself. Narcissus' preoccupation with his physical beauty and his self-love lead to his destruction: he dies as a consequence of his wish to unite with his admired mirror image in the water. Freud (1953/1914) made use of this myth in his theory and coined the term *narcissism*. In his writings, narcissism was adopted from the Greek mythology to refer to the earliest developmental stage, a stage of "primary narcissism." The infant in this stage exists in a "boundaryless state," a state of blissful union with the mother.

Freud also postulated a "secondary narcissism," a libidinal investment in the self and away from the world of external objects, which may occur later in development. Freud's contributions lie behind the currently common use of the term as a metaphor for self-absorption and self-love.

Despite the growing interest in narcissistic phenomena, there is still considerable disagreement and unclarity with respect to its conceptualization. Definitions of the terms vary from those cast in the terms of Freud's economic principles (e.g., describing narcissism as the "libidinal cathexis" of self-representation, Hartmann, 1950; Kohut, 1971) to those emphasizing the functional aspects of narcissistic activity as a measure of preserving the stability of the self (Stolorow, 1975) and to definitions which emphasize the emotional content of narcissistic phenomena as in Kernberg's (1975) emphasis on "oral rage" and Rothstein's (1980) definition of narcissism as "a felt quality of perfection." Differences of opinion are also apparent with respect to the adaptive value and ubiquitous nature of narcissism. While Kernberg (1975) seems to treat the term as equivalent to pathological character development, Kohut (1977) and Rothstein (1980) emphasize adaptive, normal narcissistic aspirations and view narcissistic personality disorders as a product of inadequate integration of narcissism with other ego functions. Kohut, furthermore, deems derogatory references to narcissism as resembling Victorian hypocrisy toward sex. Condemning self-love and strivings for admiration and recognition as "selfish," "immoral," or "immature," he claims, is similar to prohibiting sexual wishes. In both attitudes, Kohut (1977) argues, we conform to an arbitrary moral code by denying strivings that are natural and universal, and yet their manifestations are obvious everywhere.

Freud described development as the vicissitudes of drives. His developmental stages referred to the different forms of the conflict between drives and the environment. The theory of the vicissitudes of libidinal drives explained well the phenomena Freud observed in neurotic patients, especially the driven, dissociated, and restricted nature of their behavior. To account for other disorders (namely, psychotic disorders and sexual perversions), Freud postulated narcissism, a libidinal drive invested in the self, as a developmental phase on the way from autoeroticism to object love. Developmental maturity depended on giving up self-love for the mature love tie to others. This shift did not occur in sexual perversions and psychosis. Thus, in Freud's writings self-love and its expressions were assigned a semipathological status (Wolf, 1977). With a shifting clinical picture in which inhibition of sexuality seemed rare and in which neurotic symptoms, if present at all, were embedded in a global picture of despair, emptiness, and frenzied lifestyle, the view of the sexual drive per se as the bedrock of psychopathology has changed. Kohut (1971) was the first to conceptualize this seemingly new clinical picture as a defect in the cohesion of the self. In this conceptualization, the drives were encompassed in a psychology of the self. Driven or inappropriate expression of sexuality and agression was the consequence rather than the cause of a disintegrated or fragmented self. Kohut argued that self-love continued to develop in parallel with the love of others and that its various expressions—namely, the needs for recognition, admiration, and exhibitionism—have their mature forms. Development begins, Kohut postulated, with a nuclear self organized around two poles: a grandiose self and an omnipotent parent. In the normal course of events both poles are modified by the frustrations imposed by reality and by the growing ability to appraise one's true talents and limitations. The normal expectable environment should provide confirmation, mirroring, and empathy as well as moderate frustrations that channel ambitions and expectations in certain directions providing a realistic pattern that can be followed. In the normal course of events, then, the "grandiose self" is integrated with other ego functions providing for a relatively adequate although never "objective" appraisal of the self. The grandiose self remains, however, as the source of what may be labeled positive self-related affect: our ability to enjoy our accomplishments, to feel enthusiastic about our ambitions, and to "matter" to others. The "omnipotent parent" remains as the ideal towards which we strive and as the source of our ability to admire those who seem to have attained them. In the narcissistic disorders, on the other hand, the two poles retain their infantile form, unintegrated with developing talents and skills. They will be either completely repressed and unavailable to consciousness, or as is most often the case, they will continue to exist side by side with an experience of the self as insignificant and inferior.

Rothstein (1980) also emphasizes the ubiquitous nature of narcissism. He describes it as the investment in the self as perfect: "all human beings pursue these illusions [of perfection] in one or another mode." What is different is the state of integration of these pursuits along a spectrum from psychotic to normal: "What has been called normal narcissism, in contrast to normal self esteem and self regard and despite its adaptive advantages, is a mechanism for self aggrandizement and subtle self delusion that man finds necessary to assuage the insult of his true being" (p. 45).

A pursuit of illusions of perfection, which Rothstein describes as a ubiquitous narcissistic pursuit, is eloquently illustrated in Tolstoy's story of his youth (1937):

> My only real faith at the time was faith in self perfection. But in what self perfection consisted and what was the aim of it I could not have said. I tried to perfect myself mentally—I studied everything I could, anything life threw in my way,—I tried to perfect my will, I drew up rules I tried to follow, I perfected myself physically, cultivating my strength and agility by all sorts of exercises and accustoming myself to endurance and patience by all kinds of privations. And all this I considered to be the pursuit of perfection. The beginning of all was of course moral perfection but that was soon replaced by perfection in general, by the desire to be better not in my own eyes or those of God but in the eyes of other people. (p. 6)

Despite the differences in definitions and emphasis in the writings on narcissism as outlined above, and despite the unclarity that often results from them, a description of narcissistic phenomena emerges that may illuminate some of the data on religious conversion. Narcissism is a defensive focus on the self, a self-absorption that serves to bolster positive self-regard. Mental activity is narcissistic to the extent that it functions to maintain the cohesiveness, the stability, and the positive affective coloring of the self-representation. When moderate and well integrated, it is an adaptive part of our experience. For, when allowed appropriate expression, the narcissism of the child and the grandiosity and exhibitionism of childhood evolve into realistic self-esteem and pleasure with ourselves. They are expressed in the capacity to be enthusiastic and to admire the great after whose lives we can permit ourselves to model our own (Kohut, 1977).

But narcissistic mental activity may become intense and perpetuated. In the psychological disturbances which have come to be called narcissistic, an intense focus on the self is a chronic pattern.

Among the markers of this pattern of chronic narcissistic difficulties are a constant state of demand, a need to prove and glorify the self, and wild oscillations of self-esteem. Narcissistic patients seem to sway between grandiose, inflated images of their talents and convictions of their utter helplessness and inferiority. They harbor a sense of specialness and feel themselves entitled to what they want, whenever they want it and at any cost. They are preoccupied by their appearance and status. Just as they seem to entertain delusions of omnipotence, they are ravenous for the admiration and recognition of others. They constantly seek others' approval to validate their self-esteem and depend on the unconditional approval and "mirroring" environment for the maintenance of their own sense of self.

The story of Ed's conversion to the Baha'i faith provides a mild example of the behavior pattern described here. Ed's story (presented in Chapter 3) reflects a self-absorption, a preoccupation with his reflection in the eyes of others, and a need to attach himself to the semblance of power. Describing his associations with peers, Ed vacillates between perceiving himself as the successful entertainer and experiencing himself as the inadequate outsider who is likely to be the subject of ridicule and gossip. He prides himself on being the "center of attention" but reports "paranoid" fears of exposure. He seems to entertain unrealistic expectations of excellence and is constantly frustrated in attempts to align himself with those he deems powerful. Ed's conversion may have offered some resolution for these concerns. His conversion allowed an expression of grandiose expectations, of having a powerful impact, of becoming "a saint" and the messenger for the "most significant thing that has come along for our civilization." His life-long wishes to "excel" and to be admired could be expressed and partially fulfilled in the new environment, for it offered unconditional approval, freedom from "gossip," and the opportunities "to appear" and "to give lectures" which Ed identifies as the most enjoyable part of his new life. Ed's aspirations for a special mission and a powerful impact coincided with his experience of himself as inferior and helpless. Indeed, the worship of idols depends on the sense of the inferiority of the self. As Freud (1953/1914) observed, charismatic leaders depend on the repressed narcissism of their followers.

Writing about the religious conversion of a Christian divinity school student, Helfaer (1972) describes similar vacillation between expectations of irrevocable impact and a sense of inferiority:

> [He] achieved an exquisitely appropriate combining of both his profound sense of inferiority and also the sense of being special, his long standing feelings that he was to fulfill a golden future, be dominant and

achieve something great . . . . The religious symbolism allowed both these features of his personality, the feeling of inferiority and the grandiosity, to come to fruition, to achieve an active motivational salience and take a culturally valid, conscious form. (p. 164)

Consider also the following excerpt from an interview with a "born-again" Episcopal minister. Prior to his conversion he had aspired and felt entitled to power and anticipated ultimate success but had also felt deeply unworthy and unloved:

> I wanted to at least be the president of the USA. I had my picture with the mayor of the largest city, governor of the largest state, president of the country, but I wanted more. I wanted power and people and mass movements . . . and Christ was entirely different . . . I realized He loved the unloveable . . . something happened inside of me that if He loved them maybe He could love me.

The narcissistic condition is also manifested in particular difficulties in sustaining close relationships (cf. Lasch, 1979). Narcissistic people have little sense of the impact their actions have on others. When they do form emotional ties, these are often explosive and self-destructive, based on the conviction that exploitation dominates personal relationships. Their own self-representation and their images of others are split between "good," idealized, totally protective omnipotent figures and no less omnipotent malevolent persecutors. Narcissists view and treat others as extensions of themselves. They are oblivious to the interests, beliefs, or characteristics of the people they encounter who do not serve their own needs: These people matter only to the extent that they reflect the narcissists' own desires and fears.

THE WISH FOR MERGER

The person who seeks a relationship in which only one of the partners matters is bound to experience repeated disappointments in relationships with real and separate others. For, as Peter stated, most others can give only conditionally. By contrast, a merger with a transcendental perfect object may promise this person a love relationship that places no demands. This merger may be attained in the religious conversion.

In the early studies of religious conversion a sense of "giving up," of passive "self-surrender," was described as central to the religious experience. In this process the person resigns himself or herself to the crisis, puts aside the doubts and the questions plaguing him or her, and passively awaits God's guidance. Starbuck (1899) viewed "self-surrender" as an indispensable last step in the conversion experience of many of his subjects.

In many cases, he writes, "relief persistently refuses to come until the person ceases to resist or to make an effort in the direction he desires to go" (in James, 1902, p. 171). William James attributed a "well-developed subliminal self" to the person prone to experience conversions. He described the self-surrender as a process in which active awareness and a conscious sense of sin and worthlessness are overpowered by a different, positive "subconscious" system which has been incubating all along but which can emerge only via a passive surrender: "When the new center of personal energy has been subconsciously incubated so long as to be just ready to open into a flower, 'hands off' is the only word for us, it must burst forth unaided" (p. 172).

Starbuck and James describe a process similar to the crisis of doubts that preceded Peter's second conversion. Peter's resolution of this crisis, however, involved more than a passive surrender, more than a cessation of doubts and questions. It seemed to involve a surrender to another of autonomy and will. The experience is not just a "letting go" but a form of a takeover, through which the experience of the self as a separate and volitional actor is altered. There is now a new "pilot" residing inside, directing the convert's actions.

Peter wished for "utter perfection" and unconditional love that would transform him but he simultaneously avoided ties with others. These tendencies are reminiscent of the pattern of interpersonal relationship that reflects narcissistic difficulties. The person who experiences narcissistic difficulties retreats into the self, cultivating an aloofness and a shallowness in interpersonal relationships. In addition to this protective recoiling from what he or she may consider the mediocre lot, this person may also feel occasional intense attachments to powerful idols which are experienced as extensions of his or her own self. These idols are internalized and merged with the self to become the invincible suppliers of protection and power. According to Kernberg (1975), narcissistically disturbed adults, while withdrawn and guarded in most of their interpersonal ties, are constantly looking for a magical rescuer. They are searching for external omnipotent powers from whose support and approval they attempt to derive strength. They form an immediate attachment to a hero or outstanding individual and experience themselves as part of that idealized person.

Idealization of love objects and modeling oneself after the example of an admired idol are ubiquitous parts of human experience. But narcissistic emulation of idols is characterized by the extent to which there is no active choice or selection of the attributes of the object of worship. Qualities that are subsidiary are adopted as enthusiastically as the qualities that are central. Narcissistic idealization is also distinct in the degree of self-reference that permeates the idealization. Idols are perceived to the extent that they gratify or frustrate the self's wishes. The idealization is combined with an increased sensitivity to disappointments. It is readily turned into fear and hatred when the idol seems to reject or in other ways frustrate the person's needs.

A number of my interviews illustrate such religious conversions, which effect a merger in which God is experienced as an extension of the self. Describing the consequences of his conversion, Philip, a born-again Christian, says: "What is important is that the Holy Spirit takes residence inside you. You go on with guidance so that you hopefully switch on to that other pilot guiding you when you see you're falling back into anger, lust, resentment." Scott, another Evangelical Christian, describes the consequences of his conversion:

> What I began to see was that Jesus was inside of me and I was his earthly vessel, His vehicle for getting around, and when I went to my old pursuits of sleeping around, drinking, etc., it was painful for Him because He identified with me, so it was painful for me. The things He used to do, which I wouldn't have done, produced joy for Him so it began to produce joy for me.

In this merger with the perfect object, the convert's choices are guided by what is pleasurable or unpleasurable to the "other pilot" which has become an extension of the self. The reality external to the self hardly matters. At the same time the merger ameliorates the experience of the self as inferior and defective. As the "other" in the religious conversion is perfect and infallible, the experience of merger achieves the felt quality of perfection rendering the transformed self perfect as well.

The merger with God may offer an opportunity for a relationship that circumvents the demands of relationships with separate others who have wishes and needs of their own. In this conversion, the discovery of God is described as a discovery of a caterer to the self. This pattern emerges clearly in the following case of a dual religious conversion.

THE CASE OF BEN

Ben, a 26-year-old Baha'i believer who holds a PhD degree, converted twice. His first religious conversion, which he considers the most significant one, was a conversion to Christianity. The second, a year prior to my interview with him, was a conversion to the Baha'i faith. At the Baha'i fireside meeting in which I met him, he stood out in an extravagant three-piece suit and carefully matched shirt and tie. He announced that he was the "ultimate convert" and promised that I would get my "best story" interviewing him.

Ben is the middle child in a Jewish middle-class family. His childhood was a lonely and agonizing time. He describes a withdrawn father, who would disappear for long stretches of time, and an anxious, overprotective mother. He describes constant parental strife and an intense rivalry with his siblings, an older brother and a younger sister, whom he did not like nor trust. Other significant figures in Ben's childhood were scarce. He does recall several teachers toward whom he developed an "emotional attachment." He explains this attachment as a consequence of the teachers' attitudes towards him:

> My brother was in the same school and he embarrassed me, getting into fights, etc. I never felt comfortable being in the same school with him and I remember one of the teachers in the playground talked to me and felt that this was wrong of him [the brother] to make me embarrassed, that I should not have to put up with that kind of thing, so at the time I remember it strongly affected me that she was interested . . . . Then in sixth grade I was ambivalent [towards the teacher]. Sometimes I liked her but sometimes she would say things that would hurt me and I disliked her.

Similarly, he remembers as "interesting" some of his brother's friends because they took an interest in him: "Sometimes his friends, my brother's friends, were interesting. I remember one of them felt an interest in me, that I was O.K., that I was better than other people." What stands out in his memory is the experience, rare for him, of being taken seriously and of being viewed as special.

Ben's parents did not practice their Jewish religion but they sent him to Hebrew school, which he remembers with distaste:

> I went to Hebrew school but I did not feel comfortable there. I disliked it very much most of the time. But there was no concept of God in my mind, although I liked to see pictures or read stories about Christ, oh, not Christ, it was the Jewish thing. But I do remember one time I brought in the Old Testament and the New Testament, it was in one book, and they sent me to the rabbi. My parents gave me that book, but the teachers made a big thing out of it. Told me I could not read this book. That stands out in my mind, because I remember the Old Testament pictures were kind of bright and the New Testament's were soft and subtle, I enjoyed them more. They were softer and Jesus looked real nice, whereas the Hebrews—they had beards, looked kind of strong and fierce.

Ben describes his adolescence, his high school years, and his early years in college as extremely unhappy. Although his relationship with his parents had worsened he continued to live at home. He developed an ulcer, did not have any friends, and did not have any freedom. His mood was one of:

> hurried frustration, I did my work at school and I also worked at a restaurant, but that was all. There was no sense in it. Although I did it, I felt if I did not go through with college, if I quit or got fired or something that would reflect on me. So I went to school and I kept these jobs even though I did not see any sense in it . . . . I lived at home and that was terrible.

He had several intense emotional attachments with male friends, but all of them ended in disappointment:

> I remember having strong attachments to certain people, although it was unregulated, there were one or two relationships, maybe three, that I felt were strong on my part and I think this has had something to do with my later conversion. Because these people that I knew, I respected and loved very much and I, if they suggested anything, I would have done it. I cared about their opinion. Later on there were other people's opinions that I cared about and that's why I did certain things . . . because I wanted the emotional attachment . . . . It never seemed to work out, always brought a lot of pain.

During his later years in graduate school, Ben became interested in religion through the influence of a friend, his current object of admiration. This friend had been "experimenting" with religion and then left for California and wrote to inform Ben that he had become a Catholic convert and a monk. It was the friend's conversion which gave the main impetus to Ben's own conversion to Christianity:

> I thought, well I'm going to investigate this and I'm going to find out what this is all about because, when I go to visit him then I'll be up on it, so I did it, investigating on my own and I knew that if he was so strongly committed to it that there was something in it because he would not commit himself to anything, being a very rational and intelligent person that I admired, that was not good. So I started reading the Bible, etc. and not long after that, say a couple of weeks, I knew that I would be strongly attached to that.

Ben's account of his growing "attachment" to Christianity is a blatant statement of his need for an undemanding, totally protective object:

> [What attracted me] was the fact that Christ was so forgiving that all of the things that I felt were wrong with me and everything all of a sudden could be erased and that I could live a whole new life, could start a relationship with someone [Christ] who would never cause me any pain and that this relationship was something that I always knew I wanted all along because I was never physically or sexually oriented. I never felt comfortable in that regard, and this relationship seemed to me perfect because I would not have to [be sexual]. I would be getting everything I wanted and not have to do anything I did not want to do. It seemed very strong to me, a very strong thing.

Two weeks after he had learned of his friend's conversion, Ben commenced instructions to become a Catholic. The day prior to his scheduled baptism, he decided, however, not to go through with the formal conversion. This decision was the consequence of yet another powerful influence which he couldn't resist. His mother and other family members had been taking est at the time, and in an attempt to prevent his conversion, they persuaded Ben to do the same:

> I was back in my hometown, after being away for graduate school, and my mother's nephew, my cousin, was taking it [est] and the whole family was taking it and she [the mother] said she'll pay for it and it's a good thing, and I could not see how it could be a bad thing. I was Christian after all, and at the state I was in I felt anything could be helpful, and if it's not, then it's my fault.

He reports liking his experience at the est seminar, but his needs and his confusion with respect to his own goals and preferences seem to have intensified:

> Everybody was smiling and they were happy and had a lot of Christian spirit in them, even though they did not know it was Christian. It was nice. I learned an awful lot . . . . I realized that I was creating everything that was happening to me including the religious thing and I did not go through with the baptism, although that always seemed . . . they said that there was no God, and I never agreed with that although I knew that they did not really mean that. Like the whole basis for them doing what they were doing was that they believed in God. So I did not go through with the baptism, although I remained a Christian. I still consider myself Christian.

Ben's account of his more recent conversion to the Baha'i faith was strikingly casual. He told me that last spring he had met a Baha'i and had gone to fireside talks with him, and two months later he had declared himself a Baha'i. But as with his attachment to Christianity, his discovery of the new faith had not been founded upon an appreciation of any objective attributes of the faith and had resulted in no firm commitment. He offered the following explanation for this second conversion: "It seems a good religion and it does a lot to me. It seemed so easy to do that I just did it. But there was always this sneaking suspicion in my mind that I am more Christian than Baha'i." From Ben's point of view, his conversion to the Baha'i faith is justified as an "easy thing to do." Similarly, he described his conversion into Christianity as an "easy process," one that offered, with no effort on his part, instant fulfillment of his needs:

> The process of believing in God was an easy one. As I said, all my life I had a need for a strong emotional attachment, not of a physical nature, and that need was never fulfilled, so when I finally found something that fulfilled it, it did not take me long to realize that I should hold on to it. So I don't feel that it was a sudden, traumatic thing. It was an extremely nice thing that had happened in a short period of time. As I said, it gave me what I've always wanted. I feel happy about it and it was easy to get.

Ben believes that after his second conversion he developed a better understanding of other people. But he experiences frequent relapses. Last summer, for example, during a vacation in Europe, he felt that:

my conversion was tested, my religion was tested. I would revert back to selfishness and antagonism and sometimes very bad feelings towards my parents. The whole embrace of religion was very weak. I did not have a job, I had no stability, I did not have a good time in Europe, and I felt mean, very mean.

Ben's story reveals a striking superficiality of interpersonal contacts, openly expressed fears of sexuality and anger, and arbitrary vicissitudes of beliefs and lifestyle. Most patent of all is his need for a totally nondemanding, one-sided love relationship which inevitably had been frustrated in his relationships with others, and which seems to have been finally gratified in his first conversion. Ben's account of his preconversion life portrays the recurring disappointments in previous relationships and his relief at discovering one that was "easy to get." His story is remarkably self-centered. He perceives others only in terms of their ability to gratify his own wishes. His rational for the religious conversion as an easy gratification, without sacrifice or effort, brings to mind Balint's (1968) description of the interpersonal relationships of narcissistic patients:

> It is definitely a two-person relationship in which, however, only one of the partners matters; his wishes and needs are the only ones that count and must be attended to. The other partner, although felt to be immensely powerful, matters only insofar as he is willing to gratify the first partner's needs and desires or decides to frustrate them; beyond this his personal interests, needs, desires, wishes, etc. simply do not exist. (p. 23)

The unusual amount of self-reference in Ben's description of relationships with others and his view of the religious conversion as a facile fulfillment of his needs reflect a fragile self: a constant state of desire for approval and recognition and an inability to experience himself as a separate and volitional actor. His conversion, as he himself so plainly acknowledges, may be understood as an attempt to annul the pain of disappointments and rage encountered in his ties with others via an "attachment" that would guarantee unlimited and undemanding supplies.

Ben's only justification for his conversion seems to be "It does me good." He seems to feel that the belief that provides relief is the belief to be adopted. Whether or not it conforms to, is validated by, or may be useful toward understanding or action in some reality outside the self is immaterial. Reality may, in fact, become an obstacle whereas the conversion experience offers a new reality, a reality that conforms to his wishes.

Some conversions allow a retreat into a world that conforms to one's wishes by a special brand of mystical awareness. These experiences are discussed in the following section.

THE PERSONALIZED MIRACLE

In the typical religious conversion experience, a feeling of immense relief or joy is taken as the proof and as the only necessary indication of the truth of the new beliefs. No critical evaluation of them is required. The flood of emotions that the convert experiences is followed by an interpretation that endows the emotional experience with meaning. It is a religious interpretation of the experience which to the outside observer may seem arbitrary. The convert-to-be attributes his or her emotional rapture to the presence of a God, or to the presence of His divine messengers. Other possible interpretations of the experience are not attended to. Experiencing a dramatic conversion seems to depend on a suspension of intellectual scrutiny.

A temporary or partial suspension of critical and systematic evaluations may take part in experiences other than religious conversion that lead to a shift of perspective. For example, the role of nonverbal, unorganized, fleeting images or sensations in the process of artistic creation has been emphasized by many (e.g., Kris, 1952; Koestler, 1964). Creative resolutions of intellectual puzzles often emerge from a period of incubation, a period in which an active search for a solution is given up and repeated scrutiny of the problem is halted. The passive, meandering mind may then be seized by a sudden "insight," which consists in a different view of the problem which enables a resolution. The abeyance of critical evaluation which occurs in religious experiences has been similarly described as a part of an active quest for solutions resulting in new insights (see Batson and Ventis, 1982).

But for some of the religious converts in my research, the extent and the scope of the suspension of reality testing that is involved in the religious experience are striking. Their conversion experiences are studded with "mysteries" which reflect childlike beliefs in the power of wishes. In the process of their conversion, these converts perceive miracles in which commonplace occurrences are endowed with a personalized "miraculous" interpretation and are elevated to the status of a special message. A gratifying world in which wishes may be instantly granted and of which they are the center is validated in the process of their conversion by omens and signs meaningful only within their own new version of reality. Consider the following case of conversion from Judaism to Christianity.

The Case of Ken

Ken is a 24-year-old member of a charismatic church who considers himself a Jew for Jesus. The eldest of three in an upper-middle-class Jewish family, he was raised by a mother who was a Hebrew teacher and by Jewish Orthodox grandparents and thus was exposed to a great deal of Jewish teaching and practice which he had often found scary and rigid:

> Sometimes I'd like it but sometimes it was really scary, I used to be afraid if I did something wrong . . . God would be so mad at me, all kinds of terrible things would happen. Actually, I was not as afraid of condemnation from God as from the older people in the synagogue. They seemed so holy, everything you'd do you'd feel they'd say something about it and you'd get a bad year or somebody would die. I'd be really afraid that if I did not pray I'd be in a lot of trouble, [it] just seemed very oppressive.

These fears of death and condemnation were not associated with Orthodox Judaism alone. Ken's parents consistently perpetuated them. He describes both his parents as overprotective, constantly worrying and fretting over him and his younger siblings. They seemed terrified of the outside world and worried about their children's ability to take care of themselves. Ken felt closer to his father but describes him as a hypochondriac, obsessed with the dangers of cancerous agents, afraid of simple everyday situations, and overly concerned about the health of his children and the dangers awaiting them outside their home.

The parents' fear that Ken would be unable to function independently was confirmed. Ken anticipated disasters—especially the death of his parents—throughout his childhood, believing that such misfortune would be brought upon him by an angry, punitive God.

Ken's fears of dangerous, uncontrollable powers worsened during his adolescence. Around the age of 14, he stopped believing in God but continued to pray "just in case." His preoccupation with death continued: he associates it with a preoccupation with a "real" self:

> I was preoccupied with what happens to a person after death, what part of the person was real, was the real self. I had to prepare myself for that thinking about where to get buried so that the part of the person that was real would end up in something nice, becoming part of the universe, which is where you came from.

Ken's fears and his uncertainty of a "real self" fostered a defensive aloofness and an increased withdrawal from family and peers.

> [I was] depressed about everything. I did not know who I was, where I was, what I was supposed to be. All I knew was that I had not done well in school and that was why people did not like me. The competition bothered me, everybody competing all the time, everybody trying to prove that they were better than the other. I was a loner.

He looked for consolation in grandiose anticipation of future success:

> It was jealousy or pride, you know, I used to think these guys are not good enough for me. I don't need them. If they don't want [me], it's their problem. I am not even going to be looking at them . . . . I was building up images inside, you know, how good it would be when I am finally great; then they will all come to me, then they will see.

Ken describes the following six years of his life as desperate. He had managed to graduate from high school and then tried college but soon dropped out. Experimenting with drugs during his short stay at college further debilitated him, shaking his already fragile hold on reality. He spent a year at home doing nothing, infuriated and confused by his parents, relatives, and peers urging him to make something of his life. He then tried a variety of odd jobs and several living arrangements. He lived for a while with a group of young Jewish Zionists who were practicing a form of Orthodox Judaism diluted with radical politics. After his initial enthusiasm, he felt a stranger in their midst. Their practices and attitudes reminded him of his mother and of the stern religious education of his childhood.

Leaving home and receiving psychiatric help for three years helped Ken survive the emotional upheaval of his adolescence, but it did not transform him. He felt burdened by living, by trying to "relate conflicting parts of my life," by pretending to enjoy people around him, all the while presenting the facade of aloofness, and harboring feelings of rage and hurt. He recalls "lying in bed at night feeling that my head was going to explode, feeling really crazy." The only happy times were on camping trips, in nature, away from the company of people. On one of these trips, Ken was introduced to Christianity. He was told of a Jewish friend who had become a Christian after several "incredible" events:

> He was hitchhiking and really needed a ride and a truck passed him and he started praying, he said, "I don't believe in you, but I would this time and if you are there that car is going to stop." After he said that, the car brakes slammed and the driver backed up and picked him up and he was like freaking out. When I heard that I said wow, because I knew my friend, he was really intelligent and I looked up to him. I knew he would not tell me anything that was not the truth. Then he told me some other incidences, real complicated ones, and I said that's incredible. Then he asked if I believed and I said no but I thought it would be really exciting if that was real.

Ken decided he would try to test God for himself. Walking alone one night he requested a first "miracle"—to see a girl he had been working with and whom he had not seen at work for a while:

> I said, even though I thought that's ridiculous, I'm talking to nobody, I said I am going to believe in You this time, I am going to believe she is going to be at work tomorrow. And the day went by, I had forgotten that I had made that prayer. Just five minutes before I was going to leave [work] I went to the second floor to get some paper towels and just there at the desk was the girl I had asked to see. She was sitting and I went over and talked to her and it turned out that somebody had gotten sick that day and she was called in just out of the blue. So I went downstairs and then I suddenly realized, wow, I prayed to see her last night.

A month went by and Ken received another sign. Walking alone, contemplating the uniqueness and importance of individuals and thinking that "life is a drag," he recalls crying out loud, "What's the answer?" and at that moment a car drove by and a bumper sticker on its back windows read "Jesus saves." Ken was astounded by the "perfect timing." He became convinced that Somebody was listening.

A new excitement had taken over Ken's life. To his mother's astonishment and at first with her ardent blessing, he began frantically reading the Bible, looking for the prophecies which indicated Jesus was the new Messiah, as his friends had suggested. Their beliefs presented a new hope: "If there was a God, I wanted to find him because then nothing mattered. My past, He knew about it, He knew exactly who and where you were and had something planned for you." Still plagued by doubts that he was talking himself into it, and that, as his parents argued, he was being "brainwashed" into a world of fantasy, Ken set up additional "tests" to verify God's power and His personal interest in him.

Finally, another "heavy coincidence" made him a "true believer":

> One morning I said, I was excited about it but I was still thinking "am I talking myself into it?" I was thinking it's probably not true, but I was thinking "If you are the one who's doing all this stuff, if you are God, right now as a confirmation for that you could play on the radio that song that I am thinking in my head." It was an old song, 10 or 11 years old. I heard it maybe two or three times played on the radio. I said, "You could do it right now, but I'll be satisfied if I hear it later sometime this morning." I was sure I was going to dissolve this thing, go back to reality and forget about the whole thing, but then I walked into my sister's room and that song was playing. I was really happy that day.

This final "miracle" confirmed Ken's wish for a world in which everything is possible. He told his convert friend about his own growing belief and asked for his guidance in accepting Jesus. When they prayed together that night, Ken, convinced that he had been heard and would forever be protected, felt real peace and happiness:

> God loves you, cares for you just the way you are. He'll change you, it's not up to you, there is nothing that you can do, all you can do is be obedient and listen and cooperate and just trust that He has a plan. God has so much power, so much control, he knows you better than you know yourself. He knows you from birth. He died for your sins and He will deliver you from your sins, all you have to do is to acknowledge that. If God really loves you then what else do you need?

A charismatic Christian meeting marked another turning point in Ken's conversion:

When I went to the prayer meeting, listening to people praying really loudly it was making me uneasy. I was thinking this is crazy, but all of a sudden I hear people speaking languages and I recognized, it sounded like Hebrew, like a synagogue, it was amazing, I was freaking out, these people were Catholic. How come they can speak Hebrew? My friends were telling me those are the gifts of the spirit: When you become a believer you get the whole package, everything, but you do not have it manifested unless you ask for it. That really convinced me that Jesus and the God of Israel were the same, that it was the God of Israel because they were speaking what sounded like Hebrew. How could anyone except the God of Israel do that, have them speaking Hebrew?

The meeting consolidated the message Ken had been hearing from his peers. While praying and praising God with two other former Jews who had become followers of Christ, Ken had another mystical experience. Already veterans in the new faith, his friends had been guiding Ken in their version of Christian doctrine and had told him about the baptism of the Holy Spirit. They then laid their hands over his head, praying that he would receive it. Ken felt flooded with joy, which he describes as a blissful feeling of being drunk, of being fed. That night, lying in bed, he experienced again, with even greater intensity, the divine power his friends had promised him:

I said, "OK, God, if you want to do it, you can do it now." Just as I was starting to fall asleep, all this intensity started hitting me from above, like intense warmth, like a blanket of love. It was almost like it made noise, like it hit me on top of my head, surged all the way down my body and just filled it. I would have been knocked down by the power if I had not been lying down already. I could not understand where all this was coming from—who was giving me this love, all I felt was this warm love, I could not really describe it . . . I just started saying, "God, I love you." I could not express the emotion, it was so intense . . . . I never experienced that before and I was trying to find ways to express it, something said to me, telling me to speak and I opened my mouth and all of a sudden this foreign language was coming out.

In his religious conversion, Ken entered a safe, protective reality populated only by the chosen of his peers. In this reality all dangers disappeared and all tensions dissolved; no longer does Ken need to perform, compete, or invest any effort, not even in attempting to appease a fierce God, as he had done in his tormented childhood. Most striking in Ken's story is the series of "miracles" which guaranteed his re-birth as a Christian. These miracles are miraculous only in Ken's eyes. Ken does not require the splitting of the sea, the walking on water, or a sudden cure, to behold the power of God. An unexpected ride, a song played on the radio, or a car sticker are sufficiently "magical" for him. These commonplace events become personalized miracles which he interprets as signs of God's special interest in him.

Ken's religious conversion provided him with the protection of a "blanket of love," annulling the pain and dangers he had known throughout his preconversion life. The details of the new world Ken discovered had been clearly molded by the suggestions of his peers. In particular, his belief that Christ and the God of Israel are one and his initiation into manifesting the gifts of the Holy Spirit were outlined by his enthusiastic converted friends. The specifics of the religious interpretation he had placed on his experience followed their dicta.

The particular dress of the object of infatuation, the omnipotent authority, the admiring peers, or the transcendental loving object may be provided by the milieu in which the experience occurs. As was described previously, expectations present at group gatherings, imitation of other members, latent directions provided by peers and mentors, and engaging in some ritual action without justification before acquainting oneself with the new beliefs—these and other processes present at the time of conversion participate in shaping the experience and in the future maintenance of the new beliefs. But these powerful influences generated in the immediate context of the conversion affect people who are already prone to the experience. There is no evidence that Ken was "brainwashed" by peer pressures as his parents contend; his peers' expectations had fallen on fertile grounds. They resonated with Ken's lifelong resort to magical rituals in order to avert real and imagined dangers. They responded to his wish to feel powerful and to be protected in what he perceived as a menacing world. Previous exposures to peer pressures, as in the Zionist commune he had joined for a short period, did not induce a change of heart. The model which he finally responded to was one promising him a world in which he would be unconditionally loved and protected, engulfed by a "blanket of love."

Ken's tendency to impose a unique self-centered interpretation on trivial events and the earlier anxieties and "magical" counter-measures to which he had been prone prior to his conversion under-score the fragility of his reality testing. Ken's world seems to be shaped, more than is normally and inevitably the case, by his inner wishes and by the opportunities for or obstacles to gratification of these wishes. In his world, limits and reality constraints are not inevitable; they are perceived as devices imposed by harsh frustrators and designed to torment the self. Conversely, these limits and constraints are remedied by benevolent, gratifying powers.

The trivialization of the miraculous and the generation of personalized messages, miracles especially geared to the self, appear in the stories of other converts. For a woman who had been reborn for 10 years at the time of the interview, the miraculous sign of God's power had been the disappearance of a painful plantar wart:

> I had this plantar wart, I went to two doctors and it would keep coming back and it was very painful, I decided I would forget about it because the doctors could not do anything about it, it was on the bottom of my foot, week after week they'd try to dig out the root. I remember one day I was in the shower and off the top of my head I said, "God, if there is a God, take away this plantar wart and I'll really believe that You are," and the plantar wart went away so then I knew for sure there was a God.

For a male Hare Krishna devotee, the miracle had been a clairvoyant's prophecy that he would "wear robes and give his life to God," which he had recalled several months later, meeting devotees while he roamed the city streets. For a young Jewish woman who grew up contemptuous of anything religious and who became a Hassidic Orthodox Jew, the miraculous proof of God's guidance had been her meeting with a rabbi's daughter who wore a Dior dress. For this young woman, who had always valued the symbols of high social status, especially expensive clothing, the dress had been a God-sent signal that she could adopt the Hassidic way of life without completely giving up her old values.

Similarly, for Carol, a born-again Evangelical Christian, God's message apparently sanctioned her desire to pursue interests which she had previously deemed selfish:

> For seven years I was the director of state-licensed nursery school that we had in this house. Two years ago, I was praying about things and suddenly got the message from the Lord to close the school. I called all

the parents and told them exactly what happened, that the Lord had told me to close it. I've been home since then. Our children are 14, 16 and 13 and I found it was very important to have time for them. So now the Lord has me doing artwork that I never knew I could do.

Her husband similarly experienced guidance of the Lord in a way that sanctioned his former lifestyle:

Getting ahead, making money, having a good career, success, the whole American dream was important to me. Now I still have all that, the Lord has blessed me in all those ways. He hasn't made me give up my lifestyle, in fact He's even increased it. But the leap of faith that led me to accept Him and say "do with me what You will," and of course right away, I thought He was going to send me off to Africa to become a missionary and I'd get shot by a poison dart and that would be the end of it. Of course, since then I've realized He never does things like that, people may end up being missionaries but they do it with a willing heart.

For these converts, God furnishes the heart's desire. The religious practice does not center on the common good, on discipline, purity, or sacrifice as a way of life, but on a relationship which caters to the self:

The Lord is a fantastic employment agent because He can just go out and He knows where there is a great job for you and He can present it to you and then make you want to have the heart to accept it and just pull the whole thing off. He absolutely engineers the whole thing.

In his book *The Thread of Life* (1984) the philosopher Richard Wollheim draws the following distinction between beliefs and desires: "The big difference between beliefs and desires is closely connected with what has been called the difference in fit between, on the one hand, belief, on the other hand desires, and the world. We require our beliefs to fit the world but we require the world to fit our desires" (p. 53). Our attachment to our beliefs, Wollheim continues, is influenced by our hope to gain the truth through them, but what attaches us to our desires is simply that they are ours, although sometimes our attachment to desires may be influenced by our reflection upon the frustration or satisfaction that we may incur through them.

In the stories of conversion presented here the world is required to fit the beliefs, and the attachment to the new beliefs is not in the hope of gaining truth, as beliefs require, but in the hope of gaining satisfaction as befits our desires.

NARCISSISM AND SELF-WORTH

The data on religious conversion presented in this chapter point to important dimensions in the experience of the self that have only recently found their way into empirical research on self-worth.

The narcissistic elements in conversion stories draw attention to several dimensions of individual and possibly developmental differences in the experience of the self that have consequences for psychological well-being and interpersonal behavior. These include the extent to which the self is experienced as distinct from others, the extent to which positive affect is directed towards the self, the degree of integration between such affect and the accuracy of self-perceptions, the experience of the self as an agent that to some extent controls one's fate and the experience of "mattering" to others.

Recent research on newborns calls into question psychoanalytical descriptions of the infant as existing in a blissful, "boundaryless" state or, as Mahler (1968) describes it, in a state of "normal autism." As early as the first few days of life, newborns interact differently with people than with objects, show a particular interest in human faces and voices, and are ready to engage in reciprocal social interchanges with adults (Brazelton, 1976; Condon and Sandor, 1974). This research suggests that young infants have an awareness of and a special interest in others and are therefore able to somehow distinguish between themselves and others (Damon, 1983). Nevertheless, the ability to distinguish the self from others which seems to exist in some rudimentary form even at birth undergoes developmental changes throughout childhood. For example, Lewis and Brooks-Gunn (1979) describe four advances in infants' self-knowledge (focusing on visual self-recognition). During the first two years of life, infants move from an unlearned attraction to the images of others, through an ability to recognize the self through contingency cues (understanding that the self is the origin or the cause of a moving visual image on the mirror or screen), to the recognition that the self is permanent, with stable and continuous features, and to the consolidation of basic categories that describe the self, such as gender and age.

This early developmental process of acquiring self-knowledge seems a universal step in the normal development of the self as distinct from the world and from others. But the data presented here suggest that this basic experience of the self's "distinctness" should not be presupposed or taken for granted among adults as well.

Damon and Hart (1982), reintroducing William James' subjective "I" into psychological investigation, present a developmental model of self-understanding that describes shifts in the bases for understanding "selfhood" during childhood and adolescence. With respect to "distinctness" they describe a developmental shift from the child's understanding the self's distinctness as based on physical and concrete attributes (appearance, sex, age, possessions) to an understanding of distinctness as arising from the subjectivity and privacy of the self's experience that emerges during adolescence. The data presented in this chapter suggest, however, that there may be developmental as well as individual differences not only in people's understanding of "distinctness" but in their experience of it.

Furthermore, contrasting subjects' descriptions of friends and parents with self-descriptions, Hart and Damon (1985) found a striking number of self-referent descriptions (e.g., "my mother is nice because she buys me candy") in the descriptions of others made by adolescents as well as younger children. They conclude that "at least part of one's understanding of another person is concerned with how that person's qualities directly affect the self" (p. 171). The stories of conversion examined here suggest that this concern is related to the experience of distinctness and that there may be individual differences among adults in the degree and nature of this concern that affect psychological well-being and the quality of interpersonal ties. That is, there are differences among adults in the tendency to view others as extensions of the self, existing to fulfill or frustrate the self's wishes, and these differences may be related to the stability of self-representations and self-esteem as well as to one's relationships with others.

Several hypotheses are also raised by the material presented in this chapter regarding the relationship between affect, global self-worth, and a sense of volition and control.

Kohut's (1972, 1977) views of pathological self-development suggest, for example, that normal or mature development of the self includes the ability to experience positive affect that is directed towards the self (e.g., pride in oneself, enthusiasm about one's aspirations, pleasure with oneself) side by side with a growing ability to more or less realistically appraise one's talents as well as one's limitations. A problem course of development, on the other hand, may take several paths. It may consist in pervasively negative self-related affect (e.g., shame, disgust with oneself, self-hate, despair of one's aspirations) that is unintegrated and uninfluenced by one's cognitive appraisal of the self's worth or competence in specific domains. It may also consist in wild oscillations of affect that are tied to consistently unrealistic, typically inflated appraisals and aspirations in specific domains. In these cases, one would also expect a difficulty in experiencing oneself as a volitional agent that to some extent controls one's fate as well as a tendency to inaccurately appraise others, i.e., a tendency to idealize and/or devalue others.

This view has some implications for the study of self-esteem.

First, it implies that it might be useful to examine separately a global sense of worth and appraisals of worth in specific domains, as the former may not be a simple sum of the latter (cf. Rosenberg, 1979). As William James (1892) contended at the turn of the century, "there is a certain average tone of self-feeling which each one of us carries about with him and which is independent of the objective reasons which we may have for satisfaction or discontent" (p. 171). Indeed, the writings on narcissism suggest that the degree and the nature of integration or cohesiveness between the "objective reasons" and the global sense of self-worth may itself be an important dimension of developmental as well as individual differences. Secondly, this view implies that one should attempt to directly examine the affect experienced in consequence of the self's actions or appraisals (e.g., shame, pride, vanity, jealousy) as a major determinant of global self-worth. A tendency to enhance the "positive affective coloring of self representation" (Stolorow, 1975, p. 179) may be pervasive among adults, and the ability to experience positive affect directed towards the self may be an important marker of normal development. However, as Harter (1985) argued, scales that attempt to measure the self-concept or self-esteem often do not measure affects. These scales often include items that imply affect (e.g., "I worry about my homework") but there are typically no attempts to measure the affect directly or to address it separately from items that make no reference to affect (e.g., "I have a lot of friends"). Finally, the literature on narcissism presented here implies that it may be difficult to evaluate the development of self-worth without some considerations of the accuracy of self-representations. For example, high self-esteem scores may reflect unrealistic evaluations of one's successes or importance and may be coupled with dysphoric affect and an instability of self-representations.

It may be impossible to predict adjustment or psychological well-being from self-esteem measures unless one attempts an evaluation of the accuracy of self-concepts and the affect associated with them, despite the enormous difficulties of this task.

Susan Harter (1985) presents data that are relevant to some of these implications and that indicate the fruitfulness of following them. Harter's data come from the cognitive domain: She compared children's evaluation of their scholastic competence with objective indices, such as achievement scores and teachers' ratings. Developmentally, accuracy of judgments gradually increased from grade 3 through 6, dropped markedly for seventh-grade junior-high-school students, and then gradually recovered again throughout the adolescent years, to reach a peak in the ninth grade. Along with these developmental trends, there were striking individual differences leading to the identification of three groups of children: (1) those who overrate their competence; (2) those who underrate their competence; and (3) those whose ratings are congruent with teacher's judgment. An examination of these three groups separately yielded results that are consistent with the hypotheses presented here. For the accurate or congruent raters, self-perceptions in the academic domain were meaningfully related to anxiety about schoolwork, perceptions of control, and preference for challenge in this academic domain. Children who accurately perceived themselves as competent were also low in anxiety and high in preference for challenge and evidenced an understanding of the factors that had led to their successes. For the two incongruent groups, however, the pattern of correlations was noticeably weaker. In particular, for those who overrated their competence the inflated self-perception was unrelated to and unintegrated with their perceptions of anxiety, control, and preference for challenge. At least in the academic domain, then, high self-esteem per se does not predict other constructs related to psychological well-being. Furthermore, an inflated self-perception in this domain is associated with contrasting or unrelated evaluations of the self in the same domain, namely, with an incohesive or fragmented self-perception.

Differences among the accurate and inaccurate raters also emerged in actual behavior. Placed in a situation where their preference for cognitive challenge was assessed (by the use of anagrams), the overraters as well as underraters attempted to avoid challenge; that is, they selected easier tasks to perform than did the accurate raters. Again, for the overraters especially, it was not their self-evaluation of competence that predicted performance but their actual competence. Harter concludes that "at some level, the overraters are aware that they are not nearly as competent as their self reported judgements imply. Moreover, to protect what may be a fragile and distorted sense of scholastic ability, they were driven to select the easiest anagrams in order to avoid failure and its implications for the self" (p. 73).

Another set of relevant findings presented by Harter derive from the empirical investigation of "beneffectance" (Greenwald, 1980): the tendency to take credit for successes while denying one's responsibility for one's failures. Beneffectance is, then, a subtle form of self-deception that protects or enhances self-image. Greenwald marshals an array of findings that identify "beneffectance" as a frequent strategy of self-protection among adults. Harter (1985) examined developmental trends in this strategy. Her findings indicate that the two extreme groups, those who tend primarily to self-blame (take responsibility for failures but attribute successes to external factors), and those who tend to primarily exonerate the self (take responsibility for successes but blame failures on external factors), remain stable across six grade levels.

These two extreme groups were relatively rare in Harter's sample, and were virtually identical in their mean scores of scholastic anxiety (which was high) and of perceived competence and preference for challenge (which were low). These two groups may be more likely to come to the attention of clinicians and may be more highly represented among converts.

While these extreme groups remained developmentally stable, Harter found clear developmental trends in the less extreme forms of beneffactance. As they grow older, children gradually come to take less responsibility for unsuccessful outcomes while they continue to take responsibility for their academic successes. A pattern that provides a certain degree of subtle self-delusion seems, then, an adaptive pattern that characterizes normal development from childhood.

Taken together, Harter's findings present a complex pattern of relationships between self-worth, positive affective coloring of self-representations, accuracy of self-perceptions, and perceptions of the self's responsibility that is consistent with the writings on narcissism. A relatively mild form of self-deception that protects a positive view of the self seems to be an adaptive strategy that increases in frequency from childhood to adolescence. On the other hand, clear discrepancy between self-evaluations and actual competence, whether negative or positive, is associated with incohesiveness of self-perceptions and avoidance of challenge. Harter focused on the academic domain but her findings indicate the fruitfulness of examining the ties between self-worth, accuracy of self-perceptions, and perceptions of responsibility in other domains as well.

Finally, findings reported by Rosenberg (1985) identify the experience of "mattering"—that is, the sense that one's thoughts or actions have an impact and that one makes a difference to specific others—as an important dimension of psychological well-being. Summarizing large-scale studies of adolescents, Rosenberg concludes that mattering is strongly related to psychological well-being. The adolescent who does not experience the self as having an impact on others is strikingly more likely to be high on depression, unhappiness, anxiety, and tension and to express feelings of hostility, embitterment, and disenchantment.

The data presented by Rosenberg do not allow an examination of the consequences of "low mattering" in interpersonal behavior. The conversion stories presented in this chapter suggest that the experience of low mattering affects interpersonal behavior in specific ways. Most notably, the person who experiences the self as "a chip on the tide of the universe" is more likely to attach himself or herself to idols perceived as omnipotent and infallible.

6

Conversion and the Quest for Meaning

The focus of previous chapters on the search for psychological salvation, for relief and approval, raises a difficult but inevitable question: Are there motives that precipitate the religious turnabout other than the avoidance of mental anguish? Describing conversion as an infatuation geared to provide psychological relief, are we excluding the possibility of a spiritual quest? Can one, in fact, differentiate a spiritual quest from a psychological one, a search for truth from a search for relief?

There have been several attempts to draw a portrait of authentic, intrinsic truth-seeking, or—a term easier for psychologists to defend—mature religious experiences.

In Paul Tillich's theology, religious faith is the manifestation of the "ultimate concern" for "that which determines our being or not being." It is a manifestation of a most profound search for meaning. According to Tillich (1952), the ultimate concern should be distinguished from the institution of religion. Organized religion, Tillich claims, may pose a danger to the religious life for it tends to become rigid, mechanized, unquestioning. A continuous individual query is necessary for the vitality and authenticity of religion to be preserved. In this theology, religion should be a private concern about the meaning of being. When it springs from these existential concerns, the religious quest may never be gratified and the religious seeker may forever remain a seeker, whose contact with God must always be in the nature of a search and an unfulfilled ideal.

This portrait of the religious person as the seeker of ultimate truth also appears in some writings on the psychology of religion.

In his writings on the individual and his religion, Gordon Allport (1950) demarcates the "right" and the "wrong" motives for sustaining religious faith, distinguishing between the mature and the immature religious sentiments. The "wrong" motives, in Allport's terminology, rest on "viscerogenic" desires, on the needs of the body. The "right" motives emanate from "objectified" desires. When motivated by psychogenic needs, humans long for Truth, Beauty, and Good, which are located outside the self, in some realm of essences. When motivated by the viscerogenic needs, the self's own wishes are the primary concern. In Allport's view, for the intrinsically religious person, religion is not an instrumental pursuit. It is not primarily a means of handling fear nor a mode of conformity to social demands. It is rather a commitment to an ideal, unifying one's life under a conception of the nature of all existence. A religious faith, similarly to any other dominant, integrative pattern of values, may provide direction and coherence to the self, which are the *sine qua non* of psychological maturity, and without which any life seems fragmented and aimless. When integrated in the mature personality, religious faith is marked, Allport says, by increased differentiation, and by the centrality and comprehensiveness of the issues it addresses. The mature religious sentiment involves a well-differentiated, nonmonolithic belief system which comprises many subsidiary attitudes, attitudes which are critically arrived at and flexibly maintained. It is also distinguished by the autonomous nature of its motivational powers. The mature religious sentiment is guided by an appreciation of the values or goals promoted. While immature religion is concerned with self-justification and comfort, the religion of maturity guides one toward external ideals. It deals with matters which are central to all existence and it provides a consistent, comprehensive direction to life.

In this dichotomy, Allport suggests some psychological characteristics of a mature religious quest. It is the pursuit of objectified ideals that are valued intrinsically and the nonrigid, well-differentiated, critical nature of this pursuit which define the religion of maturity.

Salzman (1953) implies a similar description of the truly religious quest in his attempt to distinguish "regressive" from "progressive" conversion experiences. Progressive conversions, Salzman argues, are prompted mostly by a conscious reflection and are more gradual and integrative experiences:

> This type of conversion frequently occurs in the course of real maturing, it takes place when the person after a reasoned, thoughtful search adopts new values and goals which he has determined to be higher than those he has abandoned. It occurs in reasonably normal persons and when it is a religious conversion represents the achievement of the ultimate in the humanistic religions—the positive fulfillment of one's powers with self-awareness, concern for others and oneness with the world. (p. 178)

Fowler (1981), who attempted to integrate the theories of Piaget, Kohlberg, and Erikson into a theory of stages of faith from birth to adolescence, also contends that faith is a way of being in relation to the ultimate environment, which gives meaning to the world about us. Fowler contends that progress from one stage to another that is higher on his developmental scale depends on cognitive maturation as well as exposure to experiences that challenge our systems of meaning. Conversions may involve such developmental shifts, in which a previous world view is rendered inadequate and a new and more complex one is established in its stead.

In their book on the social psychology of religious experience, Batson and Ventis (1982) emphasize similar attributes of the religious quest. They suggest that creative problem-solving may serve as a model for understanding dramatic religious experiences. In both phenomena, Batson and Ventis argue, cognitive structures that the person employs to think about the world are changed, and a new perspective of reality is created. In both, they argue, a similar sequence, which evolves in four stages, emerges. In creative problem-solving there are first persistent but unsuccessful attempts to solve the problem by using the old structures. Encountering repeated failures, the person then gives up the active search for solutions. In the third stage, there is a sudden emergence of a new organization, a switch of

Gestalt, that enables a different view of the problem and, consequently, its resolution. Finally, there is a testing and a verification of the new view.

In religious experiences, similarly, the first stage is the "existential crisis," an unsuccessful quest for solutions to existential queries. The second stage is the giving up of this quest in despair. Then there is a religious revelation, a sudden insight that provides a sense of resolution. In the final stage, the new vision is applied to behavior. In the same manner that one may evaluate the quality of resolutions to intellectual problems, the "creative" resolution offered by the religious experience may also be judged. It may be a solution that results in a higher level of cognitive organization, or it may be a solution at a lower level, in which aspects of the problem are simplified or ignored.

In this model, the problems that beset the potential convert are "existential" problems. Batson and Ventis distinguish between such existential enigmas and the problems which may be designated as "personal" or "emotional," suggesting that an active, relentless search for meaningful answers to questions about the nature of life and death, questions that any mature, thinking person may pose, precipitates the religious experience. In this view, converts have been compelled to reexamine and reevaluate beliefs that others in their environment may take for granted. They have been asking questions about the meaning and purpose of human life which their religious experience resolves. The cognitive transformation itself may be experienced passively as an automatic resolution, like the shift that occurs in a creative insight, but it is precipitated by a very active, continuous cognitive search.

Batson and Ventis echo in their model William James' description of the twice-born character, the person prone to conversion, as tormented by the inevitable complexities of life. The religious conversion of some twice-born characters, according to James, may be an experience precipitated by a conscious, unrelenting quest for the "right" answers. Although the conversion experience usually follows a passive "self-surrender" phase in which the deliberate effort to obtain answers is relinquished, there exists, prior to the conversion, a continuous intellectual search for solutions. The solution, in these cases, is seldom a complete restitution of a previous equilibrium, a return to whatever balance there existed prior to the struggle, nor does it establish a new "healthy-minded" outlook. Rather, like these more recent theorists who emphasize the cognitive components in religious experiences, James tells us that the conversion may result in a higher level synthesis in which evil and doubt are neither ignored nor viewed as a tantalizing stumbling block but are interwoven as elements in a more complex order.

These writings advocate the possibility of an "authentic," "progressive," "intrinsic," "quest-oriented," or truth-seeking religious experience. This experience includes the following components: It is precipitated by a relatively conscious, reflective existential search. One would expect to find, in the period preceding this conversion, the manifestations of a concern for or at least an interest in what is morally right or wrong, in what is true or false, in what constitutes the common good—a concern for questions that reach beyond the particular circumstances of the individual's life. The conversion experience could be prompted, at least in part, by "choosing" the new view as a better alternative to former beliefs, rendering life more meaningful and intelligible, albeit not always more pleasant or easy. The conversion experience could be a private, even lonely, experience which does not depend upon the recognition or approval of others and which need not abolish in the convert a critical, searching attitude.

The transformation that occurred in the majority of religious conversions that I have studied seems to follow a different course. As we have seen, there is little evidence of a deliberate intellectual quandary, of an active search for answers, or even of a well-formulated puzzle, and from the point of view of the convert, the religious revelation itself centered on the experience of unprecedented love and acceptance by others. Converts and nonconverts did not differ in their interest in ideological questions throughout adolescence, nor on the various measures of tolerance of ambiguity and existential quest I have employed. They did differ in the nature and the intensity of the emotional turmoil that had dominated their previous lives. Their conversions were invariably precipitated by a flood of negative emotions and, more often than not, centered on an intense interpersonal attachment which ameliorated their experience of the self as insignificant and helpless. The aforementioned views of the mature religious quest do not incorporate these emotional components of the conversion experience.

As defined in my study, existential quest, an interest in ideological and existential questions that reach beyond the idiosyncratic circumstances of the individual's life, occurred among 27 percent of the converts. The presence of this existential quest, however, did not prove the convert superior in emotional maturity, nor did it necessarily demonstrate an especially stable, healthy, or generous temperament, as Allport's dichotomy seems to imply. At the same time, the presence of turmoil and anxiety, of underlying conflicts, and of an infatuation with a real or imagined figure that I have found among converts does not necessarily rule out a quest for truth and values and a sensitivity to the lot of others, nor does it rule out the achievement of a unified identity, as we shall see in the stories of Leo Tolstoy and Dorothy Day.

The Case of Leo Tolstoy

Leo Tolstoy's religious transformation was prompted by an upsurge of love for the common peasants, but his change of heart was preceded by a diligent if passionate, investigation of a puzzle. The autobiographical *My Confession* (1961/1884) recounts with force, directness, and eloquence the story of a spiritual crisis in a twice-born character, a crisis that was experienced as a relentless search for truth.

Tolstoy's early life exemplifies the unhappy climate reiterated in the stories of other converts. Losing his mother at the young age of two and his father a few years later, he was left to the care of relatives, guardians, and tutors. But his confession begins later, when he was a young student falling away from the religious upbringing of his childhood. His temperament then reveals the traits which would be intensified and persistent throughout his life. He was "passionate, jealous, vain but affectionate, impressionable, aspiring and truth seeking; truth telling also, to himself, if not always to others" (Noyes, 1968/ 1919, p. 9). A tension between aspirations and principles on the one hand and actual conduct on the other is a perennial theme in Tolstoy's narrative of his youthful life. As in Rothstein's (1980) description of normal narcissistic aspirations, he longs for complete synchrony with an ideal and refuses to allow imperfections. He aspires to the good but feels alone and weak in this longing, ridiculed when expressing a sincere desire for what is right and praised when, unable to resist the passions of youth, he yields to "low temptations." The world is for him a "double-storied mystery" (James, 1902, p. 140) where moral perfection lurks beneath layers of natural passions and conveniences. In all his pursuits he attempts to discover the ultimate truth but turns away in disillusionment when his merciless analysis discovers an imperfection.

As a young soldier, he burned with patriotic faith but was then disgusted by the evil of war. As a writer, he taught and hailed the merits of art for "the good of humanity" but then denounced it as a "beautiful lie." He passionately believed in human progress, but the spectacle of a public execution showed him the "emptiness of the superstition of progress." For a while, marriage and peaceful family life provided him with a haven from his nagging doubts and perpetual self-examination. Although his marriage also turned out in the end to be bitterly disappointing for him, for fifteen years he lived a life centered around his wife and children and in his literary work. For a while, he seemed content in this life. But at the age of 50, he was struck by a despair more profound than he had ever experienced. It was not as unexpected as one might think in reading Tolstoy's own account. The years preceding his "moral crisis" may not have been as secure, as stable, and as fulfilling as Tolstoy describes.

His confessions leave out the series of losses he had suffered prior to his religious conversion. In the course of about two years, Tolstoy saw five deaths. The first was the death of his youngest child, following a few days of illness. This loss was followed by the death of his 80-year-old aunt, who lived with the Tolstoys, and shortly after that by the death of another child, a 10-month-old boy. During the year that followed his wife became critically ill and gave birth to a baby girl who did not live, and this was followed by the death of another member of the household—Tolstoy's only surviving aunt (Asquith, 1969). If these deaths affected him, Tolstoy gives no evidence of it. From his point of view, the crisis came unexpectedly. The question of life's meaning became a vital, urgent problem:

> These moments of perplexity began to occur more and more often and always in the same form. They were always expressed by the ques-

tions: What is it for? What does it lead to? The questions seemed such stupid, simple childish ones but as soon as I touched them and tried to solve them I became convinced first that they are not childish and stupid, but the most important and profound of life's questions, and secondly that try as I would I could not solve them. (1961/1884, pp. 15–16).

Once he had taken this perspective, once he had become so acutely aware of the absurdity and futility of a life destined to terminate arbitrarily, Tolstoy could no longer take comfort in the joys of his everyday life. Natural happiness now seemed a deceit, founded on ignorance and distortions. His life became dominated by this dark and gloomy perception: If one cannot live by a perfect truth, life is not worth living.

But the despair which had seemingly brought his life to a standstill had also inspired a systematic search for answers. For the next two years he examined, painstakingly and protractedly, "all branches of knowledge acquired by men." His efforts, he tells us, were all in vain. He dismisses scientific knowledge and philosophical discourse as either ignoring the question or offering no solution by which he could mold his own life. He was ready to give up, at the brink of suicide. The resolution came unexpectedly, in this case as in others, by a falling in love, an infatuation and an idealization of the people, the common peasants. Observing their life he saw simplicity, warmth, and industry. His mistake, he resolved, had been his preoccupation with his own life while ignoring the life of others. His trouble had been not with life in general but with the life of the upper, intellectual, artistic class to which he personally belonged. He decided that he had been living wrongly, a conventional and artificial life, a life of personal ambition. The peasants, on the other hand, lived a life free from all ostentation, superficiality, and indulgence. He decided that for the world and for his life to resume meaning, he needed to adopt the beliefs and the lifestyle of the common peasants, and the most visible and forceful part of that simple life was religious faith. Faith, he decided, was indeed the only reply to life's questions.

But even after faith in God was firmly established in his heart, Tolstoy could not blindly follow the simple Christian faith of the peasants. His conversion did not eradicate his stance as a critical, uncompromising seeker. Inquiring into religion as professed in books and in the lives of people around him, he was, once again, horrified by imperfections. He brutally denounced the life of Orthodox Christians of his circle as a life of self-indulgence and hypocrisy. He discovered contradictions and absurdities in Christian theology and was horrified by what was done in its name. Ceremonies and dogmas appeared to him scandalous; the mutual intolerance among Christian churches and the sanction, explicit or tacit, of war and capital punishment were unacceptable. As before, once he had identified a rift with the church, he was merciless in a total rejection of it. He called the church "insanity" and a conscious "interested lie." Tolstoy proceeded to develop his own theology. In his subsequent religious views, he saw property as theft and the life of luxury as the root of all evil. In his repeated attempts to live in accordance with these views, he separated himself from his wife and children. As his wife, Sophia, could not agree to partake in a life of poverty and self-sacrifice, she seemed to him submerged in mundane, trivial concerns, removed from his spiritual quest. She, on the other hand, noted how his attempts to preserve ideals of moral perfection and his concern for the "good of humanity" had burdened the lives of those close to him. She noted, for example, how he who had built a school to educate the peasants' children did not take the slightest interest in the education of his own children. She felt his Christian life to be self-centered and accused him of not having a drop of love for his children, for her, or for anyone but himself (Golinenko, Rozanova, Shumova, Pokrovskaya, and Azarova, 1985).

Tolstoy's religious convictions were fueled by an idealization of the life of the simple peasants. But at least from his own point of view, Tolstoy's convictions did not depend on the anticipation of protection and warmth awarded by others. Albeit entangled in the losses, the vanity, the self-absorption, and the bouts of depression that gave his quest a passionate intensity, Tolstoy's religious conversion was also precipitated by a persistent, conscious pondering of ultimate questions, and by a grasping of the contradictions and insufficiencies of the available answers. Resting on a solitary revelation of a truth which provided solutions to previously insoluble questions, his change of heart was, to a certain extent, ruled by his mind.

His experience centered upon the discovery of a truth which he had found compelling. The new truth may have been founded on an idealization and a dogmatic attitude, but from Tolstoy's point of view, it provided sound solutions to tormenting questions.

In his persistent search for moral perfection, Tolstoy often adopted and advocated "all-or-nothing," dogmatic, and ultimately self-righteous attitudes. His derogatory description of his youthful life is a case in point. He describes the average life of a young man of society but, in his description, the vain, purposeless aspects of this life are painted with such extremity and force as to single him and his companions out as intentional, corrupt villains. In his religious conversion, he dichotomized the world into the parasites—the idle rich—and the creators of life—the industrious poor. Likewise, although he was continuously critical of the dogmatism of the church, in his later theological work he was himself dogmatic and vehement in his fervor against it.

It was perhaps this unwillingness to allow exceptions, the refusal to forgive imperfections in himself and in others, and the need to translate abstract principles into a way of life that were essential in the religious experience of Tolstoy. The intolerance of ambiguity combined with a need for a practical guide to life may increase the likelihood of sudden, dramatic changes. On the one hand, acknowledging ambiguities and exceptions may paralyze action, hampering the application of principles to behavior. Ambiguities therefore remain unrecognizable. But to avoid the gradual recognition and the assimilation of unclarities and exceptions into the existing structure of beliefs is to increase the likelihood of a sudden bankruptcy of the entire system. As the ambiguities accumulate without a working through, finally facing them results in an outright change of heart. Once cracks in the world view are apprehended, the entire perspective is relinquished, and a new one, in which cracks are invisible, is established in its stead.

Tolstoy's story brings to mind William James's (1902) description of the self of the person prone to experience religious conversions. James calls the potential convert the "twice-born" character and contrasts him with the "once-born" person. The former is a "divided, sick" soul who is transformed by the better grasp of "religious realities".

James does not give an account of the source of the twice-born character. His description relies, like many other psychological theories of the turn of the century, on the notion of a constitutional defect. He describes the twice-born as "having an incompletely unified moral and intellectual constitution." But describing the intricacies of the experience of religious conversion itself, James' portrayal of the "twice-born" self acquires a different tone. The flawed emotional life appears hand in hand with a view of reality that connotes psychological maturity. The "twice-born" apprehends the world as a "double-story mystery," whereas the once-born character experiences it as a sort of rectilinear, one-storied affair. The once-born may possess a healthier, undivided, optimistic nature, but his or her wholesome nature implies a simplification and an obliviousness to some aspects of reality. It perpetuates a failure to detect inevitable, real complexities. It is their different experience of the spiritual life, and not their mental health status alone, which separates the once- and the twice-born characters. In the subjective experience of the potential convert, the universe is replete with irreconcilable contradictions:

> Natural good is not simply insufficient in amount and transient, it keeps us from our own real good and renunciation and despair of it are our first steps in the direction of truth. There are two lives, the natural and the spiritual and we must lose the one before we can participate in the other. (p. 140)

The twice-born person's despair of "natural good" places him or her in the admirable company of those who relinquish ready-made solutions and simple, yet blind, unquestioning happiness in their search for the true nature of life.

This world view is reminiscent of Tillich's theology and of other existential ideas on the route to salvation. In this view, despair and a rejection of fabricated solutions to the good life are the first steps toward authenticity and dignity. To reach real maturity, one needs to confront the anguish and the dread of the human condition. Coolidge (1950) elaborated this resemblance between the twice-born's experience of spiritual life and existential views of the authentic life. Comparing the philosophical schools of the American empiricists and naturalists with the European existentialists, she argues that the first group advocates a "once-born" philosophy which assumes the basic goodness of human nature. In this view, human goodness requires tender care but it will flourish and accumulate in the right environment. The European existentialists, on the other hand, present a twice-born perspective. For them, recognition of the absurd and the futile in the human condition and despair of it are prerequisites to "salvation."

William James (1902) is unequivocal in stating where his own sympathies lie:

> There is no doubt that healthy-mindedness is inadequate as a philosophical doctrine because the evil facts which it refuses positively to account for are a genuine portion of reality and they may after all be the best key to life's significance and possibly the only openers of eyes to the deepest levels of truth. (p. 137)

Confronting the only "eye openers" to truth, the twice-born individual is tormented by existential questions which others, by virtue of their "healthy-mindedness," manage to ignore. Thus, the convert is plagued by an incompleteness of character, but he or she may also be characterized by an intellectual restlessness, a struggle to attain meaning. From an "incompleteness" of character may spring a more intense questioning. The conversion of the twice-born character is a response to true, albeit painful, aspects of a reality shared by all. The twice-born that James describes is trying to reveal truth rather than defend against it. Albeit accompanied by and, perhaps, emanating from idiosyncratic sufferings, the preoccupations of these religious seekers are "objective." Reaching beyond the circumstances of their own lives, they ponder the meaning of life in general. Their psychological and spiritual salvation is achieved by facing inevitable and real absurdities, uncertainties, and ills.

In the years following his religious conversion, Tolstoy remained a twice-born character, prone to existential torments and unsatisfied with the simple joys his life could offer. His religious conversion did not resolve all doubts and questions and did not result in an everlasting peace of mind.

Emphatic and convinced as he generally was of the soundness of his religious views, Tolstoy never claimed his was an invulnerable truth. In his reply to the synod that excommunicated him for his deviations from Christian doctrine, he wrote:

> I do not believe my faith to be the one indubitable truth for all time, but I see no other that is plainer, clearer, or answers better to all the demands of my reason and my heart. (1961/1884, p.xvi)

In a visit to Moscow a few years following his conversion, Tolstoy fell again into a state of despair which lasted for months, stirred by the horrible conditions of the poor that he saw in the city. His wife had then written to him, asking: "You used to say 'I used to want to hang myself because of my lack of faith,' now you have faith, why then are you so unhappy?" (Rolland, 1972/1911, p. 157) According to some of his biographers, the answer may lie in Tolstoy's inability to relinquish reason to bask in the ecstasy of faith: He was unhappy

> because he had not the sanctimonious, self-satisfied faith of the Pharisee, because he had not the egoism of the mystic who is too completely absorbed in the matter of his own salvation to think of the salvation of others . . . because he could no longer forget the miserable creatures he had seen, and in the passionate tenderness of his heart he felt as though he was responsible for their sufferings and their abjectness. (Rolland, 1972/1911, p. 157)

A similar soul search that results in an inability to shut one's eyes to the lot of others is patent in the religious life of Dorothy Day, the founder of the Catholic Worker movement and one of the most influential figures in the history of American Catholicism. Her conversion was a part of attaining a unified identity.

The Case of Dorothy Day

Dorothy Day was born in 1897 to Episcopalian parents, the third in a family of five children. Childhood, she tells us in her autobiography, *The Long Loneliness* (1952), had been a happy time for her, the infrequent moods of uncertainty and sadness only accentuating the joys. Her description of her parents follows a common pattern. She portrays her mother as optimistic and confident, a woman with stamina, forever available and protective of her children, and emerging happy and strong from the periods of uncertainties and hardships experienced in her life. Her father, on the other hand, is described as frequently absent, often impatient and forbidding with his children. His daughter's feelings toward him emerge from the narrative as an ambivalent mixture of longing, anger, and awe.

Throughout her childhood and adolescence Dorothy had been

intensely religious, never questioning God's presence, enthusiastic in her prayers, engrossed in reading psalms and in playing "saints" with her sister. At times, the God of her childhood had been a frightening, arbitrary, impersonal force. But, she tells us, her religiosity had been dominated by a lofty enthusiasm and had been guided by a striving for spiritual perfection and a troubling awareness of sin and imperfections: "[I] wanted to do penance for my own sins and for the sins of the whole world for I had a keen sense of natural imperfections and earthiness" (p. 24).

Her religious faith combined enthusiasm with a soul-searching, self-critical attitude and a realization of inevitable shortcomings. The emotion most clearly motivating her religious life was guilt. She tells us of a continuous conflict between "flesh" and "spirit," a guilt-ridden attitude toward her own desires, ambitions, and self-seeking. Her enthusiasm and capacity for compassion as well as her acute awareness of imperfections and sense of guilt, which were fused in her religious sentiments, also aroused in her, from age 15 on, an interest in and an affinity with the poor and the destitute: "My life was to be linked to theirs, their interests were to be mine, I had received a call, a vocation, a direction to my life" (p. 38).

In a sweeping, all-or-none, principled demand, she rejected the temporary, imperfect solutions to social injustice offered by her middle-class context:

> I wanted life and I wanted the abundant life. I wanted it for others, too. I did not want just the few, the missionary-minded people like the salvation army to be kind to the poor, as the poor. I wanted every home to be open to the lame, the halt and the blind. (p. 39)

Her first step in that direction was to join the Socialist Party when she left home to study at the University of Illinois. She was alone in this decision and subsequently felt separated from most of her peers. In her rejection of the existing social order, which would not allow the justice she was seeking, she also, temporarily, rejected religion. The revolutionary, rebellious fervor was in conflict, Day felt, with the meekness and peace preached by her religion. Although she did not lose her faith in God, she denounced religion as an institution. She speaks of the scorn she felt toward those who were so comfortably happy in the face of the misery of the world, the pious

students and the religious middle class who were at peace when they
should have been in a state of war. At the time, Day made a conscious
effort to push away the religion she saw around her:

> I felt at the time that religion would only impede my work. I wanted
> to have nothing to do with the religion of those whom I saw all about me.
> I felt it indeed to be an opiate of the people and not a very attractive one
> so I hardened my heart. It was a conscious and deliberate process. (p. 43)

Her rebelliousness was partly designed to shock and anger her
friends and her family. But in the course of several years she appeared successful in her effort to detach herself from the "opiate of
the people." Religion had become, if not entirely absent from her life,
clearly divorced from the main vein which gave her life meaning and
direction. She had become engaged in an active struggle to change
the world, protesting, reading, writing, meeting other radicals, and
wavering between socialism and anarchism. She was arrested twice,
which served only to intensify her awareness of social injustice and
her idealized view of the innocent poor. At her first imprisonment,
she tells us, she had

> lost feeling of my own identity. I would never be free again . . . when
> I knew that behind bars all over the world were men and women, young
> girls and boys suffering constraint, punishment, isolation and hardship
> for which all of us were guilty. (p. 78)

During this, her first imprisonment, she found solace in reading
the Bible but refused to use religion as a crutch in this time of
helplessness:

> I did not want to go to God in defeat and sorrow. I did not want to
> depend on Him. I was like a child that wants to walk by itself. I kept
> brushing away the hand that held me up. (p. 81)

This was not a happy time in Dorothy's life. In her autobiography, she leaves out the story of the painful, private struggle in which
she was also engaged during these years: her prolonged, passionate,
and mostly unhappy love affair with a man who persistently refused
and rejected her wish for a stable commitment, and whose child she
therefore decided to abort. She also does not say much of the short-

lived interruption of in this affair by her marriage to another man, a marriage that became oppressive and intolerable to her a few months after it had begun (Miller, 1982).

But it was at a time that she considered the happiest, the most fulfilling time of her life that she once again fully embraced religious faith and became a convert to the Catholic Church. The turn she took toward religion began at a period in which her life became private, increasingly centered on her own needs and on a dedication to and intimacy with a few others. She entered then into a common-law marriage with a man, an atheist and an anarchist, and was living with him in the country, in the company of a few friends.

For Day, this happiness was accompanied by a heightened sense of a need for prayer. Embarking on a private life may have rearoused in her the old conflict of "flesh" and "spirit" and the guilt over her own self-seeking. But whatever the undercurrents of longings and conflicts which were stirring her at that time toward religious faith, she once again refused to perceive it and to use it as a source of self-centered gratification:

> I am praying because I am happy, not because I am unhappy. I did not turn to God in unhappiness, in grief, in despair—to get consolation, to get something from Him. (p. 132)

The birth of her daughter, Tamar, deepened her happiness. At that time the simple faith of Day's childhood no longer appeared as an antithesis of her radicalism. In its present version, her religiosity became a part of the other "great love" of her life, her love for the masses. For some time she had been attracted to the Catholic church as the church of the masses, the church that would bring her closer not only to God but to the masses of Italian, Irish, and Polish workers with whom she wished to unite. This alone, the fact that in this country the Catholic church is the church of the masses, had been sufficient to draw her to this church. It became clear to her that her daughter had to be baptized in the Catholic church. She began to attend Mass regularly.

Dorothy's renewed and intense interest in religion and her wish to be baptized herself as a Catholic jeopardized the happiness she had found in her private life. It inevitably widened a rift between her and her atheist lover and interfered with that very "natural happiness" which she had claimed as the source of her reawakened faith. Her mounting interest and dedication to religion had gradually divorced her from the private life. In her autobiography she describes without bitterness, and without self-righteousness, but with compassion and pain, the tensions marring her relationship with Forester, her lover and the father of her daughter. Her life with him now created a constant dilemma: the choice between "spirit" and "flesh." When an explosion between them occurred and he left the house, she determined "to make an end once and for all to the torture we were undergoing" and refused to let him in when he came back. The next day she was baptized in the Catholic church.

But Dorothy found that, if anything, her religious conversion served only to intensify the doubts that had beset her all along. She now had to contemplate, to struggle in an attempt to integrate and reconcile her affiliation with the church and her dedication to a political struggle. She was not ready to incorporate ready-made solutions:

> I felt that the Church was the Church of the poor, that St. Patrick's had been built from the pennies of servant girls, that it cared for the emigrant, it established hospitals, orphanages, day nurseries, houses of the Good Shepherd, homes for the aged but, at the same time, I felt that it did not set its face against a social order which made so much charity in the present sense of the word necessary. I felt that charity was a word to choke over. Who wanted charity? And it was not just human pride but a strong sense of man's dignity and worth and what was due to him in justice that made me resent rather than feel proud of so mighty a sum total of Catholic institutions. (p. 150)

This struggle continued for several years. For a while she found little joy in her Catholicism as she watched the church take the wrong sides and the Catholic leadership remain silent on the injustices which she found so perturbing. Her conversion had all but weakened her fight with what she considered a need for faith as a source of personal consolation. She continued in her effort to become part of a greater cause and to relinquish self-absorption and personal comforts in service to others. Merciless in her judgment of her own imperfections, she describes as sinful her first few years as a Catholic:

> How little, how puny my work had been since becoming a Catholic, I thought. How self-centered, how in-grown, how lacking in a sense of community. My summer of quiet reading and prayer, my self-absorption

seemed sinful as I watched my brothers in their struggle not for themselves but for others. (p. 165)

This continuous soul search, perpetuated by her sense of guilt in living on the labor of others, laid the groundwork for the Catholic Worker movement, established some years later. She founded the movement with Peter Maurine, a French Catholic and communist who had become her mentor. In her association with him and in her lifelong work in the Catholic Worker movement, the two major currents of her life, her religious sentiments and her commitment to socially relevant action, were finally united.

Dorothy Day's conversion to Catholicism was not a dramatic turnabout. Her renewed religious commitment did not reverse existing currents but provided a unifying integrative direction to them. It did not evolve from a single mystical "peak" experience nor from a preplanned, deliberate intellectual search, but from a persistent and acute sense of imperfections and a practical pursuit of a utopian vision.

Dorothy was not an intensely "divided" or "sick" soul. Her doubts, self-criticism, and guilt never culminated in incapacitating despair as they did for Tolstoy. Although she, too, had experienced a troubling relationship with a remote father, she had been spared the more traumatizing losses which impaired the lives of many of the religious converts I interviewed. But like most of us, she was not spared intense conflicts and turmoil. Consider her stormy and repeatedly unsuccessful relationships with men, the failure of her final intimate bond, which was replaced by a renewed religious commitment and, later, by a relationship with a mentor. Like the twice-born of William James' writings, she had to give up "natural good" in order to participate in the "spiritual" life.

These themes, however, render more complex and more intriguing an identity united by a dedication to principles and beliefs about the common good. Day was intent on turning utopian ideals into masters rather than servants of her needs. The admiration she bestows on her lover for the objectivity and abstraction of his convictions is also duly hers:

The very fact that his suffering and rebellion against life as man had made it was an abstract thing and had little to do with what he had

> suffered personally, made me respect his ideas, as ideas honestly held
> . . . . For instance, he loved his family tenderly but he saw and suffered
> keenly at what havoc a possessive family feeling sometimes wrought. He
> personally had not suffered want but economic inequality was a terrible
> thing to him. (p. 121)

It is this capacity to enlist in causes that are not merely one's own, to extract the "objective," the common, and the universal from the particular circumstances of one's life, that stands out in the life of this Catholic woman and that renders her conversion a part of a lifelong religious quest. Thus, along with the emotional intensity which invariably accompanies it, a religious conversion may be a part of a continuous quest, may be an attempt to unify rather than divorce oneself from previous currents, and may represent a systematic reaction to the predicament of others, culminating in abiding loyalty to personal principles and to the common good.

7

The Transformed Self
Summary and Implications

William James (1902) defines conversions as "the process, gradual or sudden by which a self hitherto divided, consciously wrong, inferior and unhappy, becomes unified and consciously right, superior and happy in consequence of its firmer hold upon religious realities" (p. 157). For the majority of religious converts examined in this study, "religious realities" are quite narrowly perceived. They consist primarily of the promise of unconditional love and protection by a figure perceived as infallible. In most cases and irrespective of the particular framework in which the experience occurs, conversion is then the process through which a self threatened by intense negative emotions experiences relief and happiness as a consequence of its new attachment to a real or imagined figure.

The term *religious conversion* subsumes diverse experiences: It decribes an experience of increased devotion within the same religious framework, a shift from no religious commitment to a devout religious life, or a change from one religious affiliation to another. The present investigation was limited to the latter two types of conversion. There are two other limits to the generalizability of the present findings. One stems from the socioeconomic characteristics of the particular sample employed, the other from its embeddedness in a particular culture and age. As indicated, the bulk of this book is based on the accounts of urban, middle-class youth who experienced their religious conversion during their 20s. These converts represent a considerable and a visible segment of the contemporary population of converts but not the entire range of the phenomenon. The dynamics at work in the conversion experiences of older adults or of rural blacks or in the revival experiences of those who have been exposed to charismatic religious teachings throughout their lives may be different. On the one hand, the power of groups, relegated here to a subsidiary role, and, on the other, the search for clarity, truth and ethics, described here in the context of exceptional lives, may prove, perhaps, more prominent in other samples of converts. This is an empirical question which requires further study.

The inevitable embeddedness of this sample in a particular day and age raises another question: Some of the data presented here may be more descriptive of trends in contemporary American society than of universal characteristics of religious beliefs. There is no *a priori* theoretical reason that will lead us to question the applicability to other groups of converts within Western culture of the findings associating the absent, aggressive, or ineffectual father with the religious conversion. Nor is there a reason to question the universality of the aversive power of emotional turmoil or the potentially corrective power of the experience and anticipation of unconditional love. Those are not confined to the lives of contemporary middle-class Americans. But the tone of the stories I have heard, which seems to transform a potentially complex quest into a unidimensional and blissful haven, may not be universal.

Rudolf Otto begins his classic analysis of *The Idea of the Holy* (1923) cautioning against a view of religion in which "feeling is all, the name but sound and smoke" (Goethe, 1971/1916), where the "name" stands for conception or thought. For the converts I have interviewed, the rational and conceptual aspects that distinguish a belief from a feeling were immaterial. Furthermore, for the majority of contemporary converts the conversion emerges as an unambivalent and unambiguous guarantee of protection that simplifies basic polarities in religious life. Their conversion testimonials typically dispose of the tension between the "word" and the feeling, between the unapproachability and the dependence, between the doubt and the answer, between the impulse and the discipline.

This tone of many of the stories presented here may be attributed in part to the cultural scene which shaped the form of these self-reports. The majority of stories presented here came from individuals who were part of what is commonly known as the "me generation" (Wolfe, 1976; Lasch, 1979)—those who witnessed the aftermath of the 1960s and who were, during the 1970s, in search of self-fulfillment in lieu of social action. This social atmosphere may have influenced the description, although not necessarily the nature, of the religious experiences I studied. Along with the many groups, associations, and fads formed to enhance "personal growth," religious beliefs too are upheld in this cultural context for their promise of instant psychological salvation.

These limits of the religious experiences examined here notwithstanding, this book underscores old insights that may be brought to bear upon a general understanding of the development and function of beliefs within the self. First, it indicates that world views are adopted or rejected not as isolated systems which may or may not have internal coherence, but as congruent with the lives of persons, intertwined with their dispositions, emotions, and desires. Second, it underscores the prepotency of distress and turmoil in guiding our beliefs. Negative emotions may at times be the eye openers to the human condition and to the sufferings of others, but as a rule, and especially when intense and prolonged, they more often promote a retreat into the self and a recruitment of ideology in the service of reducing turmoil. Finally, in this book an experience that seems to involve a dramatic break from personal history emerges under scrutiny as another instance of the tyranny of the past. This tyranny is qualified, however, by the power of a new interpersonal attachment that sometimes allows, at least temporarily, a rebirth into a new self.

This book examined different avenues through which the rebirth may occur. Firstly, from a psychoanalytic perspective conversion is a search for a perfect authority that does not, in fact, allow a "rebirth." From this perspective, the experience is a localized defensive maneuver that preserves the emotional status quo by replacing one player, the biological parent, with another. Secondly, as an attachment to a new group, conversion was examined as a transformation wittingly or unwittingly induced by social influences and group process which force new behaviors and an internalization of new beliefs. Thirdly,

the transformation was also discussed as a developmental phase arising out of the internal as well as external demands of adolescence.
From yet another angle, the rebirth was viewed as the consequence of
an experience of merger with an idol which ameliorates a self experienced as fragile and incohesive. Finally, the transformation was examined as the consequence of cognitive restructuring and of a more
or less deliberate search for meaning. These different avenues all
appear in the stories of conversion examined here. The data on conversion indicate, however, that there are common components to
these different avenues. First, whether or not the conversion occurred privately or in the presence of a group, whether it involved an
attachment to authority, peers, or a transcendental object, it involved
the experience of intense negative emotions prior to the change. Secondly, the transformation itself touched upon the subjective experience of self-worth and of the self as a separate agent.

Clearly, the lives of the individuals studied here changed
markedly as a result of their conversion experience. They adopted
new beliefs and lifestyles, a new vocation, and new communities
which often substituted for their family of origin. One may still question, however, whether these changes entailed a transformation of
the self.

At the turn of the century William James (1908/1892) presented
an analysis of the self that influenced psychology's approach to the
study of the self in the years to follow. James distinguished two
aspects of the self: the self as object and the self a Subject, the "me"
and the "I." The former, which James defined as everything the persons calls his or hers, includes the material self (body and possessions), the social selves (roles, relations, and interpersonal traits), and
the spiritual self (thoughts, beliefs and values, psychological mecha-
nisms). The "I," on the other hand, was defined as "pure experience"
as "the knower" which is present in all of the person's experience and
which, in fact, constitutes experience and is therefore elusive and
difficult to examine. The study of the self in psychology typically
followed James' advice that the "I" be left to philosophical inquiry and
has indeed centered on the study of the "me," which has become
identified with the study of the self-concept. Despite his own emphasis on the elusiveness of this concept James himself identified three
types of experiences through which the person may become aware of

the "I": the experience of agency, namely, the experience of the self as the source of one's actions; the experience of distinctness, otherness, or separateness; and the experience of continuity.

It seems evident that for most religious converts important components of the "me" change in consequence of the religious conversion. In addition and perhaps more importantly, their accounts indicate that the experience involved shifts in aspects of the "I," most clearly in the experience of distinctness and separateness from others.

Whether these shifts indeed represent a marked departure from the previous experience of the self and whether they remain continuously characteristic of the person following conversion are difficult questions that require longitudinal information that is not available for these converts. The stories of conversion presented here imply, however, that these elusive aspects of the self as subject constitute important dimensions of individual as well as developmental differences and are amenable to empirical investigation through self-report (cf. Blasi, 1983; Damon and Hart, 1982; Peevers, 1986).

The data presented here point to some general directions in the study of the self. One concerns the interrelationships between the "me" and the "I." How are changes, developmental or situational, in these two aspects of the self interrelated? Another direction concerns the relationships between these aspects of the self and the experience of self-worth and psychological well-being. How are individual or developmental variations in the experiences of agency, distinctness, or continuity related to the person's functioning in other domains? Finally, the data presented here point to the centrality of the experience of emotions in precipitating changes in the self. This finding underscores the importance of incorporating the emotions in the study of developmental changes in the two aspects of the self.

Appendixes

Interview

I. Name_____   Current religion_____
   Sex_____   Former religion_____
   Age_____   Time passed since conversion_____
   Education_____ _____
   Occupation_____

As you know, I am interested in religious conversion, in how people come to change their religion and their way of life. Probably different people change for different reasons and many people never change at all. I would like to hear from you about your own conversion experience and what it meant to you. Perhaps the best way for us to proceed is to start from your childhood and proceed to the way you are now. I have a few questions about your childhood and family.

II. 1. Siblings and birth order

    2. Parents' occupations
       Parents' religion

    3. Was your family religious?
       To what extent and how was religion practiced? Were there any other strong commitments, e.g., political?

    4. What kind of people were your parents? Can you describe your mother for me? Your father?
       As a child, who did you feel closer to, your mother or your father? Why?

5. Were there other people outside your family (like teachers, friends) who were significant people for you or who influenced you? How did they influence you? Was there anybody in your childhood whom you really hated?

6. How would you summarize your childhood? Was it happy, lonely, etc.? Did anything unusual happen to you as a child (for example, serious illness, separation)? Did you have many friends? Did you think a lot about God or religion as a child?

III. Let's talk now about the time after your childhood but before you converted. I am interested in what you thought and felt at that time.

[For nonconverts: Let's talk about high school and first years in college.]

1. You said that your family was (not) religious. Did you feel the same? Did you have any strong religious or political commitments? Did you join any organization or group? Did most of your friends have the same commitments?

2. Do you remember things which were dissatisfying or confusing for you during this time? What were you preoccupied with? What was your general mood at the time? Can you describe it?

3. What did you do about these dissatisfactions (confusions, etc.) that you were experiencing? Did you try to do something to solve them? How?

[Only converts—#4]

4. Was there anything in this period that you can point to as directly influencing or leading to your conversion? What was it? How is it related to your conversion?

IV. Now I would like you to tell me in more detail about your conversion experience and the two-year period before you converted.

[Only converts—#1–3]

1. Could you tell me what happened right before you converted? Did anything unusual happen? Where were you and what were you doing then? What were you preoccupied with?

2. How did you decide to join the group that you are now in? Was it a difficult decision for you? Did something happen that helped you decide? Did other people help? How long did it take you to make the decision?

3. How did it feel right after your decision to convert?
   What exactly did the decision change for you?
   You said that there were such and such things which were disturbing (confusing, etc.) to you before your conversion.
   Did your conversion immediately solve or change these things?
   In what way?

V. We finally arrive at the present. Let's talk about the way you are now.

[Only converts—#1]

1. You said you converted (X times) ago. Since then, did you continually belong to this group or did you leave and come back?

2. Do you do any volunteer work for the group, or any paid job?

3. How often do you meet others from your group? Do you have any close friends that do not belong to the same religious group? How often do you meet them?
   Do you like talking to them about your religious beliefs? Why?
   How would you feel if someone from a different religious group would like to discuss religion with you? Why?

I would like to know to what extent things have really changed for you since you converted.

[Only converts—#4–8]

4. How do you practice your religious beliefs? What kind of duties do you have?
   To what extent did these duties change your lifestyle?

5. Do you feel like a different person now? What things have not changed in your personality, mood, or behavior? Do you think other people have noticed this change as well? Who?

6. Do you see things differently now than you did before? For example, are there things that are very important to you that were not important before?
   Do you feel that you know or understand now something that you did not know before?

7. Was there a change in your political views? In what way?

8. How important are relationships with others for you now? Is it different from what you felt before?

[All subjects]

9. Some people think that once a person is a true believer he or she does not have any more doubts or questions; everything is solved for him or her. Do you think this is true?
   Do you think other people in your group may have doubts?

Do you or did you have periods in which you had doubts about your (new) religion? What kind of questions do you still ask yourself? When you are in doubt, how do you feel?

What do you do about it?

Can you give me a recent example?

Interview Scoring

Scorer_____

Code No._____   Date_____

I. Read carefully through the interview once. For every variable, circle the alternative that seems most appropriate. If you cannot find any relevant information for a particular variable, circle X = no information. You may find, however, that the information is available later in the interview. If this is the case, go back and change your answer. Consult examples for every variable. Add comments or qualifications whenever you feel it necessary. Use backside of scoring sheet for additional comments.

II. Childhood and Family Background [all subjects]

   1. [Questions 3 and 4 of Part II, in Appendix I]

      Degree of Exposure to Religion

      None—no practicing at home, no religious education

      Moderate—some practicing at home and/or some religious education, even if parents are not described as religious people

      Strong—practicing all or most requirements and religious education

   2. [Question 4 as above, but everything in Part II may be relevant]

      Father described as:

[Choose *one* category, although *S*'s answer may include several elements. Decide by the overall tone of *S*'s description. Judge not only by *S*'s direct description of parents but also by what he or she says about childhood events involving them, his or her feelings toward their marital relationship, etc.]

Absent—death, divorce, or long-term hospitalization (over one-half year) before *S* was 10. Indicate which: _____

Psychologically absent—withdrawn, depressed, very passive, or other indications that father was not available for support and guidance, e.g., "Very quiet, withdrawn, it was difficult to get any guidance from him or even interest"; "My father was absorbed in his own problems"; "He always seemed timid and scared."

Hostile/aggressive—cold, rejecting, critical, harsh, domineering, temper tantrums, and/or indications of continuous fights and tension between *S* and father, e.g., "My father was always quite cold and very stern"; "No matter what you did it was wrong"; "Was very authoritarian, overdoing it."

Unstable—alcoholic, dramatic changes in moods, impulsive, or any clear indication that father was very unpredictable, e.g., "Was nice to us children but fell into drinking, would get intoxicated a lot."

Overprotective—always worried, concerned, domineering by protection (rather than discipline), should be perceived by *S* as negative, at least to some degree, e.g., "Always worried about us, very concerned, in some ways would like to dominate us."

Neutral—description focuses on external characteristics; no strong emotional statements or no indication of a strong emotional response to father, negative or positive; description could include personal characteristics (calm, simple) but no particular emotional tone.

Positive—overall impression is of respect, admiration, and/or affection toward father, e.g., "Very gentle"; "Easygoing, generous."

Other, nonnegative description. Indicate: _____

3. Mother described as:

[Same categories and same criteria as for father]

Absent
Psychologically absent
Hostile/aggressive
Unstable
Overprotective
Neutral
Positive
Other

4. [Especially Question 6 in Part II of Appendix I but Part II as a whole]
Traumatic Childhood: Overall
[S's judgment of his or her own childhood and his or her prevailing mood during childhood.]

Happy, no stress—basically free of fear and tension; S should say that childhood was happy or at least normal, usual, e.g., "Usual, felt happy, no problems"; "Boring, but happy"; "Was happy, I loved it."

Moderate or mixed—S describes childhood as sometimes happy, sometimes unhappy, or qualifies childhood "happiness" in any other way. e.g., "Basically happy but not without turmoil"; "No particular stress, but I was not completely satisfied."

Unhappy—S's description of childhood *focuses* on negative feelings such as fear, loneliness, misery, hostility, e.g., "I felt very unhappy, agonizing time"; "Very lonely"; "I was scared all the time."

5. Traumatic Childhood: Specific Events

Absent—S does not report any events which may be considered traumatic (even though childhood may be described as unhappy). Nonmajor accidents (e.g., breaking arm) or moving are not considered traumatic unless S indicates that the event had traumatic effects, was very disturbing. Just mentioning divorce does not score for trauma. Should be described as disturbing, difficult.

Moderate—traumatic events, violence, separation, or loss, involving close figures other than parents (grandparents, peers).

Severe—S describes events or series of events which may be considered very disturbing, especially those involving parents: death, separation, violent fights, breakdowns, e.g., "Mother attempted suicide"; "Police were constantly at our house."

6. Childhood Preoccupations with God or Religion

[Degree of interest, concern, preoccupation with religious issues and practices and/or the nature of God]

None reported—does not remember or reports no interest or involvement with religious issues.

Moderate—some interest and/or questioning but does not seem to be emotionally involved, or not very frequently, e.g., "From time to time"; "Just as it came up in a discussion"; "Once in a while I would wonder if God existed."

Strong—emotional involvement and frequent questioning and/or thinking about religious issues. Reports much prayer, desiring to be priest, rabbi, etc.; preoccupation with questions about the nature of God, e.g., "Decided pretty early that God was my father"; "Felt I wanted to become a priest"; "Worried a lot about eternity."

III. Adolescence [all subjects]

7. [Questions 1–4 of Part III in Appendix I may be relevant to all variables]

Reports Cognitive, Existential, or Religious Concerns

[Whether or not subject reports preoccupation and questioning concerning general issues—life, death, God, reality, specific questions about his own religion, or concern about justice and social order.]

Absent—when preoccupations are described only in terms of *S*'s personal life circumstances, no interest in global issues, or very vague global issues, e.g., "I was interested only in sports and my family"; "Identify who I am, stuff like that."

Present—reports particular concerns as above, e.g., "My biggest discomfort in high school was being rich or middle class, social justice issues"; "I did not know whether to accept Christ or not, could not decide on one church."

8. Reports Ideological Involvement

[Membership in political and/or religious organizations]

Absent—no membership in political or religious groups, clubs, organizations.

Present—membership in political and/or religious clubs, groups, etc., other than those demanded by practicing or school program. If present, political, religious, both, e.g., "I got involved with groups which were very political"; "Involved in starting civil rights support groups."

9. General Emotional Stress in Adolescence

a. *Overall* [see Variable 4]

Happy, no stress—prevailing mood is reported as happy, easygoing, normal, usual. No particular tensions reported, e.g., "Usual adolescence, nothing very disturbing."

Mixed, moderate—reports dissatisfaction and frustrations, but not intense ones; prevailing mood described as mixed or varying, but no intense unhappiness, e.g., "was a mixed bag"; "Can't say I was unhappy but was not happy either."

Unhappy—description focuses on negative experiences: unhappiness, loneliness, fear, anxiety, hostility, symptoms; e.g., "I was very unhappy most of the time"; "Felt very rejected"; "I know for sure I had anxiety neurosis and obsessional thoughts."

b. *Specific*—traumatic experience [see Variable 5]

Absent

Moderate

Severe

10. Drug Involvement [May appear at different points in the interview]

None—never or less than five times, tried but no involvement.

Moderate—sporadic use, not a habit but more than trying, e.g., "All my friends took drugs, so I did too, from time to time."

Strong—more than once a week, regular use of drugs for at least a year.

IV. Conversion Process [converts only]

11. *Immediate Antecedents* [Especially Questions 1 and 2] [Events reported as leading to or involved in the conversion or events which characterized the one- to two-year period prior to conversion. For some converts may be based on the same information as variables 7–9]

a. Cognitive and Existential Issues [see variable 7]

None—conversion was not preceded by a period of questioning, intellectual restlessness, etc. Investigating the new faith only after *S* was already introduced to it and/or as a part of a required "initiation" period.

Present—conversion was preceded by cognitive, existential, religious concerns. Does not have to be the only factor involved. Taking courses in religion by itself is not evidence of concern or interest; *S* should indicate particular need or motivation for taking such courses, e.g., "I was seriously questioning Catholicism"; "I thought the important question was what's wrong with the world"; "Was bothered by the diversity of religions."

b. Emotional Issues: Overall [Emotional unheaval reported by *S* as preceding the conversion which *S* sees as related or which prevailed in the one- to two-year period prior to conversion]

None—the conversion process does not seem to have started on a background of emotional upheaval, does not seem to be loaded or influenced by experiences as outlined below.

Present—emotional issues seem to be at least one of the factors leading to conversion. Process started on a background of conflicts, needs, anxieties, depression, etc. In general, seems to be emotionally loaded. Experiences of rejection, low self-esteem, intensive confusion over goals, chaotic lifestyle (promiscuity, drugs), psychiatric symptoms, e.g., "I was really depressed"; "It was really a confusing time, don't know why"; "Had suicidal thoughts"; "Was ashamed of myself,"; "Trying to get some order in my life."

c. Traumatic Events [Reports death(s), accidents, which sees as related to conversion, and/or which occurred during one to two years prior to conversion]

None, Moderate, Severe   [If same as 9b, indicate]

Specify the event _____, e.g. car accident, mother's death.

12. The Change [Consider especially S's response to Question 2 in Part IV of Appendix I]

a.   Gradual   versus   Sudden
More than one month   Less than one month
between first contact and   between first contact and
decision to join the group.   decision to join.

b.   Not dramatic   versus   Dramatic
                                                   Reports sudden relevation,
                                                   vision, miracles, and other
                                                   intense, sudden
                                                   experiences associated with
                                                   the conversion, e.g., "Had
                                                   an experience which
                                                   convinced me God existed";
                                                   "Suddenly out of the blue,
                                                   I felt what I was reading
                                                   was the only truth."

13. Evidence of Peer or Strong Group Influence
Absent—no evidence of particular involvement of peers or group in the initial contact and/or decision to convert.

Present—initial contact was dependent on close friends or same-age relatives, and/or decision to convert took place in group setting, with suggestions and support by group. Evidence of direct involvement of the group, e.g., "My roommates and his friends convinced me to come"; "This friend had such a change in his life and all his friends too; I wanted to have it too."

14. Authority Figures Involved in Conversion Process [Parents, religious leaders, older siblings, older lover seem to be directly involved in the conversion process (i.e., converted themselves, dramatic experience occurred following their suggestion)]

Yes/No   Specify whom _____

15. Immediate Consequences [Consider especially Question 3 in Part IV of Appendix I]

[The immediate results of the decision to convert or of the conversion experience as described by S. Refers to *direct* consequences of the conversion and to changes taking place right after the conversion or the decision.]

a. Cognitive solutions

Absent—does not mention solutions to particular questions or only in very vague, cliché terms, e.g., "Just everything was convincing"; "I understood the spiritual world."

Present—describes solutions to particular questions, contradictions, etc. Does not have to be the only factor but has to be seen as an important one, e.g., "It answered my questions about the unity of religions, the Trinity"; "Answered all the questions I had about social and moral issues."

b. Emotional relief

[Immediate consequences are described primarily in terms of relief from conflicts, anxieties, negative emotions, e.g., "Did not feel as depressed as before"; "All anxieties were gone"]

Absent
Present

c. Struggle with parents [Did conversion result in or involve struggle with parents—both or one?]

None—parents did not care or did not know.
Moderate—initial resistance on the part of one or both parents but no prolonged struggle.
Strong—parents very hostile, embittered by conversion, long struggle lasting at least two months, attempting to stop conversion, constant quarrels and bitterness about it.

17. Rigidity [Degree of avoidance of other views, judged particularly by last part of Appendix I but also by the interview as a whole.]

Low—tolerance and interest in other religious groups, accepts the possibility of different views, social ties outside own group.

Moderate

Strong—disdain of different beliefs, strict adherence to the letter of the law, much proselytizing during the interview, everything is interpreted in terms of present beliefs.

18. Doubts

None—reports no doubts or questioning of beliefs; questioning own ability to achieve higher levels of "spirituality," etc. does not count as doubts.

Moderate—some infrequent doubts of God's existence or nature but cannot specify question or give example, e.g., "In the beginning I used to wonder, not very often, if this is really true"; "When things don't go right, when I get depressed, I'd ask if God is really there."

Strong—specific questions about beliefs or dogma; can give examples of doubts or questions, e.g., "I have lots of questions about the church and Catholic dogma."

III

Discrete Emotions: Scoring Rules

1. Score for explicit mention of the emotion and its synonyms as outlined below.
2. Score for emotion—terms appearing in:
   a. description of mother (II, 4, 5)
   b. description of father (II, 4, 5)
   c. description of childhood (II, 6)
   d. description of adolescence (III, 2–4)
   e. description of two years preceding conversion (IV, 1,2)
   f. description of immediate consequences of conversion (IV, 3)
3. For each variable (a–f) score *once* for each emotion, even when there are several references to the same emotion, e.g., "I was very miserable, I was suffering like crazy"—scored once for distress/anguish; "very bitter, very resentful, doubting everybody"—scored once for anger/rage.
4. For each variable score once for *each* discrete emotion, e.g., "I was getting very depressed, a lot of anxieties, just a lot of anxieties and unhappiness"—scored for distress/anguish and for fear/terror (anxiety).
5. Score only for emotions *felt by S.*
6. Do not infer from description of events or behaviors about S's emotions, e.g., "I found my mother who attempted suicide"—not scored unless S indicates a particular emotional response on his or her part.
7. For emotions toward parents (a and b): score only emotions toward parents as S was growing up. Do not score for emotions describing only

relationship at present, e.g., "There is a love between us now"—not scored.

8. For emotions following conversion (f): score only emotions mentioned as direct and immediate consequences of the experience and related to the new beliefs e.g., emotions toward parents, as part of struggle with them following conversion, not scored.

Scoring for Discrete Emotions: List of Scored Terms*

a. With respect to childhood and adolescence, pre- and postconversion:

Happy/joyous: Explicit references to a state of enjoyment and pleasure: happy, joyful, delighted, cheerful, content, serene, elated. Also: blissful, gratified, carefree, relieved.

Distress/anguish: Explicit references to a state of internal pain and turmoil: sad, discouraged, depressed, desperate, unhappy. Also: tormented, morose, suffering, very upset, going crazy, miserable.

Anger/rage: Explicit references to aggressive feelings towards others: enraged, angry, mad, irritated, hate, dislike, resentment. Also: hostile, bitter, aggressive, very competitive.

Fear/terror and anxiety: Explicit references to specific fears or general apprehension: scared, fearful, afraid, terror, panic. Also: anxious, worried.

Shame/shyness: Explicit references to awareness of defects in self and painful withdrawal from others: shy, bashful, timid, embarrassed. Also: withdrawn, humiliated, inhibited, felt inferior, kept to myself.

Guilt/remorse: Explicit references to misgivings about self's actions: guilty, blamed myself, regret/remorse, repentant. Also: sinful, felt bad about (self's action).

Contempt/scorn: Explicit references to viewing others as inferior and unworthy: contemptuous, scornful, disdainful, despise, disrespect.

Interest/excitement: Explicit references to a state of arousal and a wish to approach and explore: excited, alert, attentive, enthusiastic, interested.

b. With respect to parents:

Admiration/respect: Explicit references to high esteem of parent: admired, respected, adored, looked up to. Also: my model, wanted to be like him/her.

*List based in part on Izard (1977) and on Sommers (1984).

Love/like: Explicit references to affection and warmth toward parents: loved, liked, felt great warmth.

Indifference: Explicit claims of no attachment and/or no knowledge of parent (lack of any emotional terms alone—not scored as indifference): indifferent, no attachment, did not know him/her, did not care, did not affect me in any way.

Anger/rage: Scored as in (a).

Contempt/scorn: Scored as in (a).

Fear/terror: Scored as in (a).

References

Abelin, E.L., 1975. Some further comments on the earliest role of the father. *International Journal of Psychoanalysis*, 56, 293–301.

Adams, G.R., and Gullotta, T., 1983. *Adolescent Life Experiences*, Monterey: Brooks/Cole.

Allison, J., 1968. Adaptive regression in intense religious experiences. *Journal of Nervous and Mental Disease*, 145, 452–463.

Allison, J., 1969. Religious conversion: Regression and progression. *Journal for the Scientific Study of Religion*, 8, 23–28.

Allport, G., 1950. *The Individual and His Religion*. New York: Macmillan.

Anderson, S.M., and Zimbardo, P.G., 1984. On resisting social influence. *Cultic Studies Journal*, 1(2), 196–219.

Argyle, M., 1959. *Religious Behavior*. Glencoe, Ill.: Free Press.

Argyle, M., and Beit Halahmi, B., 1975. *The Social Psychology of Religion*. Boston: Routledge and Kegan Paul.

Asquith, C.M.E., 1969. *Married to Tolstoy*. London: Hutchinson Press.

Baker-Miller, J., 1984. *The Development of Women's Sense of Self. Work in Progress Publication Series*. Wellesley, Mass.: Wellesley College.

Balint, M., 1968. *The Basic Fault*. London: Tavistock.

Bateson, C.D., and Ventis, W.L., 1982. *The Religious Experience*. New York: Oxford University Press.

Batson, C.D., 1975. Rational processing or rationalization: The effect of disconfirming information on a stated religious belief. *Journal of Personality and Social Psychology*, 32, 176–184.

Bem, D.J., 1979, Social pychology. In E.R. Hilgard, R.L. Atkinson, and R.C. Atkinson (Eds.) Introduction to Psychology. New York: Harcourt Brace Jovanich.

Bengtson, V.L., 1970. The generation gap: A review and typology of social-psychological perspectives. *Youth and Society*, 2, 7–32.

215

Biller, H., and Meredith, D., 1974. *Father Power*. New York: McKay.

Blasi, A., 1983. *The Self as Subject: Its Dimensions and Development*. Unpublished manuscript. University of Massachusetts, Boston.

Blasi, A., 1988. Identity and the development of the self. In D.K. Lapskey and F.C. Bower (Eds.), *Self, Ego and Identity: Integrative Approaches*. New York: Springer Verlag.

Blau, R., 1979. *The Guardians of the City*. Jerusalem: Idanim (in Hebrew).

Block, J.H., 1971. *Lives through Time*. Berkeley, Calif.: Bancroft Books

Blos, P., 1976. *On Adolesence*. New York: The Free Press.

Bourne, E., 1978. The state of research on ego identity: A review and appraisal, Part 1. *Journal of Youth and Adolescence*, 7, 223–251.

Braden-Johnson, A., 1977. A temple of last resorts: Youth and shared narcissism. In M.C. Nelson (Ed.), *The Narcissistic Condition*. New York: Human Sciences Press.

Brazelton, T.B., 1976. Early parent–infant reciprocity. In V.C. Vaughton and T.B. Brazelton (Eds.), *The Family: Can It Be Saved?* Chicago: Yearbook Medical Publishers.

Brittain, C., 1969. A comparison of rural and urban adolescents with respect to peer versus parent compliance. *Adolescence*, 13, 59–68.

Bromley, D., and Richardson, J. (Eds.), 1983. *The Brainwashing Deprogramming Controversy: Sociological, Psychological, Legal and Historical Perspectives*. New York: Edwin Mellen Press.

Broughton, J.M., 1978. Development of concepts of self, mind, reality and knowledge. *New Directions for Child Development*, 1, 75–100.

Broughton, J.M., 1981. The divided self in adolescence. *Human Development*, 24, 13–32.

Broughton, J.M., and Riegel, K.F., 1977. Developmental psychology and the self. *Annals of the New York Academy of Science*, 291, 149–167.

Cameron, C., 1973. *Who Is Guru Maharaj Ji?* New York: Bantam Books.

Clark, E., 1929. *The Psychology of Religious Awakening*. New York: Macmillan.

Clark, J.G., 1979. Cults. *Journal of the American Medical Association*, 242, 279–281.

Clarke-Stewart, K.A., 1978. And daddy makes three: The mother-father-infant interaction. *Child Development*, 49, 466–478.

Coe, G.A., 1900. *The Spiritual Life*. New York: Eaton and Mains.

Coleman, J.C., 1980. Friendship and the peer group in adolescence. In J. Adelson (Ed.), *Handbook of Adolescence Psychology*. New York: Wiley.

Condon, W.S., and Sandor, L., 1974. Neonate movement is synchronized with adult speech: Interactional participation and language acquisition. *Science*, 183, 99–101.

Coolidge, M., 1950. Some vicissitudes of the once born and twice born man. *Journal of Philosophical and Phenomenological Research*, 11, 75–87.

Cooley, C.H., 1902. *Human Nature and the Social Order*. New York: Scribner.

Damon, W., 1983. *Social and Personality Development*. New York: Norton.

Damon, W., and Hart, D., 1982. The development of self understanding from infancy through adolescence. *Child Development*, 53, 841–864.

Daniels, A.M., 1893. The newlife: A study of regeneration. *American Journal of Psychology*, 6, 61.

Day, D., 1952. *The Long Loneliness*. New York: Harper and Brothers.

Deutsch, A., 1975. Observations on a sidewalk ashram. *Archives of General Psychiatry*, 32, 166–174.

Douvan, F., and Adelson, J., 1966. *The Adolescent Experience*. New York: Wiley.

Elkind, D., 1967. Egocentrism in adolescence. *Child Development*, 13, 255–278.

Elkind, D., and Bowen, D., 1979. Imaginary audience behavior in children and adolescents. *Developmental Psychology*, 15, 38–44.

Enright, R.D., Lapsley, D.K., Drivas, A.E., and Fehr, L.A., 1980. Parental influences on the development of adolescent autonomy and identity. *Journal of Youth and Adolescence*, 9, 529–546.

Erikson, E.H., 1950. *Childhood and Society*. New York: Norton.

Erikson, E.H., 1956. The problem of ego identity. *Journal of the American Psychoananlytic Association*, 4, 56–122.

Erikson, E.H., 1958. *Young Man Luther*. New York: Norton.

Erikson, E.,1968. *Identity: Youth and Crisis*. New York, Norton.

Etemad, B., 1978. Extinction from cultism. *Clinical Psychiatric Therapy*, 18, 217–223.

Festinger, L., 1954. A theory of social comparison processes. *Human Relations*, 7, 117–140.

Festinger, L., Riecken, M.W., and Schachter, S., 1956. *When Prophecy Fails*. Minneapolis: University of Minnesota Press.

Fowler, J., 1981. Stages of Faith: *The Psychology of Human Development and the Quest for Meaning*. New York: Harper and Row.

Frank, J.D., 1974. *Persuasion and Healing: A Comparative Study of Psychotherapy*. Baltimore: Johns Hopkins University Press.

Fren, R., 1959. *The Psychology of Christian Conversion*. Westwood N.J.: Fleming Revell.

Freud, A., 1958. Adolescence. *The Psychoanalytical Study of the Child*, 13, 255–278.

Freud, S., 1953/1905. Three essays on the history of sexuality. In J. Starchey (Ed. and Tr.), *Standard Edition of the Complete Psychological Works of Sigmund Freud*. London: Hogarth Press.

Freud, S., 1953/1914. On narcissism: An introduction. In J. Starchey (Ed. and Tr.), *The Standard Edition of the Complete Psychological Works of Sigmund Freud*. London: Hogarth Press.

Freud, S., 1953/1928. A religious experience. In J. Starchy (Ed. and Tr.) *Standard Edition of the Complete Psychological Works of Sigmund Freud*. London: Hogarth Press.

Freud, S., 1961/1927. *The Future of an Illusion*. In J. Strachy (Ed. and Tr.), New York: Norton.

Furlong, M., 1980. *Merton: A Biography*. New York: Harper and Row.

Galanter, M., 1982. Charismatic religious sects and psychiatry: An overview. *American Journal of Psychiatry*, 139, 1539–1548.

Galanter, M., 1982. Psychological induction into the large-group: Findings from a modern religious sect. *American Journal of Psychiatry*, 137, 1574–1579.

Galanter, M., Rabkin, R., Rabkin, J., and Deutsch, A., 1979. A psychological study of conversion and membership in a contemporary religious sect. *American Journal of Psychiatry*, 136, 165–170.

Gilligan, C., 1982. *In a Different Voice*. Cambridge: Harvard University Press.

Glock, C.V., and Bellah, R. (Eds.), 1976. *The New Religious Consciousness*. Berkeley: University of California Press.

Goethe, J.W., 1916/1971. *Faust*. Middlesex: Penguin Books.

Goffman, E., 1959. *The Presentation of the Self in Everyday Life*. Garden City, N.Y.: Doubleday.

Golinenko, O.A., Rozanova, S.A., Shumova, B.M., Pokrovskaya, I.A., and Azarova, N.I. (Eds.), 1985. *The Diaries of Sophia Tolstoy*. New York: Random House.

Goodman, F., 1972. *Speaking in Tongues: A Cross Cultural Study of Glossolalia*. Chicago: Chicago University Press.

Greenson, R., 1968. Disidentifying from mother. *International Journal of Psychoanalysis*, 49, 370–374.

Greenwald, A.G., 1980. The totalitarian ego: Fabrication and revision of personal history. *American Psychologist*, 7, 603–618.

Grollman, E.A., 1963. Some sights and insights concerning the father-God mother-Goddess concepts of Judaism and Christianity. *American Imago*, 20, 187–209.

Helfaer, P.M., 1972. *The Psychology of Religious Doubt*. Boston: Beacon Press.

Hall, G.S., 1905. *Adolescence*. New York: Appleton.

Harder, M.W., Richardson, J.T., and Simmonds, R.B., Dec. 1972. Jesus people. *Psychology Today*, 6, 45–113.

Hart, D., and Damon, W., 1985. Contrasts between understanding self and understanding others. In R.L. Leahy (Ed.), *The Development of the Self*. Orlando, Fla.: Academic Press.

Harter, S., 1985. Competence as a dimension of evaluation: Toward a comprehensive model of self-worth. In R.L. Leahy (Ed.), *The Development of the Self*. Orlando, Fla.: Academic Press.

Hartmann, H., 1950. Comments on the psychoanalytic theory of the ego. *The Psychoanalytic Study of the Child*, 5, 74–96.

Hetherington, E.M., 1972. Effects of father absence on personality development in adolesecent girls. *Developmental Psychology*, 7, 313–326.

Heirich, M., 1977. Change of heart: A test of some widely held theories about religious conversion. *American Journal of Sociology*, 83, 653–679.

Hine, V., 1970. Bridge burners: Commitment and participation in religious movements. *Sociological Analysis*, 31, 61–66.

Hoffman, M., 1983. Affective and cognitive processes in moral internalization. In E.T. Higgins, D.N. Ruble, and W.W. Hartup (Eds.), *Social Cognition and Social Behavior*. New York: Cambridge University Press.

Inhelder, B., and Piaget, J., 1958. *The Growth of Logical Thinking from Childhood to Adolescence*. New York: Basic Books.

Izard, C.E., 1977. *Human Emotions*. New York: Plenum Press.

James, W., 1902. *The Varieties of Religious Experience*. New York: New American Library.

James, W., 1908/1892. *Psychology: The Briefer Course*. New York: Holt.

Josselson, R., 1980. Ego development in adolescence. In J. Adelson (Ed.), *Handbook of Adolescent Psychology*. New York: Wiley.

Kernberg, O., 1975. *Borderline Conditions and Pathological Narcissism*. New York: Aronson.

Kildhal, J.P., 1958. Personality correlates of sudden religious converts contrasted with persons of gradual religous conversions. (Doctoral dissertation, New York University, 1957). *Dissertation Abstracts*, 18, 2210–2211.

Kliegerman, C.A., 1957. Psychoanalytic study of the confessions of St. Augustine. *Journal of the American Psychoanalytic Association*, 5, 469–480.

Koestler, A., 1964. *The Act of Creation*. New York: Dell.

Kohut, H., 1971. *The Analysis of the Self*. New York: International Universities Press.

Kohut, H., 1977. *The Restoration of the Self*. New York: International Universities Press.

Kris, E., 1952. *Psychoanalytic Explorations in Art*. New York: International Universities Press.

Kundra, M., 1983. *The Unbearable Lightness of Being*. London: Faber and Faber.

Lamb, M.E., 1975. Fathers: Forgotten contributors to child development. *Human Development*, 18, 245–266.

Lamb, M.E., 1980. The development of parent-infant attachments in the first two years of life. In F.A. Pederson (Ed.), *The Father-Infant Relationship*. New York: Praeger.

Lamb, M.E., 1981. *The Role of the Father in Child Development*. New York: Wiley.

Langone, M.D., 1986. Cultism and American culture. *The Cultic Studies Journal*, 3(2), 157–172.

Lasch, C., 1979. *The Culture of Narcissism*. New York: Norton.

Leahy, R.L., and Shirk, S.R., 1985. Social cognition and the development of the self. In R.L. Leahy (Ed.), *The Development of the Self*. Orlando, Fla.: Academic Press.

Leonard, M., 1966. Fathers and daughters: The significance of fathering in the psychosexual development of the girl. *International Journal of Psychoanalysis*, 47, 325–334.

Leuba, J.H., 1912. *A Psychological Study of Religion*. New York: Macmillan.

Levine, F., 1974. *The Strange World of the Hare Krishnas*. Greenwich, Conn.: Fawcett.

Levine, S., 1984. *Radical Departures*. New York: Harcourt Brace Jovanovich.

Lewis, M., and Brooks-Gunn, J., 1979. *Social Cognition and the Acquisition of Self*. New York: Plenum Press.

Lifton, R.J., 1961. *Thought Reform and the Psychology of Totalism*. New York: Norton.

Lifton, R.J., 1979. *The Broken Connection*. New York: Simon and Schuster.

Lofland, J., 1977. Becoming a world saver revisited. *American Behavioral Scientist*, 20, 805–818.

Lofland, S., and Stark, R., 1969. Becoming a world saver: A theory of conversion to a deviant perspective. In B. Mclaughlin (Ed.), *Studies in Social Movements*. New York: Free Press.

Lynn, D.B., 1974. *The Father: His Role in Child Development*. Monterey: Brooks/Cole.

Maccoby, E., 1980. *Social Development: Psychological Growth and the Parent Child Relationship*. New York: Harcourt Brace Jovanovich.

Mahler, M.S., 1968. *On Human Symbiosis and the Vicissitudes of Individuation*. New York: International Universities Press.

Marcia, J.E., 1966. Development and validation of ego identity status. *Journal of Personality and Social Psychology*, 3, 351–358.

Marcia, J.E., 198. Identity in adolescence. In J. Adelson (Ed.), *Handbook of Adolescent Psychology*. New York: Wiley.

Mead, G.M., 1934. *Mind, Self and Society*. Chicago: University of Chicago Press.

Miller, W.D., 1982. *Dorothy Day: A Biography*. New York: Harper and Row.

Mischel, T. (Ed.), 1977. *The Self: Psychological and Philosophical Issues*. Oxford, England: Basil Blackwell.

Montemayer, R., and Eisen, M., 1977. The development of self conceptions from childhood to adolescence. *Developmental Psychology*, 13, 314–319.

Naipaul, S., 1981. *Journey to Nowhere*. New York: Simon and Schuster.

Newcomb, T.M., 1943. *Personality and Social Change*. New York: Dryden.

Norton, R., 1975. Measurement of ambiguity tolerence. *Journal of Personality Assessment*, 39(6), 607–619.

Noyes, G.R., 1968/1919. *Tolstoy*. New York: Dover.

Offer, D., 1969. *The Psychological World of the Teenager: A Study of Normal Adolescent Boys*. New York: Basic Books.

Offer, D., and Offer, J.L., 1975. *From Teenage to Young Manhood: A Psychological Study*. New York: Basic Books.

Ofshe, R., and Singer, M.T., 1986. Attacks on peripheral vs. central elements of self and the impact of thought reforming techniques. *Cultic Studies Journal*, 3, 3–24.

Otto, R., 1923. *The Idea of the Holy*. London: Oxford University Press.

Paloutzian, R.F., 1983. *Invitation to the Psychology of Religion.* Glenview, Ill.: Scott Foresman.

Parker, M.S., 1985. Identity and the development of religious thinking. *New Directions for Child Development,* 30, 43–60.

Peevers, B.H. (1984, July). The self as observer of the self: A developmental analysis of the subjective self. Paper presented at the Conference on Self and Identity, Cardiff, Wales.

Poling, T.M. (1986, August). Conversion to ISKCON: Familial antecedents. Paper presented at APA meeting, Washington, D.C.

Pratt, J.P., 1907. *The Psychology of Religious Belief.* New York: Macmillan.

Proudfoot, W., and Shaver, P., 1975. Attribution theory and the psychology of religion. *Journal for the Scientific Study of Religion,* 14(4), 317–330.

Rizzuto, A.M., 1981. *The Birth of the Living God: A Psychoanalytic Study.* Chicago: University of Chicago Press.

Rolland, R., 1972/1911. *Tolstoy.* New York: Garland Press.

Rosenberg, M., 1979. *Conceiving the Self.* New York: Basic Books.

Rosenberg, M., 1985. Self concept and psychological well being in adolescence. In R.L. Leahy (Ed.). *The Development of the Self.* Orlando, Fla.: Academic Press.

Ross, J.M., 1979. A review of psychoanalytic contributions on paternity. *International Journal of Psychoanalysis,* 60, 317–326.

Rothstein, A., 1980. *The Narcissistic Pursuit of Perfection.* New York: International Universities Press.

Salzman, L., 1953. The psychology of religious and ideological conversions. *Psychiatry,* 16, 177–187.

Schafer, R., 1960. The loving and beloved superego in Freud's structural theory. *The Psychoanalytic Study of the Child,* 15, 163–188.

Schafer, R., 1976. *A New Language for Psychoanalysis.* New Haven: Yale University Press.

Schein, E.H., 1961. *Coercive Persuasion.* New York: Norton.

Segal, J., 1957. Correlates of collaboration and resistance behavior among U.S. Army POW's in Korea. *Journal of Social Issues,* 13, 31–41.

Selman, R., 1980. *The Growth of Interpersonal Understanding.* New York: Academic Press.

Simmonds, R.B., 1977. Conversion or addiction? *American Behavioral Scientist,* 20, 909–924.

Singer, M.T., Jan. 1979. Coming out of the cults. *Psychology Today,* 72–82.

Sommers, S., 1984. Adults evaluating their emotions: A cross cultural perspective. In C.D. Malatesda and C.E. Izard (Eds.), *Emotions in Adult Development.* New York: Sage Pub.

Starbuck, E.D., 1899. *The Psychology of Religion.* New York: Scribner.

Stolorow, R.D., 1975. Toward a functional definition of narcissism. *International Journal of Psychoanalysis,* 56, 179–186.

Tillich, P., 1952. *The Courage to Be.* New Haven: Yale University Press.

Tolstoy, L., 1961/1884. *A Confession.* London: Oxford University Press.

Ullman, C., 1982. Change of mind, change of heart: Some cognitive and emotional antecedents of religious conversion. *Journal of Personality and Social Psychology,* 42, 183–192.

Ullman, C., 1987. From sincerity to authenticity: Adolescents' view of the true self. *Journal of Personality,* 55, 4, 583–596.

Ullman, C., 1988. Psychological well being among converts in traditional and nontraditional religious groups. *Psychiatry,* 51, 312–322.

Waterman, A.S., 1982. Identity development from adolescence to adulthood: An extension of theory and a review of research. *Developmental Psychology*, 18, 341–358.

Waterman, A.S., 1985. Identity in the context of adolescent psychology. In A.S. Waterman (Ed.), Identity in adolescence: Processes and contents. *New Directions for Child Development*, 30, 5–24.

Wolf, E.S., 1977. Irrationality in a psychoanalytic psychology of the self. In T. Mischel (Ed.), *The Self: Psychological and Philosophical Issues*. Oxford, England: Basil Blackwell.

Wolfe, T. (1976, August 23). The "me" decade and the third great awakening. *New York Magazine*, 26–40.

Wollheim, R., 1984. *The Thread of Life*. Cambridge, Mass.: Harvard University Press.

Zimbardo, P.G., and Hartley, C.F., 1985. Cults go to high school: A theoretical and empirical analysis of the initial stage in the recruitment process. *Cultic Studies Journal*, 2(2) 91–147.

Index

223